...ore the

HITLER'S TRAITORS

HITLER'S TRAITORS

by
Susan Ottaway

LEO COOPER

First published in Great Britain in 2003 by
LEO COOPER
an imprint of Pen & Sword Books
47 Church Street
Barnsley
South Yorkshire
S70 2AS

ISBN 1 84415 021 6

A catalogue record for this book
is available from the British Library

Typeset in 11/13pt Sabon by
Phoenix Typesetting, Burley-in-Wharfedale, West Yorkshire

Printed by CPI UK.

For Ben, Chris, Ed, James, John and William

Contents

Acknowledgements

The research for this book was done over a long period of time, not with a book in mind but just from a personal interest in the subject itself. My acknowledgements are not, therefore, as straightforward as they might have been.

It has been impossible to acknowledge the people who, over the years, kindly sent me the photos included in this book. At the times they were sent they were purely for my own interest and I apologise if anyone is offended by my use of them here without a proper credit.

My thanks, as always, go to librarian Audrey Ford for her unfailing kindness and help, to the staff of the National Archives at Kew (formerly the Public Record Office), who are always helpful and efficient, Dr Johannes Tuchel, Director of the German Resistance Memorial Centre in Berlin, and to David Chacksfield, Lewis George, Ian Ottaway, Linda Taylor, Y.R. Todd and, of course, my partner, Nick.

Introduction

Contrary to popular belief, there were a significant number of German citizens who abhorred the 'principles' of the Nazi party and who did their utmost to rid Germany of its evil regime. The task that they set themselves was not an easy one. Not only were they fighting the party, the government and all its servants, but they could not know which of their neighbours, casual acquaintances, even friends and family, would turn against them and betray them. In Nazi Germany 'tale-telling' was encouraged. It was one's civic duty to inform on anyone who did not swallow the party line and all its obscenities. Anyone who made even the most casual remark against the party ran the risk of being overheard and betrayed. Arrest, imprisonment and even death often followed.

It was useless to appeal to reason – there was no reason in Nazi Germany, at least none that a civilized society could accept. This, of course, begs the question, how could it have happened? Germany had, after all, a highly civilized, cultured society.

There are many theories; the most simple and, perhaps, the most logical is that the German people as a whole are an ordered people, used to obeying their 'masters' whether they be parents, bosses or heads of state. Hitler and his uniformed thugs played upon the tendency of the population to be law-abiding and then backed this up with threats and reprisals to anyone who was out of line. There were many German people who thoroughly disliked the Nazi regime but who, nonetheless, acknowledged that it was the government of their country and regarded those who tried to fight it as traitors.

It is perhaps easy for us, in the early twenty-first century, to criticize.

We would all like to imagine that we would be different. Wouldn't we behave like Miep Gies, the young, Austrian-born woman who looked after Anne Frank and her family during their time in hiding from the Nazis or, perhaps, Oskar Schindler, protecting his band of Jewish factory workers, or the Swedish diplomat, Raoul Wallenberg, who, it is believed, saved up to 100,000 Jews from Nazi tyranny? Probably not. It is a disappointing fact that people are usually much more courageous in theory than in practice. It is hard to go against the general trends, to stand out from others for our beliefs; much easier to follow everyone else and toe the line.

How many of us would have acted had we known that our husbands, wives or children would be made to suffer for our actions, that they would be arrested and imprisoned simply because they belonged to the family of a dissenter? No one was exempt. Even young unmarried men and women knew that their parents, brothers and sisters would be made to suffer if they were discovered. It takes a very brave person with unshakeable ideals to stand up for their principles knowing all that might result.

The book is in two parts. It is not a scholarly work, nor was it ever meant to be a definitive history of the German opposition to Hitler and the Nazi party – that would take too many volumes. I have simply tried to present the stories of some of the brave individuals and groups who risked their lives in an effort to free both themselves and their country from tyranny.

Part One covers Hitler's background and his rise to prominence with the NSDAP. It also describes the first part of the Third Reich from Hitler becoming Chancellor in 1933 to the declaration of war in September 1939. There are so many books about the Second World War that I did not feel it necessary to describe these events, other than where they have relevance to the German resistance movement.

Part Two chronicles the history of a number of resistance groups and tells the stories of some of the brave individuals, both men and women, who risked their lives for the sake of humanity, hoping that their sacrifices would eventually bring about the fall of the party that had done so much to damage their country. Sadly very few of them lived to see the dawn of freedom in Germany but, perhaps, thanks to their actions, the people who did survive to live on in post-war Germany did so with the knowledge that not all Germans had shamed their nation as the Nazis had done.

Part One

Adolf Hitler
and
the Nazi Party

Chapter One

The Birth of a Dictator

Adolf Hitler was born on 20 April 1889 in the Austrian border town of Braunau am Inn where his fifty-two-year-old father, Alois, was a customs officer.

Alois's parents, Johann Georg Hiedler and Maria Anna Schicklgruber, were not married when their son was born in 1837 and he was given his mother's surname. Five years after his birth, his parents did marry but never lived together and Alois was mainly brought up by an uncle.

When he was ten years old his mother died and his father left home, not telling anyone where he was going. He didn't return until his son was nearly forty. By then he had changed the spelling of his name to Hitler and, eventually and rather belatedly, acknowledged Alois as his son, enabling him to change his name from Schicklgruber to Hitler.

Alois had trained as a shoemaker but soon tired of it and at the age of eighteen joined the border police, which was part of the customs service, and went to work near Salzburg. When he eventually became a customs officer himself at the age of twenty-seven, he married the daughter of another customs official.

His marriage to Anna Glasl-Hoerer, who was fourteen years his senior, was not happy, although they remained together for sixteen years, before separating three years before Anna's death. Alois was not a faithful husband and even before his separation from Anna he had been having an affair with a young woman called Franziska Matzelsberger who was a cook in a hotel. She gave him his first child, a boy also named Alois, in 1882. One month after the death of his wife in 1883, Alois married his mistress who was, by then, pregnant again. She gave birth to their daughter, Angela, three months after their wedding. This marriage did not last either, Alois becoming a widower for the second time a year later when Franziska succumbed to tuberculosis.

It would appear that Alois was not particularly upset at losing his wife; she too, had separated from him before her death. Six months later he married his second cousin, Klara Pölzel. The third Mrs Hitler was twenty-three years younger than her husband and had, at one time, lived with Alois and his first wife before going to Vienna to work as a maid. She returned when Alois's second wife left him and he was in need of a housekeeper. By the time they married Klara was pregnant. She gave birth to a boy they named Gustav in 1885 just four months after the wedding. Sadly the child died in infancy as did his sister, Ida, who was born the following year. Their third child was a boy. They named him Adolf. Another boy, Edmund, who lived to be just six years old, followed him in 1894 and, in 1896, their fifth and last child, a girl named Paula, was born. She, like her brother, Adolf, lived to adulthood.

Adolf Hitler began his schooling in 1895 at the village school of Fischlham. He enjoyed school and did well at his lessons, but, because his father found it hard to settle in one place, he was sent to many different schools before the family finally settled in Linz. At one point in his education he was taught by monks in a monastery where he developed a desire to become a priest. This ambition did not last long and by the time he was due to begin his secondary education he had decided to become an artist. He went to the secondary school in Linz where his father was happy for him to study art until he realized that his son intended to make it his career. Alois Hitler was determined that his son should follow him into the civil service. As Adolf later disclosed in his book *Mein Kampf*:

> It was simply inconceivable to him that I might reject what had become the content of his whole life. Consequently, my father's decision was simple, definite and clear; in his own eyes I mean, of course. Finally, a whole lifetime spent in the bitter struggle for existence had given him a domineering nature, and it would have seemed intolerable to him to leave the final

decision in such matters to an inexperienced boy, having as yet no sense of responsibility. Moreover, this would have seemed a sinful and reprehensible weakness in the exercise of his proper parental authority and responsibility for the future life of his child, and as such, absolutely incompatible with his concept of duty.

Young Adolf was just as determined as his father and at the age of eleven decided that rather than try to reason with him he would try other methods to get his own way. Although he had started his schooling as a promising student he decided to stop working in all the subjects that did not interest him. He felt that once his father saw that he was not doing well enough to join the civil service, he would let him do what he wanted.

In the end his father took no part in his son's choice of career. At the age of sixty-five, just before Adolf's fourteenth birthday, Alois died. This made the question of Adolf's future employment easier for him to handle, but, although his mother made sure that his education continued in the manner his father had wished, she had problems of her own.

After her husband's death Klara had moved from their house to a small apartment on the outskirts of Linz, but she had financial worries and struggled to keep her small family clothed and fed. Adolf, though he professed to love his mother, never lifted a finger to help her, thinking only of what *he* wanted:

My mother, to be sure, felt obliged to continue my education in accordance with my father's wish; in other words, to have me study for the civil servant's career. I, for my part, was more than ever determined absolutely not to undertake this career. In proportion as my schooling departed from my ideal in subject matter and curriculum, I became more indifferent at heart. Then suddenly an illness came to my help and in a few weeks decided my future and the eternal domestic quarrel. As a result of my serious lung ailment, a physician advised my mother in most urgent terms never to send me into an office. My attendance at the Realschule had furthermore to be interrupted for at least a year. The goal for which I had so long silently yearned, for which I had always fought, had through this event suddenly become reality almost of its own accord.

5

>Concerned over my illness, my mother finally consented to take me out of the Realschule and let me attend the Academy.

He left school in 1905, not having graduated, but before he took the entrance exam for the Vienna Academy of Fine Arts Adolf decided that he deserved some time to himself. He left the family apartment and with money provided by his downtrodden mother he went to Vienna, intent upon enjoying himself for a few months. He refused to look for paid employment. Instead he wandered the streets of Vienna taking in all the sights and visiting the museums and galleries. He had, by this time, developed a hatred for the Austro-Hungarian Empire and fervently wished for the Germanic people within it to form a union with Germany and remove all 'foreigners' from within its borders.

In spite of his political awakenings Adolf still intended to become an artist and, in 1907, submitted drawings that, if satisfactory, would allow him to take the entrance examination for the Vienna Academy of Fine Arts. He passed the first test, but, following the entrance exam, was shocked to learn that he had failed to gain a place at the Academy. A year later he was back in Vienna, but this time the drawings he submitted were so bad that he was not even allowed to sit the examination. Failure was an option he had never considered. He had always had supreme confidence in his artistic ability and so he questioned the decision of the Academy. He was told that, while his painting was not of an acceptable standard, he might be able to study architecture at the School of Architecture. It was then that Adolf realized that his plan to force his father into allowing him to become an artist had backfired. Because he had not studied, he had not finished his course work and had, therefore, not graduated. Without his graduation he was not eligible to obtain a place at the School of Architecture. Unable to accept that his failure was his own fault, he blamed his teachers for his lack of education. This attitude remained with him for the rest of his life. While it is quite understandable for an eleven-year-old boy to be lazy about his schoolwork, it is quite strange that a grown man should still be justifying the decisions he made as a child but blame the results on other people.

With his life's dream in tatters he did not know what to do. He still wanted to become an architect but knew that, if he were to achieve his ambition, it would take a huge amount of hard work and money. He was not prepared to work for a living, still relying on his mother to keep him, and so his days of aimless wandering continued. He was later to say of this time:

> These were the happiest days of my life and seemed to me almost a dream; and a mere dream it was to remain. Two years later, the death of my mother put a sudden end to all my high-flown plans. It was the conclusion of a long and painful illness, which from the beginning left little hope of recovery. Yet it was a dreadful blow, particularly for me. I had honoured my father, but my mother I had loved.

Klara Hitler died of cancer just before Christmas 1908. She was fifty-one years old. Her life had been one of hardship: marriage to a much older, allegedly violent man and the financial worries which followed his death, the early death of three of her five children, the utter selfishness of her only surviving son and finally her own painful death at a relatively early age. Adolf Hitler may have loved his mother but her death hit him more in his pocket than in his heart. While he had described the previous years of aimless wandering, financed by his mother, as the happiest days of his life, he regarded the next five years, fending for himself, as a time of hardship and misery. He was later to say of that time:

> I owe it to that period that I grew hard and am still capable of being hard. And even more, I exalt it for tearing me away from the hollowness of comfortable life; for drawing the mother's darling out of his soft downy bed and giving him 'Dame Care' for a new mother; for hurling me, despite all resistance, into a world of misery and poverty, thus making me acquainted with those for whom I was later to fight.

What he was less willing to admit was that not only did he receive an orphan's allowance, he was also supported to a great extent by his aunt, Johanna Pölzel, who regularly sent him money. On her death in 1911, she left him a large inheritance. It does not seem to have fitted with his own mood of self-pity to admit that he was still being financed in his wanderings by others and not by his own efforts and he maintained that he worked as a labourer for much of the time.

7

It has often been said that Hitler's anti-Semitism stemmed from a belief that he had Jewish blood, perhaps from his grandfather. However, it would seem that this was not true, as he states:

> In this period my eyes were opened to two menaces of which I had previously scarcely known the names, and whose terrible importance for the existence of the German people I certainly did not understand: Marxism and Jewry.

For Adolf the seeds of hate were sown in those years in Vienna, following the death of his mother. He also developed what he believed was an understanding of people and their patterns of behaviour:

> . . . the higher classes feel less constraint in their dealings with the lowest of their fellow men than seems possible to the 'upstart'.
>
> For anyone is an upstart who rises by his own efforts from his previous position in life to a higher one.
>
> Ultimately this struggle, which is often so hard, kills all pity. Our own painful struggle for existence destroys our feeling for the misery of those who have remained behind.
>
> In this respect Fate was kind to me. By forcing me to return to this world of poverty and insecurity, from which my father had risen in the course of his life, it removed the blinkers of a narrow petty-bourgeois upbringing from my eyes. Only now did I learn to know humanity, learning to distinguish between empty appearances or brutal externals and the inner being.

His journey of discovery in Vienna came to an abrupt end in 1913 when he fled to Bavaria to escape having to serve in the Austrian army. He settled in Munich, but in February 1914 was recalled to Austria to begin his military service. However, after a medical examination, he was rejected as being unfit and so was able to return to Munich. He was living there when, in August 1914, the First World War broke out.

Although he had been reluctant to enlist in the Austrian army and was, presumably, relieved at being rejected, he felt no such qualms about serving with its Bavarian counterpart. He wrote to the King of Bavaria and begged to be allowed to fight. He was assigned to

Kingston College LRC

Customer name: MR Min Myat
Customer ID: MYA08075092

Title: Hitler's traitors
ID: 00120148
Due: 22/02/2010

Total items: 1
Total fines: £1.20
25/01/2010
Issued: 3
Overdue: 0
Hold requests: 0
Ready for pickup: 0

Items that you already have on loan

Title: An introduction to AutoCAD 2004: 2D and
3D design
ID: 00124360
Due: 20100208   000000

Title: Advanced automotive fault diagnosis
ID: 00140654
Due: 20100211   000000

Thank you for using the
3M SelfCheck™ System

the 16th Bavarian Reserve Regiment and ultimately achieved the rank of lance corporal.

Surprisingly he proved to be a good soldier, although he was not popular with his fellow soldiers. He was sent to the front in 1914 as an orderly, a position he retained for two years until he became a despatch bearer in 1916. He took part in many battles during the First World War and was decorated twice, receiving the Iron Cross, Second Class, in 1914. In 1918 he captured an enemy officer and fifteen men and, for this action, was awarded the Iron Cross, First Class, a very unusual award for an ordinary soldier.

He was wounded twice. In October 1916 he received a leg injury for which he was hospitalized. Just a few weeks before the end of the war he was gassed very badly and spent three months in a hospital on the outskirts of Berlin. In spite of this he declared that the war had been the greatest and most unforgettable time of his life.

In January 1918 the American President, Woodrow Wilson, had made a speech to the US Congress setting out his 'Fourteen Points' for world peace. These covered such things as borders, sovereignty and reparations but also included a demand for 'general association of nations', a concept which eventually led to the formation of the League of Nations, the forerunner of the present United Nations. The Allies did not universally support Wilson. French Prime Minister Georges Clemenceau is said to have sneered at Wilson's efforts, declaring:

> President Wilson and his Fourteen Points bore me. Even God Almighty had only ten!

Clemenceau, an acknowledged hater of the Germans, was over-ruled and copies of the Fourteen Points were dropped over enemy territory. The German people were becoming increasingly hostile to their leaders and more and more anxious for the war to end. By September 1918 the Austro-Hungarian government sent a note to the Allies requesting that peace negotiations begin, but the request was rejected.

The following month a joint German and Austrian request for an armistice was received by President Wilson. Notes were sent back and forth between Germany and the USA. Wilson was anxious that the Germans should vacate the lands that they had occupied and that, in future, European boundaries should be organized by nationality rather than by occupation. He wanted Germany to pay reparations to the countries whose territory had most been damaged, namely France and Belgium and suggested that Germany should be included in the peace negotiations provided that their representatives truly spoke for the people.

By the end of October the Germans had agreed to suspend submarine warfare, prohibit the use of poison gas and to withdraw their troops from foreign territory. Wilson was satisfied that his terms for peace had largely been met and he agreed to put their request to the Allies.

The armistice ending the First World War was signed in a railway carriage in the forest of Compiègne north of Paris at 5 a.m. on 11 November 1918. Hostilities formally ended at 11 a.m.

On 18 January 1919, the forty-eighth anniversary of the formation of the German Empire, the Peace Conference began in Paris. A total of thirty-two nations took part in the conference which was held in the Palace of Versailles, but it was dominated by the 'Big Four', British Prime Minister David Lloyd George, French Prime Minister Georges Clemenceau, Italian Prime Minister Vittorio Orlando and US President Woodrow Wilson. In spite of Wilson's belief that Germany should be included, she was not and immediately the German people felt that Wilson had betrayed them.

Each member of the 'Big Four' had their own agenda and their aims differed widely. France wanted to weaken Germany on all fronts, militarily, politically and economically. Clemenceau argued that the Rhineland and the Ruhr, Germany's industrial heartland, should become a semi-autonomous state with leanings towards France. This would make it more difficult for the Germans to invade France again. He also wanted to form an alliance with Poland and the states of the Austro-Hungarian Empire to form a buffer zone in the east. Clemenceau also argued for very heavy reparations to pay off France's war debt and rebuild the country.

Italy laid claim to the territory she had been promised in return for joining the Allies, the south Tyrol and the Trentino, which is in modern-day Slovenia.

Britain was keen for Germany to demilitarize and wanted the German battle fleet and to control its merchant navy. She also laid claim to Germany's African colonies. Although Britain demanded her share of reparations, she did envisage a time when Germany would recover economically and become a full trading partner again.

Wilson wanted to set up the League of Nations, which, he believed, would enable states to resolve their differences at the conference table rather than on the battlefield. He also felt that, if nothing were to be done in this regard, it would leave the way clear for the Bolsheviks to infiltrate the workers and spread communism throughout Europe. He wanted to weaken Germany's military might to ensure that she would not instigate further conflicts but he was not in favour of breaking her economically.

The delegates at the Paris Conference, after much haggling and argument, eventually produced a draft peace treaty, which was shown to the Germans on 7 May 1919. Although Woodrow Wilson's Fourteen Points had been the basis for Germany's surrender, the peace terms did not fully adhere to these points. Germany was held to be entirely responsible for the war and was instructed to pay an immediate sum of five billion US dollars to the Allies with more, undisclosed amounts, to follow. She was also to be prevented from rearming. The west bank of the Rhine was to be occupied by Allied troops for up to fifteen years and the Saar basin, which held huge coalfields vital to the German iron and steel industry, was to be administered by the League of Nations. In addition France was given the control of the coalmines as recompense for the damage done to French coalfields by the Germans during the war. Not content with that, the Treaty also made the port of Danzig a free city and gave Alsace Lorraine to France. The terms meant that Germany would lose approximately 87,000 square miles of territory, which amounted to thirteen per cent of the country's total and, with the land, the seven million people (ten per cent of the population) who lived there. Alsace being ceded to France also meant that Germany lost her entire potash and textile industries.

At the same time that the conference was beginning its deliberations, Germany held an election to form an assembly that would draw up a new constitution. All males over the age of twenty were eligible to vote. Of the 421 seats in the assembly, 236 were won by various small political groups, 163 by the Socialists and 22 by independents. The National Assembly convened in Weimar to the south-west of Berlin on 6 February 1919 and the Weimar Republic was born. Its constitution, which was adopted on 31 July, provided for two legislative chambers, the *Reichstag* and the *Reichsrat*, and a president who would serve for seven years. The *Reichstag* was based on a system of proportional representation, with one member for every 60,000 votes and the *Reichsrat* had representatives from each of the seventeen German states.

The first president to be elected was Friedrich Ebert who served until his death in February 1925. He asked Philipp Scheidemann to form a government. Although the Weimar constitution was considered to be very forward-thinking and fair it had one fatal flaw – Article 48. This was the clause that permitted the president to suspend temporarily the rights of citizens guaranteed under the constitution, if he deemed it necessary. It was to be the clause that allowed Hitler to govern quite legally while doing exactly as he wanted, without regard for the rights or the wishes of the German people.

Chapter Two

The Rise of the Nazis

On 20 June 1919, one week before the Treaty of Versailles was signed, the German chancellor Philipp Scheidemann resigned. He felt unable to put his name to a document that imposed such punitive measures against his homeland, so the Socialist politician Gustav Bauer took his place. The following day the German Navy scuttled most of its fleet, which was being held at the British naval base of Scapa Flow, rather than hand the ships over to the British.

The peace treaty was signed in the Hall of Mirrors in the Palace of Versailles, near Paris, on 28 June and, by agreeing to its terms, the Weimar government had sealed its own fate.

The German people felt betrayed both by President Wilson and, more so, by their own government who seemed to accept the terms without a fight. The people were crushed. Throughout the war they had been led to believe that they would triumph in the end and it came as a shock to them when they finally understood that they weren't going to win. The Imperial government had promised that they would make the Allies pay huge reparations to help repay its war expenditure. The figures that they promised amounted to four times that which the Allies eventually demanded from Germany.

After their defeat in 1918 the German people found themselves hungry, short of money and other resources, with their economy at the point of near collapse and their territory invaded by the victorious Allies, who not only continued to blockade their beleaguered land but also demanded their own crippling reparations. In addition they had not been asked or allowed to participate in the peace talks and were not invited to belong to the League of Nations.

13

Although unfairly, the Weimar Republic was accorded most of the blame for these ills.

Following the revolution in Russia, a large number of German citizens looked to communism as a way out of their problems. In the early days of the Weimar Republic the Communists organized riots, strikes and demonstrations in Bremen, Cuxhaven, Düsseldorf, Halle, Mülheim and Wilhelmshaven, in an effort to gain power. These were followed by a strike in Berlin that led to street fighting and assaults on policemen. The Communists wanted Germany to be governed along the same lines as Soviet Russia. The government's answer to this insurrection was to send in the *Freikorps* (Free Corps), a group of former officers, soldiers, nationalists and unemployed, all with right-wing political views, who regarded the Social Democrats and the Jews as being responsible for the plight of Germany. Their aim was to rid the Fatherland of its 'traitors'.

The Communist demonstrations led to the *Freikorps* being tasked with shooting anyone who was found with a gun. They took on this assignment with great enthusiasm and, in just a few days, shot and killed over 1,000 people, including thirty sailors who were peacefully queueing for their wages. They were also used to quell uprisings in other German towns such as Braunschweig, Magdeburg, Dresden, Leipzig and Munich.

There was political unrest all over Germany; many small political parties were formed, one of which was the *Deutsche Arbeiterpartei* (German Workers' Party), founded in Munich in January 1919 by journalist Dietrich Eckart and Anton Drexler, a toolmaker. Munich had by this time become a centre of political activity. Initially the party had only a handful of members, but these figures grew steadily over the next few months.

At the end of the war Hitler had remained in the army. Following his discharge from hospital he was given the task of spying on the ever-increasing number of political parties.

In September 1919 it was the turn of the *Deutsche Arbeiterpartei* to be investigated. Hitler found it to be a very small nationalist party with few members, no constitution, no funds and no definite objectives. The only view that was common to all its members was a hatred of the government and, it would seem, of Jews. These views coincided exactly with those of Hitler and, rather than

14

investigate the party and report back to the army, he decided to join it himself. He was member no. 55 and soon advanced to no. 7 of the Executive Committee. He rapidly became very active within the party and whenever he had the opportunity would speak to whoever would listen about his vision for the future of Germany. He developed an almost laughable style of oration in which he ranted and screamed, waving his arms about and making extravagant gestures, but his message appealed to all those who felt that they had been badly served by the Weimar government and who blamed the Jews for the state in which Germany found itself.

On 19 February 1920 he and Anton Drexler had a hastily arranged meeting during which they drafted their Twenty-Five Points document. (See appendix 1) The following day Hitler delivered a speech at the *Hofbräuhaus* in Munich in which he set out the aims and objectives of the Twenty-Five Points.

Before long Hitler had become the most prominent member of the party and, two years after joining it, he became its leader. One of his first tasks was to change the name of the party from *Deutsche Arbeiterpartei* to *Nationalsozialistische Deutsche Arbeiterpartei* – NSDAP (National Socialist German Workers' Party). The name Nazi was taken from the first two letters of **National** and the third and fourth letters of *Sozialistische*. Having become leader of the party, Hitler decided to leave the army to devote himself full time to building up a following and, ultimately, to making a name for himself in the world of politics.

When he became leader Hitler also took control of a newspaper, the *Völkischer Beobachter*, which had been acquired with the help of an army officer, Major General von Epp, at the end of 1920. Before the war the paper had been called *Münchener Beobachter* and had appeared weekly, but its name was changed in 1919 when it began to be produced twice weekly. Even before being acquired by the NSDAP, the paper was rampantly anti-Semitic, publishing articles about clearing out the Jews from German society and building camps in which to house them away from decent German people. It was music to the ears of the party members, one of whom, Ernst Roehm, persuaded his commanding officer, von Epp, to raise the money to buy the paper. Von Epp did as he was asked and soon found the money both from donations from like-minded friends and, it was said, from secret army funds. By 1923 the paper was being published on a daily basis. Its editor was Alfred Rosenberg and it came under the financial control of Max Amman who was also treasurer of the NSDAP. Rosenberg was anxious to use the paper to promote Nazi ideas whilst Amman wanted to sell as many copies as possible to bolster party funds. It would seem that Hitler agreed with Rosenberg as the articles published became steadily more racist and offensive to right-thinking people.

To guard against any trouble from political opponents, particularly at party meetings, Hitler set up a group called the *Sturmabteilung or* SA (Storm Troopers) and put them under the control of his friend, Ernst Roehm, an army veteran of the First World War. The group was composed mainly of thugs and criminals and was very effective in curbing opposition to the party. Over the next few years the SA became an important force in promoting Hitler's rise to power. Hitler was extremely grateful to Roehm for his assistance and said of him:

> I want to thank Heaven for having given me the right to call
> a man like you my friend and comrade-in-arms.

He also organized his own personal bodyguards, the *Schutzstaffel* or SS (Elite Guard) which came under the control of Heinrich Himmler. Although the *Schutzstaffel* began its existence as a small force of bodyguards, it eventually became the main police force of the NSDAP.

By the middle of 1922 the German government claimed itself unable to meet the war reparations payments. This led French newspapers to suggest that France should suspend payments of her war debts to Britain, a move totally rejected by Britain who still had to meet payments to the USA for the arms she had supplied during the war.

On 15 September 1922 the German Chancellor, Josef Wirth, in a speech in Berlin, declared, 'Bread first, reparations second', but the government was having problems in providing anything at all, bread or reparations payments alike.

In January 1923 France lost patience with Germany and occupied the Ruhr, Germany's main industrial area. The government decided on a policy of peaceful resistance to the occupation but the situation caused inflation to rise at an alarming rate and, almost overnight, even wealthy Germans lost all their money. It was extremely bad for the country but to Hitler it seemed to provide a way for him to further his political aims.

Ernst Roehm had been working tirelessly to form alliances with other small nationalist parties and by November 1923 the NSDAP had enough allies for Hitler to believe that he could make an attempt to take over the Bavarian government. These small parties had united under the name of the *Kampfbund* (Militant Association) with Hitler as its leader. The Bavarian government tried to ban the organization and its public meetings and demonstrations, but they had little effect on the new association.

Hitler decided to publish some inflammatory articles about central government in the *Völkischer Beobachter* and, in doing so, managed to create a rift between the Central and the Bavarian governments. The Central government in Berlin, under its new Chancellor, Gustav Stresemann, who had come to power on 13 August, demanded that the newspaper be closed down, but the Bavarian Commissioner for Public Order, Gustav von Kahr, refused to take orders from Berlin and, instead, formed an alliance with the Bavarian army commander, General Otto von Lossow, and with the head of the provincial police force, Hans Ritter von Seisser. Although von Kahr let it be known that he intended to form a national government, he did nothing about it. Hitler became nervous about the situation and fearful that von Kahr might try to restore the Bavarian monarchy, as he was known to be a monarchist.

A meeting had been arranged for 8 November 1923 at the *Bürgerbräukeller* and Hitler, with the backing of the ultra-right wing General Erich Ludendorff, decided to seize power himself. Positioning a large number of SA around the beer cellar, Hitler burst in and, waving a pistol, proclaimed the establishment of a new national government. He and Ludendorff coerced von Kahr, von Lossow and von Seisser into agreeing to be part of the new government, but during that night, while Hitler and Ludendorff were making their plans, the others had second thoughts and retook control of the Bavarian government and of the army. When Hitler discovered this treachery the following day he and his supporters marched to von Lossow's headquarters. Von Kahr had, in the meantime, issued a proclamation outlawing the Nazi party and the *Kampfbund* and when Hitler and his mob arrived at the

17

headquarters the Munich police stopped them. In the ensuing scuffles sixteen Nazis and three police officers were killed and several others were injured, including Hermann Goering, the air ace of the First World War who was later to become head of the Luftwaffe. Hitler, himself, was not hurt but seemed to be utterly defeated by this setback and disappeared into the crowd. Three days later he was arrested.

In spite of being able to bring the Bavarian government into line once more, there was unrest in the ranks of the national government and when, at the end of November 1923, the Social Democrats decided to leave the coalition government, Chancellor Stresemann was forced to resign. He had been in power for only three months and ten days.

On 26 February 1924 Adolf Hitler was in court, charged with high treason. There were nine other defendants also charged with treason, including Erich Ludendorff and Ernst Roehm. A panel of judges, three lay and three professional, tried the ten men. The lay judges were blatantly pro-Nazi while the professionals, although feigning impartiality, allowed Hitler to use the trial to further his own ends by letting him conduct his own defence. Seizing upon the political turmoil that was still evident in Germany, Hitler turned his defence into a propaganda campaign and made speeches which brought him to the forefront of public opinion throughout the country. Although to the foreign press, which was present in great numbers at the trial, he represented the worst of extremist views, to the German people he became something of a hero. He used the trial to highlight everything that he believed to be wrong with the government and the way it had ruled Germany since the Treaty of Versailles. The chief prosecution witnesses were von Lossow, von Kahr and von Seisser, whom Hitler also accused of treason, saying that if he was guilty as charged then they must also be guilty since their views had been the same as his prior to his arrest. The trial lasted for twenty-four days and the verdict was announced on 1 April 1924. Hitler and eight of the other nine were found guilty; only Ludendorff was acquitted. Hitler proclaimed that, although the court might find him guilty, history would not do so. He was sentenced to five years' imprisonment, which was the minimum for a charge of treason, the maximum being life.

He was imprisoned at Landsberg am Lech in Bavaria. From the start his sentence was more like a time at a rest home than a punishment. He ate breakfast in bed and went for walks in the grounds. Photos of Hitler during his time in Landsberg show him wearing *lederhosen* rather than prison uniform and sitting in a comfortable room with pictures on the wall and furnished with a cloth-covered table and a vase of flowers. He was allowed to have visitors whenever he wanted and was given his choice of books to read. It was during this time that he wrote the first part of *Mein Kampf*, dictating this curious book, in the fashion of an eccentric novelist, to his faithful supporter Rudolf Hess. In it he laid out the story of his life thus far and his political aims and ideology. He dedicated the work to the sixteen Nazis who had given their lives for the cause in the following foreword:

On November 9, 1923, at 12.30 in the afternoon, in front of the *Feldherrnhalle* as well as in the courtyard of the former War Ministry the following men fell, with loyal faith in the resurrection of their people:

ALFARTH, FELIX, businessman, b. July 5, 1901
BAURIEDL, ANDREAS, hatter, b. May 4, 1879
CASELLA, THEODOR, bank clerk, b. August 8, 1900
EHRLICH, WILHELM, bank clerk, b. August 19, 1894
FAUST, MARTIN, bank clerk, b. January 27, 1901
HECHENBERGER, ANTON, locksmith, b. September 28, 1902
KÖRNER, OSKAR, businessman, b. January 4, 1875
KUHN, KARL, headwaiter, b. July 26, 1897
LAFORCE, KARL, student of engineering, b. October 28, 1904
NEUBAUER, KURT, valet, b. March 27, 1899
PAPE, CLAUS VON, businessman, b. August 16, 1904
PFORDTEN, THEODOR VON DER, County Court Councillor, b. May 14, 1873
RICKMERS, JOHANN, retired Cavalry Captain, b. May 7, 1881
SCHEUBNER-RICHTER, MAX ERWIN VON, Doctor of Engineering, b. January 9, 1884

STRANSKY, LORENZ RITTER VON, engineer, b. March
  14, 1889
WOLF, WILHELM, businessman, b. October 19, 1898

So-called national authorities denied these dead heroes a
common grave.
  Therefore I dedicate to them, for common memory, the first
volume of this work. As its blood witnesses, may they shine
forever, a glowing example to the followers of our movement.
                                                  Adolf Hitler

  Landsberg am Lech
  Fortress Prison
  October 16, 1924

Serving only nine months of his sentence, Hitler was released in
December 1924 following an amnesty. He emerged from the prison
at Landsberg to the task of rebuilding the Nazi party. In this task
he had the support of two friends, Josef Goebbels, later to become
propaganda minister in Hitler's government and Hermann
Goering, who had recovered from his injuries following the
abortive *putsch*.
  The Bavarian government tried to deport Hitler to Austria,
following his release from prison – in spite of his fierce pride in
Germany, he was still an Austrian citizen – but the government
in Vienna refused to accept him, stating that because of his service
with the German army he had ceased to be Austrian.

Chapter Three

The Road to Power

Learning from mistakes made in the unsuccessful *putsch*, Hitler decided that the only way to gain power was to do so legally. He was so insistent upon gaining power through legal means that he was given the nickname of Adolf Légalité (Adolf the Legal). In reality Hitler had little regard for the justice system but wanted to be seen to be abiding by the law. It was a good piece of PR as he came to be regarded as an upright, sincere party leader.

He vowed that if there was ever another chance of other political groups wanting to form an alliance with the NSDAP they would have to do so on his terms, namely join the NSDAP and renounce membership of all other parties. In this way he felt that there was less likelihood of last-minute cold feet and betrayal. He also decided that it was pointless to try to come to power until he had the wherewithal to carry it through in terms of organization and manpower.

Although Hitler was at the head of the National Socialist party, the two elements, nationalists and socialists, held very different views. They were also divided geographically, with most of the nationalists in Munich and other southern towns and the socialists in the north, particularly Berlin. It was Hitler's task to unite the different factions and he used his talents as a public speaker to this end. By carefully constructed speeches, he managed to appeal to both the lower and upper classes, the socialists and the nationalists.

On 14 February 1924 Hitler called a meeting of party district leaders in the southern town of Bamberg, in an attempt to iron out the difficulties between the northern and southern factions. Although he wanted to appeal to all, his own real opinion was against the socialist northerners who wanted to adopt some communist principles and he scheduled the Bamberg meeting for a weekday when it was difficult for northerners to attend. Two leaders who did manage to get to the conference were Gregor Strasser and his protégé Josef Goebbels. Strasser was of the opinion that capitalism must be stamped out at all costs and that Germany should cooperate with communist Russia. He saw himself as being more intellectual than Hitler and envisaged a time when he would take over from the Austrian upstart: the two argued. Goebbels, sensing that he would be better served in the party by switching sides, did just that and abandoned his mentor Strasser. By October 1924 Hitler had appointed Goebbels as *Gauleiter* (District Leader) of Berlin, a position that started him on his rise to fame within the party.

By this time Germany was more settled. Everyday life was becoming easier, supplies of consumer goods were more plentiful, inflation was down and the mark was stable. During the mid-1920s Weimar culture became apparent: new art and music, poetry and literature, architecture and design flourished. Musicians, writers and artists were encouraged by the Weimar government to pursue their art. Hitler viewed this attitude with scorn, decrying the policy as having created an artistic junkyard. One wonders what his attitude might have been had he been able to enrol at the Vienna Academy of Fine Arts and pursue his wish to become an artist. If he had been one of the artists enjoying the freedom of the new age would he still have regarded it as a junkyard? Perhaps so. Even the artists and intellectuals who benefited from the liberal policy of the Weimar regime seem to have felt no loyalty to the government that gave them their artistic freedom. As Gordon A. Craig says in his book, *Germany 1866-1945*:

> It is interesting to note how few of them seemed to feel any reciprocal obligation or any inclination to come to the Republic's defence when, in the years of the great depression, its many foes gathered for their final assault upon German democracy.

In the 1928 *Reichstag* elections the NSDAP won twelve seats compared with the fifty-four seats of the Communists. Neither party came even remotely close to gaining a majority of votes. In 1929, however, depression hit Germany along with the rest of the world and the country again found itself in the grip of poverty and unemployment. The people, looking for someone to deliver them from this unhappy situation, turned to Hitler and the NSDAP. In the *Reichstag* elections of 14 September 1930 the Communists gained a further twenty-three seats, giving them a total of seventy-seven, while the NSDAP's total rose from twelve to 107, gaining 6 million votes and making it the second largest party in the country. Chancellor Heinrich Brüning, with the approval of President von Hindenburg, brought in Article 48 of the Weimar constitution that allowed him to suspend all the rights of a citizen and rule by decree. It was an action that was to be copied by Hitler not long after.

On 25 February 1932 Hitler eventually succeeded in becoming a German citizen. Being now eligible for higher office, he decided to run for President against the Communist Ernst Thälmann, the army officer Theodor Duesterberg, and the incumbent Paul von Hindenburg. The presidential election, which was held on 13 March 1932, gained Hitler thirty per cent of the votes but did not produce an outright winner. Another election was held on 10 April when von Hindenburg won fifty-three per cent of the votes and held on to his position as President. His votes were 19,359,650 compared with Hitler's 13,418,011. Thälmann received just over 3½ million votes.

This was proving a turbulent time for the government. Although Brüning had succeeded in ending reparations payments and had also made some headway in trying to have the terms of the Treaty of Versailles modified, the unemployment figure had risen to 6 million and von Hindenburg was becoming disenchanted with his chancellor. Spurred on by General Kurt von Schleicher, von Hindenburg asked for Brüning's resignation on 30 May 1932. He replaced him with Franz von Papen and made von Schleicher Minister of Defence.

At the next elections, held in July 1932, the NSDAP won 230 seats in the *Reichstag*, becoming for the first time the largest party in the country. It was, however, a difficult time for all political parties for in the elections of November 1932 the NSDAP lost thirty-four of the seats it had gained in July, while the Communists increased their figure by twenty-three to 100.

On 3 December 1932 von Schleicher replaced von Papen as Chancellor. Both von Papen and von Schleicher saw in Hitler and the NSDAP a way to further their own careers. Von Schleicher offered to support Hitler if he would guarantee him a place in his cabinet and a position in charge of the army. Von Papen had a secret meeting with Hitler on 4 January 1933 during which he promised to obtain the support of wealthy businessmen and industrialists in return for positions of power for his friends within Hitler's government when he came to power. Hitler and von Papen agreed to exclude Jews, Communists and Social Democrats from politics altogether.

Although Hitler was satisfied with the deal he had made with von Papen, the former chancellor now had to convince von Hindenburg. This proved to be a very difficult task, accomplished eventually only by the intervention of von Hindenburg's son, Oskar, and a wealthy financier, Kurt Freiherr von Schroeder. On 30 January 1933 the aged president eventually acceded to their wishes and appointed Hitler Chancellor of Germany, with von Papen as his deputy.

Since he still did not have a majority in the *Reichstag*, Hitler, with the agreement of von Hindenburg, called for yet more elections. These were due to take place on 5 March 1933 when Hitler hoped to gain a lot of the seats at present taken by the Communists.

On 27 February he was given a huge helping hand when the *Reichstag* building caught fire. Exactly how this happened was, and has remained, a mystery.

The building was huge, constructed of sandstone blocks with a 130-foot tower at each corner and a massive glass dome in the centre. It was located on Königsplatz, opposite the Brandenburg Gate. Berliners hated the building from the moment it was completed in 1894 at a cost of 87 million gold marks. To them it became known as the 'biggest round cheese in Europe'.

On the evening of 27 February 1933 one of the caretakers, Rudolf Scholz, was making his rounds when he heard footsteps. They belonged to a secretary, Anna Rehme, who worked for the communist deputies. Twenty minutes later Scholz said goodbye to

Rehme, who was accompanied by two communist deputies, Ernst Torgler and Wilhelm Koenen. The time was approximately 8.40 p.m. A few minutes after 9 p.m. a man was seen on one of the building's balconies carrying a burning torch. He disappeared into the building and was seen to be lighting fires in many of the rooms. The fire brigade was called and a policeman named Poeschel, along with the House Inspector Alexander Scranowitz, apprehended the arsonist as he emerged from the rear of the Sessions Chamber in the *Reichstag* building. He was carrying his passport that identified him as Marinus van der Lubbe, a twenty-four-year-old Communist from Leiden in Holland. He said that he had worked alone and had started the fire as a protest against the government. In a statement given to police when he was interviewed on 3 March 1933 he said:

I myself am a Leftist, and was a member of the Communist Party until 1929. I had heard that a Communist demonstration was disbanded by the leaders on the approach of the police. In my opinion something absolutely had to be done in protest against this system. Since the workers would do nothing, I had to do something myself. I considered arson a suitable method. I did not wish to harm private people but something belonging to the system itself. I decided on the Reichstag. As to the question of whether I acted alone, I declare emphatically that this was the case.

Hitler and other leading members of the NSDAP were delighted with the arson attempt and saw it as a great opportunity to suppress the communist opposition. Sefton Delmer, head of the Berlin bureau of the *Daily Express*, was at the scene of the fire when Hitler arrived and Delmer wrote the following report for his paper:

The arson of the German parliament building was allegedly the work of a Communist-sympathizing Dutchman, van der Lubbe. More probably, the fire was started by the Nazis, who used the incident as a pretext to outlaw political opposition and impose dictatorship.
'This is a God-given signal! If this fire, as I believe, turns out to be the handiwork of Communists then there is nothing that shall stop us now crushing out this murder pest with an iron fist.' Adolf Hitler, Fascist Chancellor of Germany, made this

dramatic declaration in my presence tonight in the hall of the burning Reichstag building.

The fire broke out at 9.45 tonight in the Assembly Hall of the Reichstag.

It had been laid in five different corners and there is no doubt whatever that it was the handiwork of incendiaries. One of the incendiaries, a man aged thirty, was arrested by the police as he came rushing out of the building, clad only in shoes and trousers, without shirt or coat, despite the icy cold in Berlin tonight.

Five minutes after the fire had broken out I was outside the Reichstag watching the flames licking their way up the great dome into the tower.

A cordon had been flung round the building and no one was allowed to pass it.

After about twenty minutes of fascinated watching I suddenly saw the famous black motor car of Adolf Hitler slide past, followed by another car containing his personal body-guard. I rushed after them and was just in time to attach myself to the fringe of Hitler's party as they entered the Reichstag.

Never have I seen Hitler with such a grim and determined expression. His eyes, always a little protuberant, were almost bulging out of his head.

Captain Goering, his right-hand man, who is the Prussian Minister of the Interior and responsible for all police affairs, joined us in the lobby. He had a very flushed and excited face.

'This is undoubtedly the work of Communists, Herr Chancellor,' he said. 'A number of Communist deputies were present here in the Reichstag twenty minutes before the fire broke out. We have succeeded in arresting one of the incendiaries.'

'Who is he?' Dr Goebbels, the propaganda chief of the Nazi Party, threw in.

'We do not know yet,' Captain Goering answered, with an ominously determined look around his thin, sensitive mouth. 'But we shall squeeze it out of him, have no doubt, doctor.'

We went into a room. 'Here you can see for yourself, Herr Chancellor, the way they started the fire,' said Captain

Goering, pointing out the charred remains of some beautiful oak panelling.

'They hung cloths soaked in petrol over the furniture here and set it alight.'

We strode across another lobby filled with smoke. The police barred the way. 'The candelabra may crash any moment, Herr Chancellor,' said a captain of the police, with his arms outstretched.

By a detour we next reached a part of the building which was actually in flames. Firemen were pouring water into the red mass.

Hitler watched them for a few moments, a savage fury blazing from his pale blue eyes. Then we came upon Herr von Papen, urbane and debonair as ever. Hitler stretched out his hand and uttered the threat against the Communists which I have already quoted. He then turned to Captain Goering. 'Are all the other public buildings safe?' he questioned.

'I have taken every precaution,' answered Captain Goering. 'The police are in the highest state of alarm, and every public building has been specially garrisoned. We are waiting for anything.'

It was then that Hitler turned to me. 'God grant,' he said, 'that this is the work of the Communists. You are witnessing the beginning of a great new epoch in German history. This fire is the beginning.' And then something touched the rhetorical spring in his brain. 'You see this flaming building,' he said, sweeping his hand dramatically around him. 'If this Communist spirit got hold of Europe for but two months it would be all aflame like this building.'

By 12.30 the fire had been got under control. Two Press rooms were still alight, but there was no danger of the fire spreading. Although the glass of the dome has burst and crashed to the ground the dome still stands.

So far it has not been possible to disentangle the charred debris and see whether the bodies of any incendiaries, who may have been trapped in the building, are among it.

At the Prussian Ministry of the Interior a special meeting was called late tonight by Captain Goering to discuss measures to be taken as a consequence of the fire.

The entire district from the Brandenburg Gate, on the west, to the River Spree, on the east, is isolated tonight by numerous cordons of police.

Within days of the fire the arrests of Communists began. They continued over the next few months with one-third of the *Reichstag* representatives disappearing and by July the Communists were admitting that over 11,000 of their members had been arrested. This would seem to be a conservative estimate and the Nazis claimed that they had disposed of many more than 11,000 Communists. Still others disappeared from the political scene, either into hiding or in to exile outside of Germany.

In response to the *Reichstag* fire the following emergency measures were decreed on 28 February:

Article 1. In virtue of paragraph 2, Article 48*, of the German Constitution, the following is decreed as a defensive measure against communist acts of violence, endangering the state:

Sections 114, 115, 117, 118, 123, 124, and 153 of the Constitution of the German Reich are suspended until further notice. Thus, restrictions on personal liberty [114], on the right of free expression of opinion, including freedom of the press [118], on the right of assembly and the right of association [124], and violations of the privacy of postal, telegraphic and telephonic communications [117], and warrants for house-searches [115], orders for confiscation as well as restrictions on property [153], are also permissible beyond the legal limits otherwise prescribed.

In addition to van der Lubbe, four other Communists were arrested and accused of starting the *Reichstag* fire. One of the defendants was Ernst Torgler, who had been one of the last people to leave the building that night. The other three were Bulgarians – Georgi

Article 48 of the German Constitution of 11 August, 1919:
If public safety and order in Germany are materially disturbed or endangered, the President may take the necessary measures to restore public safety and order, and, if necessary, to intervene with the help of the armed forces. To this end he may temporarily suspend, in whole or in part, the fundamental rights established in Articles 114, 115, 117, 118, 123, 124, and 153.

Dimitrov, a forty-six-year-old writer, Blagoi Popov, a student aged thirty, and Vassili Tanev, a thirty-five-year-old shoemaker. Everyone agreed that the fire had been too well planned and executed for it to have been the work of only one man.

The trial began on 21 September before the Fourth Penal Chamber of the Supreme Court in Leipzig, with Dr Wilhelm Bünger in charge, and continued for fifty-seven days until 23 December 1933. In spite of all the evidence that it had been the work of several people, only Marinus van der Lubbe was convicted of the crime, the others all being acquitted. Van der Lubbe was beheaded on 10 January 1934, three days before his twenty-fifth birthday. He was buried in Leipzig against the wishes of his family, who wanted to take his body back to Holland for burial.

Hitler was furious with the verdict. He had wanted clear-cut communist guilt to be established. He decided that in future all cases of treason were to be removed from the jurisdiction of the Supreme Court to be tried at a new facility, the People's Court, which would be manned entirely by members of the NSDAP.

There was a strong suspicion that the fire itself had been the work of the NSDAP. There was even evidence to suggest that Hermann Goering had been heard to say that there was only one person who knew the truth about the fire and that person was him, as he was the one who had started it. Whether or not he was claiming to have actually lit the match is not known. He is more likely to have been claiming that he was responsible for having planned the whole affair. Henry Gilfond said of the Nuremberg trials in his book *The Reichstag Fire*:

> Gestapo Chief Rudolf Diels and Goering's Secretary of State Gritzbach testified that Goering knew the Reichstag was to be set afire. They also said that well in advance of the arson he had prepared lists of the people he was going to arrest.

Goering, of course, denied the charge but no one has been able to ascertain the actual truth of what happened that night. It is most likely to have been a Nazi plot, both to help Hitler eliminate his communist opponents and to enable him to invoke Article 48 of the constitution.

Whatever the truth of the *Reichstag* fire it did bring Hitler the result he wanted. When the elections were held on 5 March the

Nazis gained another ninety-two seats, bringing their total to 288. Their actual votes increased from 11,737,000 to 17,277,200 or forty-four per cent of the total votes cast. With support from the Nationalists, Hitler had his desired majority – fifty-two per cent.

The arrests of the Communists continued and on 20 March Heinrich Himmler announced that a camp to house these political prisoners had been set up. It was located on the River Amper, twelve miles north-west of Munich and was called Dachau. This was quickly followed by two other camps – Buchenwald, in central Germany, located on a hill four miles from the city of Weimar, and Sachsenhausen, near Oranienberg, to the north of Berlin. Over the twelve-year Nazi reign many more such camps would be established.

Following on from the Article 48 decree, Hitler managed to push through an act in the *Reichstag* called *Gesetz zur Erhebung der Not von Volk und Reich* (The law to remove the Distress of People and State or Enabling Act). This change in the Weimar constitution was passed on 24 March 1933. It is worth examining the text of the Act here, as it formed the basis for Hitler's reign of terror. The Act came into force with a vote of 441 to 94 and states:

> The Reichstag has resolved the following law, which is, with the approval of the National Council, herewith promulgated, after it has been established that the requirements have been satisfied for legislation altering the Constitution.
>
> Article 1. National laws can be enacted by the National Cabinet as well as in accordance with the procedure established in the Constitution. This applies also to the laws referred to in Article 85, paragraph 2, and in Article 87 of the Constitution.
>
> Article 2. The national laws enacted by the National Cabinet may deviate from the Constitution so far as they do not affect the position of the Reichstag and National Council. The powers of the President remain undisturbed.
>
> Article 3. The national laws enacted by the National Cabinet are prepared by the Chancellor and published in the *Reichsgesetzblatt*. They come into effect, unless otherwise specified, upon the day following their publication. Articles

68 to 77 of the Constitution do not apply to the laws enacted by the National Cabinet.

Article 4. Treaties of the Reich with foreign states which concern matters of national legislation do not require the consent of the bodies participating in legislation. The National Cabinet is empowered to issue the necessary provisions for the execution of these treaties.

Article 5. This law becomes effective on the day of publication. It becomes invalid on April 1, 1937; it further becomes invalid when the present National Cabinet is replaced by another.

Berlin, March 24, 1933

(Signed)
Reich President – Von Hindenburg
Reich Chancellor – Adolf Hitler
Reich Minister of the Interior – Frick
Reich Minister for Foreign Affairs – Baron von Neurath
Reich Minister of Finance – Count Schwerin von Krosigk

In effect this gave Hitler the power to do whatever he wanted.

Chapter Four

Dictatorship

During the remainder of 1933 the new government was very busy doing the groundwork for the eventual complete domination of the country by the NSDAP.

In March Hitler appointed Josef Goebbels as *Reichsminister für Volkserklärung und Propaganda* (Reich Minister for Public Enlightenment and Propaganda). He was given the task of indoctrinating every element of national life with Nazi ideals – films, theatre, music, the press, books, employment, church, sport and the family. Goebbels had learned his trade from observing American advertising techniques and became almost as hypnotic a speaker as Hitler himself. He saved his most vicious attacks for the Jews. The majority of the German population loved it.

Encouraged by Goebbels, groups of young people stormed libraries and bookshops on 10 May and threw piles of books written by Jews and Communists and other so called undesirables out into the street. Huge bonfires were built and, surrounded by groups of supporters giving the Nazi salute, the books were burnt. It is interesting to note that, although Goebbels was happy to promote such behaviour and, it seems, the German population was happy to accept it, when it came to the reporting of this book burning, Goebbels told the press to play down the event, not wanting to incur adverse publicity abroad. In spite of the 'dumbing down' the foreign press did pick up the story and declared the book burning to be barbaric. The German poet Heinrich Heine had prophetically declared in 1823, '*Dort, wo man Bücher verbrennt, verbrennt man auch am Ende Menschen*' (Where one burns books, in the end one will also burn people). But very few Germans cared about what Heine had said; anyway he was a Jew.

At the beginning of May Hitler banned all trade unions and within a matter of days Nazi forces had occupied the offices of 169 trades unions and brought them all under NSDAP control. On the same day as the book burning, 10 May, Hitler announced the formation of the *Deutsche Arbeitsfront* (German Labour Front). All German workers, whatever their trade or level of responsibility, had to belong to the Labour Front. It was a huge organization with over 20 million members and it sought to promote Nazi ideals within the labour force. Workers were given financial assistance, education and leisure facilities all financed by the organization. Nazi party members were rewarded with holidays, paid for by the *Deutsche Arbeitsfront*. After years of financial instability and widespread unemployment, many German workers felt that they were at last being looked after by the government.

A massive building programme addressed some of the unemployment problems. The positive side to this policy was that Germany gained an impressive network of *autobahnen* or motorways, which, although not planned exclusively for the people but rather for troop movements and the transport of supplies, benefited them nonetheless. The building of concentration camps to house political opponents, Jews, gypsies and other 'undesirables', also gave employment to a large number of workers.

Following the takeover of the trade unions and their subsequent absorption into the *Deutsche Arbeitsfront*, the Nazis next targeted political parties. Throughout June and July 1933 all other parties were closed down and membership of any except the NSDAP was banned. The *Sozialdemokratische Partei Deutschlands* (German Social Democratic party) refused to be disbanded and went into exile in the Czechoslovakian capital, Prague. Thousands of members of other parties were arrested and thrown into concentration camps.

Believing that the way to ensure total obedience to the state was to target young people at their most formative stage, a youth group called *Hitler Jugend* (Hitler Youth) had been set up in the 1920s by a party member called Kurt Gruber. In 1926 Rudolf Hess suggested the name *Hitler Jugend*, and that same year control of the organization was given to Franz von Pfeffer of the SA. In 1930 Ernst

33

Roehm took over responsibility for the programme and it remained with him until the entire youth programme passed to Baldur von Schirach in 1934.

Prior to joining the Hitler Youth an investigation was made of each young boy and his family to ensure that the child was worthy of belonging to the group. The investigation concerning race was particularly stringent. Having been deemed acceptable, young boys between the ages of ten and thirteen years were accepted into the *Jungvolk* (Young People) each year on 20 April, Adolf Hitler's birthday. Upon reaching the age of fourteen years they transferred to the Hitler Youth itself and remained there until eighteen when they became adult members of the SA.

Hitler often spoke of the virtues of German youth and his hopes for their future and set out these hopes in speeches such as the following:

> We older ones are used up. Yes, we are old already . . . We are cowardly and sentimental . . . But my magnificent youngsters? Are there finer ones anywhere in the world? Look at these young men and boys. What material! With them I can make a new world. . . . A violently active, dominating, intrepid, brutal youth – that is what I am after. Youth must be all those things. It must be indifferent to pain. There must be no weakness or tenderness in it. I want to see once more in its eyes the gleam of pride and independence of the beast of prey. . . . I intend to have an athletic youth – that is the first and the chief thing . . . I will have no intellectual training. Knowledge is ruin to my young men.

Girls also had an organization to which they could belong. This was the *Bund Deutscher Mädel* (League of German Girls) and was run along the same lines as the Hitler Youth. Girls between the ages of ten and fourteen years were enrolled in the *Jungmädel* (Young Girls) and transferred to the *Bund Deutscher Mädel* proper at the age of fifteen. They remained members until they were twenty-one years old. While the boys were instilled with discipline, obedience to the state and complete loyalty to Adolf Hitler above all others including their own families, the girls were prepared for motherhood and domestic tasks. The boys wore a uniform similar to that of the Boy Scouts while the girls wore white blouses, navy blue skirts and brown jackets. They were encouraged to grow their hair and wear it in two plaits, in much the same way as German peasant women wore their hair.

Strangely enough, children didn't find these youth organizations at all restrictive. They had a lot of fun and went hiking and camping. There was a big emphasis on physical fitness. They had their own flags and their own songs, such as this Hitler Youth anthem entitled *Vorwärts, Vorwärts* (Forwards, Forwards):

Forwards! Forwards! The bright trumpets flare.
Forwards! Forwards! Youth knows no dangers.
Germany, you will shine brightly,
though we may perish.
Forwards! Forwards! The bright trumpets flare.
Forwards! Forwards! Youth knows no dangers.
Is the goal still so high?
Youth is up to it, though!

(Refrain):

Our flag flutters before us.
In the future we'll pull man for man.
We march for Hitler through night and through hardship
With the flag of youth for freedom and sustenance.
Our flag flutters before us.
Our flag represents the new era.
And the flag carries us into eternity!
Yes, the flag is greater than death!

Youth! Youth! We are the future soldiers.
Youth! Youth! The doers of coming deeds.
Yes, though our fists fall
On those who oppose us.
Youth! Youth! We are the future soldiers.
Youth! Youth! The doers of coming deeds.
Führer, we belong to you,
We are comrades to you!

Both boys and girls were taught that their main responsibility was to the state and not to their parents. For some children rebelling against parental authority this was a godsend. More sinister was the way in which they were encouraged to betray their families if they believed that they were not following Nazi party doctrine.

Erika Mann, in her book *School for Barbarians*, described what it was like to be a child in Nazi Germany:

> Every child says 'Heil Hitler!' from 50 to 150 times a day, immeasurably more often than the old neutral greetings. The formula is required by law; if you meet a friend on the way to school, you say it; study periods are opened and closed with 'Heil Hitler!' 'Heil Hitler!' says the postman, the street-car conductor, the girl who sells you notebooks at the stationery store; and if your parents' first words when you come home to lunch are not 'Heil Hitler!' they have been guilty of a punishable offence and can be denounced. 'Heil Hitler!' they shout in the Jungvolk and Hitler Youth. 'Heil Hitler!' cry the girls in the League of German Girls. Your evening prayers must close with 'Heil Hitler!' if you take your devotions seriously.
>
> Officially, when you say hello to your superiors in school or in a group, the words are accompanied by the act of throwing the right arm high; but an unofficial greeting among equals requires only a comparatively lax lifting of the forearm, with the fingers closed and pointing forward. This Hitler greeting, this 'German' greeting, repeated countless times from morning to bedtime, stamps the whole day.
>
> 'Heil' really means salvation and used to be applied to relations between man and his God; one would speak of *ewiges Heil* (eternal salvation), and the adjective 'holy' derives from the noun. But now there is the new usage . . .
>
> You leave the house in the morning, 'Heil Hitler' on your lips; and on the stairs of your apartment house you meet the *Blockwart*. A person of great importance and some danger, the *Blockwart* has been installed by the government as a Nazi guardian. He controls the block, reporting on it regularly, checking up on the behaviour of its residents. It's worth it to face right about, military style, and to give him the 'big' Hitler salute, with the right arm as high as it will go. All the way down the street the flags are waving, every window coloured with red banners, and the black swastika in the middle of

each. You don't stop to ask why; it's bound to be some national event. Not a week passes without an occasion on which families are given one reason or another to hang out the swastikas. . . .

The German child breathes this air. There is no other condition wherever Nazis are in power; and here in Germany they do rule everywhere, and their supremacy over the German child, as he learns and eats, marches, grows up, breathes, is complete.

By December 1936 membership of the Hitler Youth and its associated organizations became compulsory. It was regarded as being far more important than any formal education and probably produced a whole generation of youngsters who had no idea of anything except Nazi ideology and the Nazi way of life.

Hitler realized that Nazi values, including anti-Semitism, might incur opposition from the largest established church groups in Germany. Christians after all worshipped Jesus Christ, a Jew. Germany was a country of mixed denominations with the majority group, the Protestants, being concentrated mainly in the northern part of the country and the Roman Catholics in the south. The Protestant churches generally accepted the rise of the Nazis without protest. The NSDAP worked hard to perpetuate the belief that they would govern the country in a way of which the Church would approve. In spite of the fact that Germany had become an anti-Semitic, one-party state that imprisoned its opponents in concentration camps, the Protestant Churches, as a whole, initially displayed no animosity towards the Nazis.

Having always been in a minority and, therefore, generally in opposition to previous governments, the Catholic Church still had to be won over to Nazism. It exerted an influence over its members not only in their religious lives but also in education, politics and labour organizations. Seeking to eliminate Church opposition without antagonizing German Catholics, Hitler sent his Vice Chancellor, Franz von Papen to negotiate a treaty with Rome to ensure that relations between the two parties remained amicable. Discussions went on between von Papen and the Papal Secretary of State, Eugenio Pacelli, from April to July of 1933. Finally on

20 July von Papen and Pacelli signed the treaty in a ceremony in the Vatican. In essence the treaty, which was known as the Concordat of 1933, guaranteed the Catholic Church freedom to administer its own affairs and granted its members the right to worship as they saw fit. The Church, in return, gave the government an assurance that it would not interfere in German politics.

It is debateable whether or not the Vatican ever truly believed, or merely just hoped, that the treaty would safeguard the interests of the Church or its German members. Since the fall of the Nazi regime there have been fiercely opposing views about the role of Eugenio Pacelli who, after the death of Pope Pius XI, became Pope Pius XII. The debate about whether he was pro- or anti-Nazi continues to this day.

The Concordat gave Hitler a great advantage in world opinion. He was perceived as being a tolerant, open-minded leader. At that time, however, the world was not to know that Hitler's word was just so much hot air and that, although he had made guarantees, he was unlikely to abide by any of them.

Although many Protestant priests had supported the rise of Nazism, some became wary when they learnt of the Nazi doctrine of Positive Christianity. Alfred Rosenberg, editor of the *Völkischer Beobachter*, had put forward this doctrine even before the Nazis came to power. It broadly rejected all forms of traditional Christian belief and instead promoted the purification of the German Nordic race and the harmonization of belief in Christ with the laws of '*Blut und Boden*' (blood and soil). This was the theory that life should revolve around the land and that intellectual pursuits were of less importance. City workers were encouraged to devote some of their free time to working with farmers in the country as a way of pursuing the laws. The aim of Positive Christianity was to restore pagan values and traditions and promote the spirit of the hero rather than Jesus Christ and, once Hitler had been confirmed as German Chancellor, the *Deutsche Glaubensbewegung* (German Faith Movement) came into being and promoted its values.

Having restructured the constitution, banned all other political parties and trade unions and silenced the church, Hitler next turned his attention momentarily to foreign policy.

Germany had not been allowed to join the League of Nations when it was set up in 1920 and did not gain membership until

8 September 1926 when she became a permanent Member of the Council. On 14 October 1933, no doubt with the idea of a future war in mind, she withdrew from the Conference for the Reduction and Limitation of Armaments and, on 21 October, gave notice of her intention to withdraw totally from the League itself. This withdrawal came into effect two years later on 21 October 1935.

Slowly but surely the stage was being set not only for Nazi domination of Germany but of the world.

By the middle of 1934, having eliminated virtually all outside opposition to his policies, Hitler turned his attention to what he regarded as the stumbling blocks within the Nazi organization. In a purge that became known as *Die Nacht der langen Messer* (Night of the Long Knives), he set about removing powerful elements of the SA (Storm Troopers).

Ernst Roehm, leader of the SA, had been a staunch supporter and friend to Adolf Hitler. To a large extent it was through his efforts that Hitler had come to power. The SA under Roehm's leadership had provided the security force that had disposed of many of the enemies of the Nazi party and he had built it up to an organization of about 3 million members. Composed largely of petty criminals and bullies, it had, through physical violence, fought off challenges from other political parties and had cleared the way for Hitler to establish his Nazi dictatorship.

Roehm was hopeful that one day his organization would be absorbed into the regular army, no doubt with him still at its head. He felt that the SA had earned that right. Unfortunately for him not all NSDAP supporters were as grateful to him as Hitler seemed to be and the high command of the army was horrified at the thought of having to accept a bunch of thugs in their midst. Furthermore the NSDAP was always in need of funds and the wealthy industrialists who could provide that financial aid were diametrically opposed to the socialist Storm Troopers and their leader, Ernst Roehm. Hitler had always been aware of the need to balance the nationalists' view with that of the socialists in a party that called itself 'National Socialists', but found his task more and more difficult because Roehm had formed an alliance with the left-wing Gregor Strasser, former mentor of Josef Goebbels, and was pushing for a second revolution to gain ultimate power for the workers. Hitler tried to reason with his friend, telling him of the delicate balance that he had to maintain between the different factions, but Roehm would not be silenced.

Taking a pragmatic approach, Hitler decided, along with his colleagues Goering, Goebbels and Himmler, that Roehm had to be permanently silenced. On 29 June Hitler called SA *Obergruppenführer* Viktor Lutze and informed him that he had been promoted to *Stabchef* (Chief of Staff) of the SA. Hitler was staying at Bad Godesberg at the time and he then received a visit from Goebbels who had arrived from Berlin. He told Hitler that the Berlin chief of the SA, Karl Ernst, was, at that very minute, planning a coup against the government. This was quite clearly a lie and was not believed for a moment. Ernst had, a few days before, got married and was on his way to board a ship in Bremen that would take him to Madeira for his honeymoon. The Nazi hierarchy knew that the story of the coup was a complete fabrication because Goering had attended Karl Ernst's wedding! It did, however, give Hitler the excuse he had been looking for to silence the left-wing elements of the SA.

In the middle of the night of 30 June Hitler flew to Munich and, in the company of Goebbels and the new SA Chief, Viktor Lutze, went directly to the Ministry of the Interior. Having alerted Goering in Berlin, the bloodbath in Munich, the political heartland of the nation, began. Prominent SA members were arrested and taken to Stadelheim prison. Hitler, meanwhile, had gone on to Bad Wiessee, where Ernst Roehm was attending a conference of SA leaders. Hammering on his hotel door, Hitler woke his friend and demanded entry into his room. Having gained access, Hitler told the astounded Roehm that he was being arrested and would be taken back to Munich.

In Berlin the same thing was happening. Scores of prominent SA members had been arrested and taken to the Lichtefelde SS Cadet School barracks where they were shot, four at a time. They did not know why this was happening. Some even swore allegiance to Hitler, thinking that he was being overthrown; most did not realize that he was responsible for their fate.

Roehm was put in a cell in Munich and, on Hitler's orders, was given a gun so that he could 'do the honourable thing' and shoot himself. He was given ten minutes to commit suicide. Refusing to believe that this directive had come from Hitler, Roehm asked to see him but was shot while still in his cell, his request unfulfilled.

It was not just SA leaders that were killed that night. Former Chancellor Kurt von Schleicher and his wife were also shot, along with some of Vice Chancellor Franz von Papen's close colleagues, including the head of the Press Office, Herbert von Bose. Other victims were Gregor Strasser and Gustav Ritter von Kahr, who had figured heavily in the failed 1923 *putsch*. He was not shot but beaten to death, his body being dumped in a swamp. Karl Ernst had the shortest honeymoon on record when he was dragged from the ship that was about to sail for Madeira and taken back to Berlin and shot.

It is believed that about 200 people were executed during the night of 30 June 1934. The event sent shockwaves throughout Germany. The public were horrified by the bloodthirsty way in which these people had been dispatched.

Although Hitler had always boasted of being law-abiding, he was now showing himself in his true colours, having a complete disregard for the law. In spite of their horror at the methods used to get rid of so many SA figures, there can have been very few who mourned their loss. The SA had become known as a band of vicious thugs and was feared by the majority of the population.

For a short while after the Night of the Long Knives Hitler was concerned about the reaction of the army. While most senior army officers had done nothing to stop the purge, they were concerned about its ferocity and Hitler feared a backlash. His fears proved to be unfounded and he returned to Berlin ten days later. On 13 July he delivered a speech to the *Reichstag* outlining what had happened on the night of 30 June. He claimed that there had been four disruptive influences who were plotting against his government; Communists supported by Jews, left-wing revolutionaries led by Ernst Roehm, leaders from the old, banned political parties and rumour-mongers of whom he said:

> Though worthless in themselves, they are, nevertheless, dangerous because they are veritable bacillus-carriers of unrest and uncertainty, of rumours, assertions, lies and suspicion, of slanders and fear.

The hypocrisy of this statement is astounding. Hitler finished his speech by saying;

In this hour I was responsible for the fate of the German people, and therefore I became the supreme justiciar of the German people. Everyone must know that in all future time that if he raises his hand to strike at the state, then certain death will be his lot.

It was a bleak warning of what was to come.

Chapter Five

The Death of Democracy

Paul Ludwig Hans Anton von Beneckendorff und Hindenburg became President of Germany in 1925 following the death of President Friedrich Ebert. Born in 1847, von Hindenburg had a successful army career before retiring in 1911 at the age of sixty-four. With the advent of war he was persuaded to come out of retirement and served throughout the First World War with distinction, retiring once more in 1918.

When he became President, von Hindenburg declared that he intended to be totally impartial. He was, however, a part of the German aristocracy and as such, could not help but be influenced by his peers. In 1927, on his eightieth birthday, von Hindenburg was presented with the estate of Neudeck, in Rosenberg, East Prussia, by the members of the Nationalist ex-servicemen's organization, the *Stahlhelm* (Steel Helmet), of which he was the president. In order to avoid paying taxes the property was registered in the name of his son Oskar.

Von Hindenburg had no time at all for Hitler, who he described as 'that Austrian corporal'. He thought him uncouth and ignorant and said that when he spoke he sounded like a peasant. It was he, however, who appointed Hitler Chancellor in 1933. By the time Hitler became Chancellor, von Hindenburg was eighty-six years old and rapidly losing his faculties. Hitler knew about the tax evasion on the property in East Prussia, so Oskar persuaded his father to make Hitler Chancellor because he was frightened that the latter might disclose what he knew and discredit both him and his father.

43

It became clear in the summer of 1934 that von Hindenburg did not have long to live. He died on 2 August, just two months before his eighty-seventh birthday and on the same day Hitler produced a new oath of loyalty, obviously already prepared for this occasion, which Werner von Blomberg, Minister of Defence, ordered the German armed forces to take. It stated:

> I swear by Almighty God this sacred oath:
> I will render unconditional obedience to the Führer of the German Reich and people, Adolf Hitler, Supreme Commander of the Wehmacht, and, as a brave soldier, I will be ready to stake my life for this oath at any time.

Upon von Hindenburg's death Adolf Hitler assumed his mantle, calling himself, not *Reichspräsident*, but *Führer* and *Reichskanzler*. Although Hitler adopted the title of *Führer* to show that his position was greater than that of any of his predecessors, his official explanation was that the title of *Reichspräsident* should die with its rightful owner, Paul von Hindenburg. He further decreed that his assumption of presidential powers should be sanctioned by a vote of the people on 19 August. On 18 August Oskar von Hindenburg made a radio broadcast on behalf of Hitler in which he said:

> The late Reich President and General Field Marshal, having concluded his compact with Adolf Hitler on January 30 of last year and having confirmed it during that sacred hour in the *Garnisonkirche* at Potsdam on March 21, always supported Adolf Hitler and approved all the important decisions of Hitler's Government. . . . My father himself saw in Adolf Hitler his direct successor as head of the German state, and I am acting in accordance with my father's wishes when I call upon all German men and women to vote for the transfer of my father's office to the Führer and Chancellor.

This piece of treachery to the memory of his illustrious father must have had the old man turning in his grave but it did ensure the safety of his son, who lived until 1960.

With the final vestige of democracy gone, Hitler had achieved his goal. He was the ruler of the Reich, which he declared would last for 1,000 years. Josef Goebbels, Propaganda Minister, had begun a programme of 'Führer worship'. In promoting his leader to the German people he also had to compete with other high-ranking Nazis in the quest to become chief sycophant. Had it not been so serious, this Führer worship would have been quite amusing. It is hard to imagine at a distance of nearly seventy years how so many grown men could have sucked up, in such a ridiculous fashion, to the little Austrian corporal. He was described by Goebbels as being 'like a great star above us.' He also declared that, 'We are witnessing the greatest miracle in history. A genius is building the world.' Rudolf Hess was of the opinion that, 'Clearly the Führer has divine blessing'. Catholic Cardinal Michael von Faulhaber believed that Hitler had 'greater diplomatic finesse and social grace than a true-born king', while one leader of the *Deutsche Glaubensbewegung* (German Faith Movement), the organization set up to replace the established church, declared, 'God has manifested himself not in Jesus Christ but in Adolf Hitler'. It is difficult to reconcile these opinions with those of President von Hindenburg who thought him an ignorant, uncouth peasant.

Children were taught to worship Hitler, particularly those who belonged to the Hitler Youth, whose songs and posters extolled his virtues. It is also said that women found him very attractive. Quite what was wrong with large numbers of German women in the 1930s and 1940s is unclear.

Photos and posters of Hitler appeared all over Germany. Wherever one looked Hitler's cold stare gazed down on the people. It was almost as if the posters were put in prominent places to remind the population to adhere to party doctrine and to prove to them that, wherever they were, he could see what they were doing. In a sense he could see because he had spies everywhere keeping an eye open for dissenters, and because the population were taught that it was their moral duty to report to the authorities any resistance to Hitler and the Nazis. It is difficult to understand whether ordinary Germans who did betray their families and friends did so out of conviction or fear. It would certainly appear that it is in the German nature to be obedient to the laws of the land, but, as will be shown in Part Two, there were many honest, decent Germans who, in spite of this national characteristic, felt unable to abide by the dictates of this corrupt regime.

From the moment that Hitler gained complete control over Germany until the beginning of the Second World War the Nazis set about promoting their aims with vigour.

The Treaty of Versailles had stripped the German people of their national pride, their wealth and their standing with the rest of the world. Hitler was determined to restore that pride and make Germany into a powerful state.

Erhard Milch, founder of the civilian airline *Deutsche Luft Hansa*, (which changed its name in January 1934 to *Lufthansa*, a name that it still retains) had long been suspected of using the airline as a way to reintroduce a German air force. This was confirmed on 9 March 1935 when it was announced in Berlin that the Luftwaffe had been formed and had been put under the control of Hermann Goering. The new organization already had 11,000 men and 1,800 aircraft. New types of military aircraft were on the drawing board, designed by manufacturers such as Heinkel, Messerschmitt, Junkers and Dornier. This was blatantly against Article 199 of the Treaty of Versailles, which stated:

> Within two months from the coming into force of the present Treaty the personnel of air forces on the rolls of the German land and sea forces shall be demobilized. Up to 1 October 1919, however, Germany may keep and maintain a total number of one thousand men, including officers, for the whole of the cadres and personnel, flying and non-flying, of all formations and establishments.

There was also a clause which banned the manufacture of aircraft, parts of aircraft or engines anywhere within German territory.

Nine days after the announcement of the formation of the Luftwaffe conscription was reintroduced, again in complete contravention of the Treaty of Versailles. Article 173 delared that:

> Universal compulsory military service shall be abolished in Germany. The German Army may only be constituted and recruited by means of voluntary enlistment.

Almost a year later, on 7 March 1936, Hitler sent his troops into the Rhineland, this time against Articles 42, 43 and 44 of the Treaty:

Article 42.
Germany is forbidden to maintain or construct any fortifications either on the left bank of the Rhine or on the right bank to the west of a line drawn 50 kilometres to the east of the Rhine.
Article 43.
In the area defined above the maintenance and the assembly of armed forces, either permanently or temporarily, and military manoeuvres of any kind, as well as the upkeep of all permanent works for mobilization, are in the same way forbidden.
Article 44.
In case Germany violates in any manner whatever the provisions of Articles 42 and 43, she shall be regarded as committing a hostile act against the Powers signatory of the present Treaty and as calculated to disturb the peace of the world.

Finding that the Allied powers did nothing to stop him gave Hitler confidence to continue doing exactly as he pleased. Their bluff had been called and they had been found wanting.

While, in the past, Nazi anti-Semitism had manifested itself in offensive press articles, the burning of books by Jewish authors, the boycotting of Jewish shops and businesses and other similar activities, it took on a new and more sinister form in the late summer of 1935 when, on 15 September, the Nuremberg Laws came into being. These stripped Jews of their citizenship and severely restricted the way in which they were able to live their lives.

In order to maintain and promote racial purity, laws had also been passed in the early days of Hitler's government enabling the state to sterilize individuals of childbearing age who had hereditary diseases such as Huntington's chorea, schizophrenia, congenital epilepsy, deafness, blindness or anyone with other physical or mental 'defects'. Not only were people sterilized to stop the spread of hereditary diseases, some of those who had already been born were sent to special 'clinics' to be killed, usually by lethal injections. Dr Pfannmüller, who also killed children by slow starvation, ran one such clinic at Eglfing-Haar, near Munich. His explanation for this shameful practise was simple:

As a National Socialist, these creatures represent for me only a burden on our nation. We do not kill by poison injections because foreign newspapers and certain gentlemen from Switzerland – the Red Cross – would get new material for their propaganda. Our method is much simpler and more natural.

How on earth could anyone, especially a doctor, describe killing a child at all, let alone by starvation, as being 'natural'?

By December 1935 SS leader Heinrich Himmler had set up an organization called *Lebensborn*, (Spring of Life). A number of nursing homes, initially for the use of wives of SS officers when having their babies, were set up. Later on they served as homes for the breeding of 'racially pure' children. The nursing homes were luxurious places and the women were very well treated and well fed. Fathers were not allowed on the premises in order to avoid *Lebensborn* homes being regarded as SS brothels.

German girls were told that it was a duty and an honour to provide the Reich, and the Führer, with racially pure babies. They were encouraged to become pregnant by SS officers whether or not they were married to each other. Married SS officers were also encouraged to have children by other women and if they and their wives, or the mothers, did not want to bring up the children they could be handed over to the SS to be looked after in the homes especially set up for the purpose. The children were given a silver mug and spoon by the SS at birth and on each birthday they received candles manufactured by inmates of Dachau concentration camp. For every fourth child that a German woman produced she would receive a silver candlestick that was engraved, 'You are only a link in the clan's endless chain'.

Many mothers of boys called their sons Heinrich after Heinrich Himmler, who was said to be delighted at having so many 'godsons' and it was believed to be such an honour to produce a child for the Führer that some mothers refused any painkillers while in labour, preferring to gaze at a picture of Hitler instead.

Although large numbers of young girls also participated in this programme, by the end of the 1930s it was felt that not enough Aryan babies were being born and the SS stepped up the *Lebensborn* programme in a disgusting manner.

Misguided though they may have been, at least most of the women participating in this sordid programme did so willingly. In 1939, however, it was decided to kidnap racially pure children from other countries and bring them into the *Lebensborn* programme. The children were usually very young as it was thought to be easier to get them to adapt to the Nazi way of life than if they were older. Consequently most kidnapped children were under six years of age when they were forcibly removed from their parents and taken back to Germany to be re-educated and finally placed with SS families for adoption. From the start they were lied to and were told that their parents did not want them. It is hard to imagine how unhappy these poor little ones would have been to have been separated from their parents and siblings, and harder still to understand how any adult could make them suffer in this way. Those children who proved to be too difficult to handle were sent, not back to their parents, but to camps to be murdered.

When Czech resistance fighters in Prague killed Deputy Protector of Bohemia and Moravia, Reinhard Heydrich, in 1942, the tiny village of Lidice was razed to the ground in retaliation. Ninety-one children from Lidice were taken to Germany as part of the *Lebensborn* programme; all the others who did not come up to Nazi Aryan standards were murdered, along with their families.

By the time the Nazi reign of terror was finally at an end, it was estimated that around a quarter of a million children had been forcibly removed from their homes and sent to Germany. Only a small number of them, perhaps 25,000, were ever returned to their parents.

While no right-minded person could support the barbaric ways in which the Nazis sought to perpetuate the Aryan race, it is perhaps worth noting that the Germans were not the only people to believe in white supremacy. The Eugenics movement, which flourished in the 1920s and 1930s, promoted the ideas of racial superiority and inferiority and the compulsory sterilization of handicapped people. Margaret Sanger, the American woman who founded Planned Parenthood said in 1934:

Feeble-minded persons, habitual congenital criminals, those afflicted with inheritable diseases, and others found biologically unfit should be sterilized or in cases of doubt be isolated

49

so as to prevent the perpetuation of their afflictions by breeding.

She also said:

> Those least fit to carry on the race are increasing most rapidly. . . . Funds that should be used to raise the standard of our civilization are diverted to maintenance of those who should never have been born.

Britain also had a Eugenics movement, which dated back to the 1860s, to Charles Darwin's disciple, Francis Galton. Known as the Galton Institute, it exists to this day. The American Society also flourishes, although it no longer calls itself the Eugenics Society, having changed its name in 1973 to the Society for the Study of Social Biology. It is, perhaps, easy to blame all the ills of the world in the 1930s and 1940s on the Nazis, but it should be remembered that the so-called civilized world also had, and still has, its share of deviants.

In 1931 the International Olympic Committee awarded the 1936 Olympic Games to the city of Berlin, a decision that announced to the world that the Germany of the First World War had been forgiven and was being re-admitted to the fold. The Nazi press had criticized the Weimar government for wanting to participate in what they described as a 'Jewish festival', but Hitler saw the Games as a perfect opportunity to show the rest of the world how successful he had been in creating a peaceful, prosperous state. In reality the Games cost money that the country could ill afford, but that was a small price to pay for the prestige that the Games would bring. Part of the fund was raised by the German *Reichspost*, which donated 1 million *Reichsmarks* and imposed a surcharge on special Olympic stamps to raise yet more money. The facilities provided were modern and stylish, guaranteed to provide a favourable impression of the rejuvenated German state.

In order not to offend the representatives of the many nations competing, the Nazis removed their anti-Semitic posters from all public places for the duration of the Games. They also managed to convince two German Jews, both living abroad, to come back to Germany to compete for the Fatherland. Rudi Ball, an ice hockey player agreed to return for the Winter Olympics, which were held in Garmisch-Partenkirchen, but insisted on leaving again the moment they were over. Helene Mayer came from her home in California to represent Germany in the fencing event at which she won a silver medal for her former homeland. It was a propaganda coup for Germany.

Many countries threatened to boycott the Games, but in the end the only one to carry out its threat was the Soviet Union. This was not a specific snub to the Nazis; the Soviet Union had boycotted all previous games and saw no reason to change their views in 1936.

The first gold medal of the Games was won by German shot putter, Hans Woellke, who was invited to Hitler's box to meet the Führer. On the same day the German javelin champion, Tilly Fleischer, won a gold medal and was also invited to meet Hitler. However, Hitler, much as he wanted favourable press coverage, could not bring himself to meet any black athletes and when the black American Jesse Owens won a spectacular total of four gold medals for the 100 metres, 200 metres, 4 x100 metres relay and the long jump, Hitler refused to have anything to do with him and pointedly left the stadium on each occasion. Curiously the crowds went wild with enthusiasm at Owens' performance, which does perhaps suggest that the German people were less enamoured of Hitler's racial theories than he would have wished.

At the end of the Games Germany had won eighty-nine medals, the highest total of any nation and an added bonus for Hitler.

During 1937 and 1938 events moved rapidly towards war. Hitler now wanted to put into operation his plans for more *Lebensraum* (Living Space) into which the German nation could expand.

No doubt hoping to give the Luftwaffe some real practice, Hitler sent aircraft of the Condor Legion to Spain to support General Franco in the Spanish Civil War. On 27 April 1937 the German aircraft bombed the Spanish town of Guernica for over four hours, reducing it to a pile of smoking ruins. It was not a military target but a religious centre and the Luftwaffe later claimed that the bombing had been accidental.

By November 1937 Hitler had announced his intentions towards Czechoslovakia and Austria to the Foreign Minister and the leaders of the military, and the following February he created the

Oberkommando der Wehrmacht, or OKW (High Command of the Armed Forces). Wilhelm Keitel was put in charge of the OKW and Walther von Brauchitsch was named Commander-in-Chief of the army. Hitler himself became Supreme Commander of the entire armed forces.

Inviting Austrian chancellor, Kurt von Schuschnigg, to his Bavarian mountain retreat of Berchtesgaden, Hitler demanded special privileges for Austrian Nazis. Realizing that the aim was really to unite the two countries and aware that he was not able to resist the might of the German Nazi party, von Schuschnigg agreed, hoping that he would be able to stall a takeover of his country. He organized a referendum to find out the opinions of the Austrian population on the question of a union with Germany. Hitler then demanded Schuschnigg's resignation, further demanding that the Austrian Nazi, Artur Seyss-Inquart, replace him. To ensure he got his own way he sent troops to the Austrian border. Schuschnigg capitulated; he cancelled the referendum and resigned. With Seyss-Inquart installed as chancellor, Hermann Goering contacted him and ordered him to send a telegram to the German government requesting an immediate invasion to assist him in 'restoring order' to the nation. The resulting absorption of Austria into the German Reich was known as the *Anschluss* (Union).

Hitler's next target was Czechoslovakia. The Sudetenland was an area of the country that had a majority German population and Hitler wanted it to become part of the Reich. Britain's prime minister, Neville Chamberlain, flew to Germany on 15 September to try to persuade Hitler not to invade Czechoslovakia. A week later he went again to talk to Herr Hitler, as he liked to call him. On 26 September Hitler made a speech in Berlin saying that his last claim to land in Europe would be the Sudetenland. In a disgraceful act of appeasement that convinced Hitler he would have no further opposition from his former enemies, the Munich Agreement was signed three days later. Chamberlain flew back to England proudly waving a worthless piece of paper and declaring 'Peace for our time'. One wonders how the betrayed people of Czechoslovakia regarded this precious peace.

The year ended on a sinister note for the Jews. In 1936 Hitler had given enough respect to international opinion to have his anti-Semitic activities suspended for the duration of the Berlin Olympic

Games. He had even managed to get two German Jews to compete in the Games. Two years later he no longer cared about international opinion. On the night of 9 November 1938, a night that came to be known as *Kristallnacht* (literally Crystal Night, but more commonly known as the Night of Broken Glass), Hitler unleashed a wave of terror against the Jewish people of Germany.

Two days before *Kristallnacht* Ernst von Rath, an official at the German embassy in Paris was murdered by a Polish Jew, Herschel Grynszpan. The Nazis had been looking for an excuse to implement a programme of terror that had long been planned and this murder provided them with a perfect opportunity. Reinhard Heydrich who was, at that time, the head of the *Sicherheitsdienst* or SD (Security Service) ordered the destruction of synagogues and Jewish businesses in Austria and Germany. It is strange that a regime with no sense of humanity, who flagrantly ignored human rights and inflicted unspeakable atrocities on so many of its nationals, should have felt that it needed a valid excuse for its behaviour on *Kristallnacht*.

In a fifteen-hour wave of terror 177 synagogues were destroyed, 101 by fire and the remainder by demolition. Catholic Cardinal Michael von Faulhaber, the same man who had claimed that Hitler had 'greater diplomatic finesse and social grace than a true-born king', disapproved of this destruction and provided a truck in which the Chief Rabbi of Munich was able to remove sacred objects from his synagogue before it was destroyed. Jewish shops were not spared either and a total of 7,500 were attacked and looted. The international press were unanimous in their condemnation of the events of *Kristallnacht*, but the Nazis were unrepentant. The appeasement of Munich had taught them that they didn't have to worry about the opinions of the international community.

In March 1939 Britain and France signed an agreement with Poland guaranteeing to come to its assistance in the case of aggression by Germany. Over the next five months the American President, Franklin D. Roosevelt, appealed twice to Hitler to respect the sovereignty of other nations. Edouard Daladier of France also made appeals to the German dictator, as did the former Papal Secretary of State, Eugenio Pacelli, now Pope Pius XII. It was all to no avail.

At the beginning of August Chief of the *Sicherheitsdienst*, Reinhard Heydrich sent for a young SS officer, *Sturmbannführer* Alfred Naujocks, and gave him a special task. He told him to attack a small German radio station at Gleiwitz on the German-Polish frontier and make it look as if the attack had come from the Polish side of the border. This, he said, would give Hitler an excuse for his proposed attack on Poland. Naujocks did as he was asked on 31 August and one day later Germany invaded Poland. Hitler was confident that nothing would be done to stop him in his quest for *Lebensraum*. The French and British appeasers, Daladier and Chamberlain, realized that the time for talking and compromise was over and on 3 September both nations declared war on Germany.

Part Two

Resistance

Chapter Six

Politics and Workers

The earliest resistance to Hitler and his Nazi regime came from the *Sozialdemokratische Partei Deutschlands* or SPD (Social Democrats) and the *Kommunistische Partei Deutschlands* or KPD (German Communist Party) who, only one day after Hitler became Chancellor, registered their protest at the new government.

The SPD was founded in Germany in 1875 and was based on the ideas of Ferdinand Lasselle and Karl Marx. Lasselle had set up an organization in Leipzig called the Universal German Working Men's Association, which was a forerunner of the SPD.

In the general election of 1877 the SPD won twelve seats. Chancellor Otto von Bismarck was concerned about the growing influence of the new party and in 1878 he banned all its political meetings and publications. The ban extended for the next twelve years, being lifted in 1890, from which time the party expanded rapidly. By 1912 the SPD held 110 seats in the *Reichstag*, becoming the largest political party in Germany.

Towards the end of the First World War some members of the SPD, led by Kurt Eisner, left the party to set up the *Unabhängige Sozialdemokratische Partei Deutschlands* or USPD (German Independent Social Democratic Party), but Eisner was assassinated on 21 February 1919 by a fanatical nationalist, Anton Graf Arco, and the party never really developed after that. It remained a separate entity until it merged with the SPD again in 1922.

At its 1920 conference in Halle a serious split occurred in the SPD, with a number of left-wing members breaking away to join the KPD which had been set up at the end of 1918 by a group of radicals who included Karl Liebknecht, Rosa Luxemburg and Klara Zetkin.

In spite of these setbacks the SPD's support grew. In successive elections for the ten years between 1920 and 1930 the SPD won the largest number of seats in the *Reichstag*, the most successful being at the election of May 1928 when they secured 153 seats. Their closest rival at this election was the Catholic Centre Party, the BVD, with only seventy-eight seats. This was, however, the first election that the NSDAP returned any members to the *Reichstag*, twelve in total, and from that time forward, while their total increased, that of the SPD declined. It was by no means a complete downturn, though. In the last election in which the SPD were able to put forward candidates, March 1933, although the NSDAP came top with 288 seats, they still returned a respectable 120. It was too much competition for Hitler and when the SPD voted against the Enabling Act, he had the excuse he needed to ban the party. The trade unions, who had strong links with the SPD, were banned at the beginning of May, in spite of having sworn allegiance to the new government and in June 1933 the SPD itself ceased to exist within Germany. Most of its leaders were arrested and thrown into prison or one of the new concentration camps. Others fled into exile in countries with liberal asylum laws such as France and Czechoslovakia where they attempted to carry on their fight against the NSDAP.

Otto Wels, the SPD leader, fled to Prague where he helped to set up the SPD in exile. It became known as SOPADE. The organization remained in Czechoslovakia until the situation there became too difficult when it relocated to Paris. Following the Nazi occupation of France SOPADE moved its headquarters to London.

Otto Wels never left mainland Europe with his exiled party. He died in Paris on 16 September 1939, one day after his sixty-sixth birthday. It would be twenty more years before the *Sozialdemokratische Partei Deutschlands* was able to resurrect itself and once more become a leading force in German politics.

On 23 March 2003, the seventieth anniversary of the speech made in the *Reichstag* by Otto Wels against the Enabling Act, the present SPD Chancellor, Gerhard Schröder, remembered his predecessor's impassioned outburst in which he had stated, 'They can take away our freedom and our lives but not our honour' when he said:

> Otto Wels's speech belongs not only to the history of German social democracy but also to the history of Germany as a whole.

The fragments of the SPD that were left in exile quickly formed themselves into groups which produced underground newspapers and articles that were smuggled into Germany through sixteen border points, manned by SOPADE members. They also used these border points to smuggle out reports from within Germany for distribution to the outside world. One such report, which was made in February 1938, states:

> To the extent that the attitude of a whole nation can ever be reduced to a formula, we can assert roughly the following three points:
> 1. Hitler has got the approval of a majority of the nation on two vital questions: he has created work and he has made Germany strong.
> 2. There is widespread dissatisfaction with prevailing conditions, but it affects only the worries of daily life and has not so far led to fundamental hostility to the regime as far as most people are concerned.
> 3. Doubts about the continued survival of the regime are widespread, but so is the sense of helplessness as to what might replace it.
>
> The third point seems to us to be the most significant, as far as the present situation in Germany is concerned. Despite the regime's enlargement of its political and economic power, and despite the far-reaching approval this has gained for it among wide sections of the nation, there is a feeling of uncertainty about the future. Whether this feeling springs from worries about a war, or is a result of shortages, the regime has not so far succeeded in eradicating the idea that its rule may only mark a period of transition. This point is more important, as far as the regime's inner strength is concerned, than the recording of temporary oscillations between satisfaction and dissatisfaction. Nor does it contradict our

observations that the political indifference of the masses is on the increase.

From its very beginning the KPD courted trouble. Following the quelling of the Spartakist Rising, a left-wing rebellion in Berlin, and the short-lived Bavarian Socialist Republic, Karl Liebknecht and Rosa Luxemburg were arrested, imprisoned without trial and executed.

The Russian head of the Comintern, Gregory Zinoviev, addressed the first congress of the KPD and the party was under heavy Russian influence especially throughout the first ten years of its existence. It became the largest Communist party in the world outside of the Soviet Union.

In the presidential elections of March 1932 the KPD put forward its leader, Ernst Thälmann, as a candidate. His slogan for the election was 'Whoever votes for Hindenburg, votes for Hitler; whoever votes for Hitler, votes for war'. Thälmann gained 13.2 per cent of the votes compared with Hitler's 30.1 per cent and von Hindenburg's 49.6 per cent. Because no one had a clear majority another election was held in which Hindenburg won with 53 per cent and Hitler increased his total to 36.8 per cent.

In the years since its establishment, the KPD was successful in gaining seats in the *Reichstag* in successive elections, attaining the highest number, 100, in the elections of November 1932. Klara Zetkin, who had first been elected to the *Reichstag* in 1920, also won a seat in 1932 and, being the oldest member of the *Reichstag* aged seventy-five years, she was entitled to make a speech at the first session of parliament. In her speech she strongly rejected the policies of the upcoming Nazi party and severely criticized the NSDAP leader, Adolf Hitler.

In spite of the relatively high level of support that the KPD received from the German people, by the time that Hitler had been Chancellor for only a few weeks it had virtually ceased to exist and was no longer a serious threat to the Nazis. The fates of the most prominent leaders of the KPD – Klara Zetkin, Ernst Thälmann, Willi Munzenberg, Ludwig Renn, John Heartfield and Walther Ulbricht – were very different, but by the end of the Nazi era only three of the six were still alive and, of the three deceased, only Klara Zetkin died of natural causes on 20 June 1933, five months after

Hitler became Chancellor. Her ashes were placed in the wall of the Kremlin in Moscow, her spiritual home.

Ernst Thälmann, a native of Hamburg, was born on 16 April 1886, the son of Jan Thälmann and his wife Maria. Having been Hitler's rival in the presidential election of March 1932, he was fiercely hated by the new Chancellor. He had been a member of the *Reichstag* since 1924 and chairman of the Communist party since 1925, but his political career ended on 28 February 1933, the day after the *Reichstag* fire, when, along with many other Communists, he was arrested and imprisoned. He spent many months in solitary confinement in Moabit prison in Berlin before being transferred to Hanover and then to a prison in Bautzen. On 14 August 1944 Hitler decided that Thälmann had been kept in prison for too long and that it was time to rid himself for good of the Communist he despised so much. Thälmann was taken to the concentration camp of Buchenwald where, four days later, on 18 August 1944, he was shot.

Willi Munzenberg, who was born in 1888, was a journalist and the owner of the *Neuer Deutsche Verlag* (New German Press) in Berlin. He had joined the KPD in 1919 and, like Thälmann, had been a member of the *Reichstag* from 1924 to 1933. When Hitler began to imprison members of the Communist party in the spring of 1933 after the *Reichstag* fire, Munzenberg left Germany and went to Paris where many Germans were trying to continue their fight against the Nazis. There he became a leading figure on the Central Committee of the KPD and sought to influence many prominent intellectuals including Ernest Hemingway, Lillian Hellman, André Gide, Dorothy Parker, Alger Hiss, Sinclair Lewis, Pablo Picasso, Felix Frankfurter and Bertolt Brecht.

In the spring of 1940 he disappeared. On 22 October some hunters found his body near the French village of Montagne near Grenoble. He had been strangled; his eyes were bulging and he had a rope around his neck. He may have been hanged but when found he was sitting beneath a tree, his knees drawn up and his badly decomposed body covered with fallen leaves. To this day the circumstances of his death remain a mystery.

Arnold Friedrich Vieth von Golsseneau was the given name of writer Ludwig Renn. He was a career soldier who during the strikes of 1918 refused to carry out the order he had been given to open fire on striking workers. After the First World War he left the army and studied law, political economy, history of art and Russian philology in Göttingen and Munich. After a time travelling within Europe Renn settled in Vienna where he spent two years studying archaeology and East Asian history before returning to Germany.

He had become interested in politics during his travels and joined the KPD in 1928. In 1933, following his outspoken condemnation of Hitler, he was arrested and imprisoned until 1935 when he went into exile in Switzerland.

With the outbreak of the Spanish Civil War, Renn travelled to Spain to join the International Brigade in their fight against the supporters of General Franco. He also went to America to raise funds for the cause, but at the end of the war was again arrested, this time by the French authorities following Franco's victory. He spent the next few years in prison and on his release in 1940 went to Mexico where he became Professor of European History at the University of Morelia.

His interest in politics remained strong and he became president of the Latin American Committee for Free Germans. After the end of the Second World War and the demise of the Nazi party, Renn returned to his native land where he became Professor of Anthropology at the University of Dresden. He died in Berlin on 21 July 1979 at the age of ninety.

Another Communist who lived under a different name from that which his parents had given him was the writer, illustrator and committed pacifist, John Heartfield. In 1916, at the age of twenty-five, he changed his name from Helmut Herzfelde as a protest against the war and German nationalism.

Working on satirical and political magazines such as *Der Knöppel* and *AIZ,* Heartfield used his artistic talent to vilify the Nazi regime. By the time the Nazis came to power in Germany Heartfield knew that his time in his homeland was coming to an end. In 1933 he escaped to Prague where he remained, still producing his anti-Nazi work, until Hitler's troops invaded Czechoslovakia. He went from Prague to London where he lived until 1950 organizing anti-Fascist rallies and speaking at political meetings. He then decided to return to Germany and made his home in the *Deutsche Demokratische Republik* or DDR (German Democratic Republic). He died in Berlin on 26 April 1968.

Of all the early leaders of the KPD, Walther Ulbricht was perhaps the only one who lived to see his dream come to fruition. Although he did not succeed in removing the Nazis from his homeland he did contribute significantly to the formation of a German communist government within at least part of Germany, becoming a founding father of the DDR in 1949.

Ulbricht was born in Leipzig on 30 June 1893, the son of a tailor. His parents were interested in politics and he grew up to be politically active. After the end of the First World War he joined the KPD and went to Russia where he received intensive training. After his return he gained a seat in the *Reichstag* election of 1928 as a representative for South Westphalia. He managed to escape arrest in 1933 by obtaining a set of counterfeit identity documents and fleeing to France. He established himself, along with many other Communists, in Paris where he became leader of the *Auslandskomitee* (Foreign Committee).

At the start of the Spanish Civil War Ulbricht went to Spain, where he not only fought against Franco, he 'disposed of' Communist party members who were suspected of not toeing the party line. In 1938 he went back to Russia where he remained until 1945 when he returned to Germany as a Soviet army colonel. He was instrumental in setting up a Communist state in the Soviet occupied part of Germany.

A dedicated party member, he was, nonetheless, despised and hated by both the West and by the Russians who kept him in his position of power as East German head of state as a matter of expediency. He is probably best remembered as being the man who ordered the building of the Berlin Wall in 1961. He died on 1 February 1973. An article in *The Times* soon afterwards summed up Walther Ulbricht quite neatly. It said:

> It is difficult to mourn Herr Ulbricht as a politician because he added little or nothing to the sum of human happiness. It is difficult to mourn him as a human being because he showed so few signs of being one.

In addition to the leadership of the various political parties, many rank and file members were arrested on very flimsy grounds or forced to flee the country to avoid imprisonment.

The distinction between what constituted a workers' resistance group and what a political resistance group became very blurred at grass roots level. By their very nature trade unions tended to be politically driven and many of the members of resistance organizations still held to the original beliefs of their former trade unions, including those that were church-inspired.

As with all forms of resistance there were too many political groups opposed to the government of the time to detail every one here. It is, however, possible to examine a few of them.

Robert Uhrig was born on 8 March 1903 in Leipzig. He became a toolmaker and settled in Berlin where he became a member of the Communist party. Following the rise of the NSDAP and Hitler, he continued his communist activities, but was arrested in June 1934 and in November was sentenced to twenty-one months' imprisonment in Luckau, a small town south-east of Berlin. His crime was that he had taken part in 'illegal activities', a euphemism for having been a Communist. He was released in 1936 and continued his communist activities along with a number of his former colleagues from the Osram light bulb factory in the Wedding district of Berlin.

The Uhrig group, as they became known, maintained contacts within a number of different factories not only in Berlin but also in towns right across Germany. They also stayed in touch with some members of the KPD who had fled the country and settled outside of the Reich. Not all members of the Uhrig group were Communists. Robert Uhrig was convinced that if the resistance to Hitler was to be effective all opponents to the regime must co-operate with each other to bring about the downfall of the Nazis. During 1941 Uhrig met, and developed a relationship with, Josef 'Beppo' Römer who had set up his own resistance group.

Another Communist party member, Römer was born in 1892. He was a lawyer and the publisher of a Communist party magazine called *Aufbruch* (Awakening), which started in 1932. He was arrested in 1933 and again in 1934 when he was sent to Dachau concentration camp. He remained there until 1939 before being released and returning to his home in Munich. He immediately started resistance work again and this time expanded his activities to include a group of colleagues in Berlin. In 1940 he began publishing a monthly newspaper that he called *Informationsdienst* (Information Service), which was aimed at opponents of Hitler.

In September 1941 Robert Uhrig and Josef Römer joined forces to become the Uhrig-Römer group. They continued to produce the *Informationsdienst*, now published twice a month. Although its leaders had slightly different methods, the groups worked well together. Uhrig was concerned about developing contacts with other resistance groups and wanted to educate the general public about the evils of Nazism by producing and distributing leaflets. Römer was more interested in forming a cohesive policy to overthrow the government and take power once the Nazis had been ousted.

Members of the group were encouraged to carry out acts of sabotage in their places of work, especially those who laboured in armament factories and other establishments that contributed to the German war effort. Those not involved in such pursuits distributed leaflets and gave covert assistance to slave labourers.

By 1942 there were many members of the Uhrig-Römer group working together for a better Germany and, although they were very careful to maintain security, in an organization of the size the group had become this was difficult. Inevitably mistakes were made and the Gestapo found an opportunity to infiltrate the group. Massive arrests were made, with more than 200 members being sent to concentration camps. Many were not even given the opportunity to try to defend themselves, even in a 'show trial', but were shipped off to the camps where they languished without any certain knowledge of what their fate might be.

Eventually, in November 1942, the trials began, although they were too late for some group members who had already been murdered. Between the end of 1942 and October 1944 over 100 members of the Uhrig-Römer group were brought to trial, including their leaders, Robert Uhrig and Josef Römer. Uhrig was sentenced to death and was executed on 21 August 1944. Römer followed him a month later on 25 September.

Although the Gestapo had made a huge dent in the numbers of resistance fighters when they infiltrated the Uhrig-Römer group, they had not managed to destroy the group totally and when the dust had settled the remaining members joined other organizations.

Founded in Hamburg in 1940, the Jacob-Bästlein group was another Communist-led resistance movement that operated throughout the northern part of Germany, including the cities of

Bremen, Lübeck, Kiel, Rostock and Flensburg. It took its name from two of its founding members, thirty-four-year-old Franz Jacob and his forty-six-year-old colleague, Bernhard Bästlein. Its members came mainly from the building trades, the shipbuilding yards and the docks of Hamburg. The group had contacts with the Uhrig-Römer group and with another group, the Red Orchestra. Their activities were similar to those of the Uhrig-Römer group, producing leaflets, sabotaging vital war work and helping slave labourers and prisoners of war.

On 15 October 1942 the group was betrayed and mass arrests of its members began. Jacob and Bästlein were arrested on 17 October. Franz Jacob managed to escape and went to Berlin to continue his resistance work. Bästlein was incarcerated in the Plötzensee prison in Berlin until 1944 from where, during an air raid on 30 January, he also managed to escape, joining his old friend once more. Many of the other members of the group, nearly eighty in total, ended their days in concentration camps such as Neuengamme near Hamburg, where they were brutally murdered.

Following Franz Jacob's escape to Berlin he made contact with Anton Saefkow who was the leader of a resistance group that was to become one of the largest in Germany.

Saefkow, a lorry driver, was born in 1903. He joined the KPD in 1924 and held various positions within the party until it was banned in 1933 when he was arrested and imprisoned. He was released in 1939 and made contact with many of his former colleagues in an effort to set up a resistance organization. He co-operated with the Uhrig-Römer group and, when it was infiltrated and its members either arrested or in hiding, several of those who managed to escape joined Saefkow. Franz Jacob, who had escaped from custody in Hamburg, also joined Saefkow on his arrival in Berlin and together they formed the Saefkow-Jacob group.

They set up a large network of agents in various factories and other work facilities whose task it was to sabotage equipment, produce and distribute leaflets denouncing the Nazi government and seeking an end to the war, forge documents, arrange meetings and ensure that the organization remained secure.

In July 1943 the NKFD (National Committee, Free Germany) had been set up in Russia in part to train agents to be sent to Germany to unite all the anti-Nazi factions. It was composed of exiled German Communists and German prisoners of war, captured after the Battle of Stalingrad. Saefkow was in accord with the aims of the NKPD and his group, although communist in essence, also included members from the banned SPD and former trade unionists. Part of the task that they set themselves was not only to increase their membership, but also to establish contact with as many other groups as possible so that a united resistance force could be set up. They sometimes signed off their leaflets, 'NKFD, Berlin Committee'.

Although there were many discussions both within the group and with other groups and individuals, including former SPD members Dr Julius Leber and Adolf Reichwein, about a coordinated resistance to Hitler, nothing was really put into practice as they were caught up in a round of arrests in July 1944. Sent to trial at the People's Court on 5 September 1944, Anton Saefkow, Franz Jacob and Bernhard Bästlein were all sentenced to death. Thirteen days after their trial the sentence was carried out in Brandenburg-Görden prison.

When Hitler and his thugs had begun their purge of the Communists following the *Reichstag* fire, most of the communist leaders who had managed to escape arrest fled to other parts of Europe.

One of these was Wilhelm Knöchel, a member of the Central Committee of the Communist party. He escaped to Holland with his wife, Cilly Hansmann, from where at the beginning of 1942 Knöchel returned to Germany to become the only senior communist leader living in Germany. His wife remained in Amsterdam, maintaining contact with Dutch supporters and receiving copies of her husband's written articles, which were then forwarded to Moscow.

Knöchel himself produced an underground newspaper, *Der Friedenskämpfer* (The Peace Crusader), which was distributed on a monthly basis to German workers and encouraged them to disrupt communications, distribution services and armament production and to 'work to rule' in their factories. Knöchel's organization also gave out leaflets and stickers to factory workers and ordinary German residents.

At every opportunity Knöchel made reports on the state of the country and the morale of the people and sent these back to Holland to be forwarded to Russia.

The organization grew in numbers over the next year and by January 1943 Cilly Hansmann decided to join her husband in Germany. She had just reached the Dutch-German border when she received word that the organization had collapsed following a raid by the Gestapo. She managed to send word to her colleagues in Amsterdam and remained in Holland herself. Her husband was not so lucky. He was taken into custody and in mid-1944 was executed in Brandenburg. Many of his organization suffered the same fate, but, because Knöchel had not contacted other resistance groups, preferring to work alone, the damage was contained.

Although there were many other resistance groups spread throughout Germany, perhaps one of the best known was the *Rote Kapelle* (Red Orchestra). The Red Orchestra was the name given by the German authorities to a number of different groups which spied for Soviet Russia. These were located all over Europe and beyond and included such well-known spies as Sandor Rado, Richard Sorge and Ruth Kusczynski, also known as Ruth Werner, Ursula Hamburger and Ursula Beurton, probably best known by her code name, Sonia. It was she who ran the atomic bomb spy Klaus Fuchs when she lived in England after the Second World War and she was regarded by her spymasters in the Soviet Union as being the most productive spy of her generation. These people, however, were concerned only with passing information to the Soviets and were quite clearly different from the branch of the Red Orchestra that operated in Germany in the 1930s and 1940s. Although they did pass information and would have been happy had the whole of Germany become a communist state, their main driving force at that time was the desire to rid their country of the Nazis.

The members of the Red Orchestra that we are most concerned with here were two married couples, Harro Schulze-Boysen and his wife, Libertas, and Arvid and Mildred Harnack.

Arvid Harnack was born in Darmstadt on 25 May 1901, the son of historian Otto Harnack and nephew of Adolf Harnack, the renowned theologian. He studied at the University of Berlin and, when he graduated in 1926, went to the University of Wisconsin in

Madison on a Rockefeller Scholarship to study economics and labour history under Professor John Commons, the celebrated American economist who was at the forefront of labour reform policy-making within the United States for the first half of the twentieth century.

While he was in Madison Arvid met and fell in love with an American girl, Mildred Fish, who was studying for her Master's degree in English literature. Born on 16 September 1902, she was the youngest of four children and came from Milwaukee, a city famed for its production of beer and for being 'the most German' of all American cities. It was said that one in every four people living in Milwaukee was of German origin and Mildred herself spoke fluent German.

The couple married in 1926 and remained in Madison until 1928 when Arvid returned to Germany. Mildred followed him in 1929, at first to the University of Jena, south-west of Leipzig, and then to Berlin where she taught literature at Humboldt University.

Arvid also obtained a teaching post and was instrumental in helping to set up 'Arplan', a working group for the study of the Soviet economy with a view to adopting some of the Soviet planning methods and forming a link between the communist east and the capitalist west. In 1932 he went to the Soviet Union to study the Soviet system at first hand.

During the early part of the 1930s the Harnacks had a busy social life and developed a circle of likeminded friends. Artists, students, professors all met at regular intervals at the Harnacks' home to discuss art, literature, poetry and politics and they often entertained overseas visitors. Their friends included Martha Dodds, daughter of the US ambassador to Berlin and mistress of Soviet diplomat, Boris Vinogradov, Greta Kuckhoff, whom they had met when they were all studying at the University of Wisconsin and former Prussian Minister of Culture, Adolf Grimme.

In 1935 Arvid went to work in the Ministry of Economics, a position that enabled him to make contact with foreign embassy officials without arousing too much suspicion. He made use of this facility and contacted both American and Soviet diplomats. To further allay suspicion, in 1937 he joined the Nazi party and the following year he formed a friendship with Donald Heath, First Secretary at the American Embassy. By this time Arvid had access to information about Hitler's plans for a war and was able to pass these on to Heath.

Greta Kuckhoff, who had also studied under Professor John Commons, introduced the Harnacks to some other friends in 1939. These were the Schulze-Boysens and they were to become as important as the Harnacks in the running of the resistance group.

Like Arvid Harnack, Harro and Libertas Schulze-Boysen both came from distinguished German families. Paradoxically many Germans with communist principles came from the upper classes.

Harro was born on 2 September 1909 in the north German naval city of Kiel, the great nephew of German naval commander Admiral Alfred von Tirpitz. His father was *Kapitänleutnant* Erich Schulze and his mother was Luise Boysen. In 1922 the family moved to Duisburg where Harro attended a grammar school. He went on to study law at the universities of both Freiburg and Berlin, but never became a lawyer. Instead, in 1932, he was appointed editor of a magazine called *Der Gegner* (The Enemy), a position he held until joining the Ministry of Aviation in April 1934.

Libertas Haas-Heye, the girl that Harro Schulze-Boysen married in 1936, was born on 20 November 1913 in Paris. She was the youngest of the three children of Professor Haas-Heye and his wife, Countess Victoria zu Eulenberg and Hertefeld. Her grandfather, a close friend of Kaiser Wilhelm II, was Prince Philip von Eulenberg and it was on his estate, Liebenberg, north of Berlin, that Libertas grew up. She was sent to a Swiss finishing school and when she returned home took up a position as a press agent with Metro-Goldwyn-Mayer in Berlin. Although she had initially supported the Nazis, she quickly converted to her husband's views and for the next few years they too developed a circle of likeminded friends and colleagues in much the same way as the Harnacks had. When the two couples met in 1939 they joined forces and brought together their own circles, thus establishing a large group of anti-Nazis.

The Nazis were fanatical about documenting all their actions in writing, photos and films and Libertas used her position with MGM, and the fact that she also wrote a film column for an Essen newspaper, to collect and pass on information about Nazi war crimes taking place on the eastern front.

Because of their positions in the civil service, both Arvid and

Harro were able to obtain information about the proposed German invasion of the Soviet Union, which they passed to Alexander Korotkov, the Berlin representative of the NKVD, forerunner of the KGB.

When, in June 1941, the invasion codenamed Operation Barbarossa began, Harro passed on vital information concerning Luftwaffe strategy to the Soviet Union.

Like other resistance groups, the Red Orchestra produced leaflets and underground newspapers decrying the Nazis and their corruption and encouraging citizens to demonstrate against them. They also tried to help Jewish victims of the regime whenever possible. In the last year of their existence they cooperated with many other groups of varying political persuasions in an attempt to form a united front against the Nazis, but before they could make really significant progress they ran into difficulties.

They had obtained several radio transmitters to enable them to send their information more rapidly to Moscow and it was said that each was coded with the name of a musical instrument, hence the name Red Orchestra. Unfortunately, because the Soviets were very sloppy in the way they contacted Harnack and Schulze-Boysen, the Gestapo found out about the group and had the leaders' telephones tapped for a while in order to obtain the names of more of the resisters.

In August 1942 Harro Schulze-Boysen was arrested while at work in his office at the Ministry of Aviation. Libertas tried to warn all their friends about her husband's arrest but did not succeed in saving them. Arvid and Mildred Harnack were arrested on 7 September and the following day, as she was getting on to a train to take her out of Berlin, Libertas herself was arrested.

Following a trial in December 1942 only Mildred was spared a death sentence. She was ordered to complete six years' hard labour at a concentration camp. Arvid and Harro were executed at Plötzensee prison on 22 December by being hung on meat hooks, obtained from a local butcher, and slowly strangled. The same day Libertas was beheaded, also at Plötzensee.

When Hitler heard about the custodial sentence handed down to Mildred Harnack he was furious and personally intervened and ordered the court to retry her. The result of this 'trial' was a foregone conclusion and this time she was sentenced to death. She spent the last few weeks of her life translating the poems of Goethe into English. She was beheaded in Plötzensee prison on 16 February 1943, the only American to face the death penalty in Nazi Germany. As she went to the guillotine her last words were said to have been, 'I loved Germany so much'.

Chapter Seven

Church Opposition

Although as a boy Hitler had briefly had an ambition to take religious orders, by the time he became Chancellor of Germany his views of religion had radically changed. He had no further interest in the teachings of the Church but understood that he had to try to unite believers under a common banner, that of the NSDAP if possible, to ensure that he eliminated any opposition to his government.

Initially most Christian church leaders showed very little opposition to the Nazi regime. Some openly supported it, but came to realize the error of their ways when the Nazis passed several measures restricting their religious freedoms. Others continued to support it throughout the life of the government and defiantly defended their stance afterwards. There was also a group of the faithful from many different denominations who, in spite of being in a minority, chose to uphold their beliefs regardless of the cost to themselves. They were the shining examples of Christianity as it was meant to be.

It is surprising that so many people who called themselves Christians did so little to oppose the Nazi regime or to help those most oppressed by it, considering that one of the main principles of Christianity is to help others. Christ himself taught that whatever was done to help another person was done for Him. The gospel of St Matthew, chapter 25, verse 40, says:

Verily I say unto you, inasmuch as ye have done it unto one of the least of these my brethren, ye have done it unto me.

73

When, in July 1933, the Nazis and the Roman Catholic Church signed the Concordat, it was hoped that German Catholics would be left in peace to worship according to their consciences. But the Catholic Church did not just provide places of worship for its followers. It provided other organizations such as schools, youth groups, medical facilities, newspapers and trade unions, looking after every aspect of daily life. The Concordat was signed to ensure that the Catholic way of life was preserved, but all it really guaranteed was the right to worship and soon the government banned all Catholic organizations except the places of worship themselves. Perhaps grateful that the Nazis had not tried to ban them altogether, they accepted this without question. It was to be a grave mistake: the Nazis were determined to restrict the way all churches operated within Germany.

There was, for example, a clause in the agreement that said:

Catholic clerics who hold an ecclesiastical office in Germany or who exercise pastoral or educational functions must:
(a) Be German citizens.
(b) Have matriculated from a German secondary school.
(c) Have studied philosophy and theology for at least three years at a German State University, a German ecclesiastical college, or a papal college in Rome.

This, in itself was not a major point of contention, but, in view of later developments, it did have an impact on the way the Church was allowed to run its own affairs and also on its perceived acceptance of Nazi doctrine.

Within the Catholic Church there were some converts from Judaism; there were also people who numbered Jews among their ancestors. When, in September 1935, the Nuremberg Laws came into being, these people were denied German citizenship. That effectively removed them from the priesthood of the Catholic Church because of the clause in the Concordat stating that clerics must be German citizens. It also removed all foreigners and those the Nazis did not regard as being of pure Aryan blood. Although, at the time that the Concordat was signed, the Catholic Church did not know that the Nazis would bring in the Nuremberg Laws, it is interesting that they should have agreed to anything that restricted their powers over their own organization. It is also interesting to note that, although the Church objected to the restrictions imposed upon it, there was very little protest about the controls imposed on other groups. This led to claims that the Catholic Church was unconcerned about anything except its own welfare.

There were, however, some exceptions and, as time went on and it became clear how evil the Nazi regime was, these numbers increased.

One of the first to speak out against the Nazis was Clemens August, Count von Galen, who was Bishop of Münster. Born on 16 March 1878 at Dinklage Castle near Münster, he was the son of Count Ferdinand von Galen and his wife, Elisabeth, Countess of Spee. Educated by Jesuits, von Galen went on to study philosophy in Switzerland, where he decided to become a priest. He studied theology in both Innsbruck and Münster before being ordained a priest in the cathedral of Münster on 28 May 1904. He served in a number of parishes in Münster and in Berlin before being appointed Bishop of Münster by Pope Pius XI in September 1933, a position to which Cardinal Schulte, Archbishop of Cologne, consecrated him on 28 October that year. He was a good and popular bishop who always tried to stay true to his chosen motto, *Nec laudibus, Nec timore* (neither for praise nor out of fear).

By the beginning of 1934 von Galen had already delivered sermons condemning both Nazi racial policies and their behaviour towards the Catholic Church. The behaviour towards the Church worried him greatly and in 1937 he became an advisor to Pope Pius XI on his encyclical, *Mit brennender Sorge* (With burning anxiety), which was issued on 14 March. The encyclical addressed the problems being experienced by German Catholics and detailed the Pope's grave concerns about the way the Nazi government had ignored the terms of the Concordat of 1933 and was persecuting Catholics in the Reich. It also sent many messages to German Catholics and their clergy about the way in which they should behave. The eighth point made in *Mit brennender Sorge* states:

Whoever exalts race, or the people, or the State, or a particular form of State, or the depositories of power, or any other fundamental value of the human community – however necessary and honourable be their function in worldly things – whoever raises these notions above their standard value and divinizes them to an idolatrous level, distorts and perverts an order of the world planned and created by God; he is far from the true faith in God and from the concept of life which that faith upholds.

By 1941 it became clear that the government was intent upon killing all those it considered to be sub-human, all the mentally ill and all those with physical disabilities. The papal encyclical had had little or no effect on the government or, indeed, on many Catholics, and the Nazis were still persecuting them and taking over Church property, which they used for such things as brothels and movie theatres. Von Galen could keep silent no longer and, holding fast to his motto, he delivered three now famous sermons on 13 and 20 July and 3 August 1941. The contents of the sermons were printed and distributed throughout the country. They even found their way overseas. In von Galen's condemnation of the practice of euthanasia he said:

If the principle that man is entitled to kill his unproductive fellow man is established and applied, then woe to all of us when we become aged and infirm! Then no man will be safe: some committee or other will be able to put him on the list of 'unproductive' persons, who in their judgment have become 'unworthy to live'. And there will be no police to protect him, no court to avenge his murder and bring his murderers to justice. Who could then have any confidence in a doctor? He might report a patient as unproductive and then be given instructions to kill him! It does not bear thinking of, the moral depravity, the universal mistrust, which will spread even in the bosom of the family, if this terrible doctrine is tolerated, accepted and put into practice. Woe to mankind! Woe to our German people, if the divine commandment 'Thou shalt not kill', which the Lord proclaimed on Sinai amid thunder and lightning, which God our Creator wrote into man's conscience from the beginning, if this commandment is not merely violated but the violation is tolerated and remains unpunished!

And of the Nazi behaviour towards members of the Catholic Church, von Galen declared:

I am conscious that as a bishop, a promulgator and defender of the legal and moral order willed by God and granting to each individual rights and freedoms to which, by God's will, all human claims must give way, I am called upon courageously to assert the authority of the law and to denounce the condemnation of innocent men, who are without any defence, as an injustice crying out to heaven. My Christians! The imprisonment of many blameless persons without any opportunity for defence or any judgment of a court compels me today to publicly recall an old and unshakeable truth: *'Justitia est fundamentum regnorum'*, Justice is the only solid foundation of any state.

The right to life, to inviolability, to freedom is an indispensable part of the moral order of society. It is true that the state is entitled to restrict these rights as a penal measure against its citizens, but the state is only entitled to do so against those who have broken the law and whose guilt has been established in an impartial judicial process. A state which transgresses this boundary laid down by God and permits or causes innocent persons to be punished is undermining its own authority and the respect for its sovereignty in the conscience of its citizens.

These sermons and their powerful messages led to von Galen being called the Lion of Münster. Although he assumed that their publication would lead to his arrest this did not happen. Hitler was furious at the attack on his government and wanted to arrest von Galen immediately but was persuaded that it would not be a good idea as the bishop had many supporters. The Bishop of Münster survived the Nazi regime and the Second World War, although his home, his belongings and much of his cathedral did not.

On 18 February 1946 Pope Pius XII created him a cardinal. He returned to Münster from Rome on 16 March but four days later he died. He was buried on 28 March in the Ludgerus Chapel in the ruined cathedral, mourned by thousands.

Von Galen's cousin, Konrad, Count von Preysing, was also a Catholic bishop. Born on 30 August 1880, two years after von Galen, von Preysing studied law in both Munich and Würzburg and became a civil servant in Bavaria in 1906. He soon decided that this was not what he wanted from his life and in 1908 went to Innsbruck to study theology. He was ordained in 1912 and in 1913 became a Doctor of Theology and Personal Secretary to the Bishop of Munich. From 1917 to 1932 von Preysing served in various Munich churches before being made Bishop of Eichstätt.

When Hitler became Chancellor in 1933 von Preysing voiced his opposition to the NSDAP leader. He also criticized the Catholic clergy who gave their support to the Nazi regime, in particular Cardinal Bertram, and constantly spoke out against the way in which the Nazis were directing the way the Church conducted its affairs. In spite of this he was named as Bishop of Berlin on 6 July 1935. Along with his cousin, he was one of the five advisors to the Pope on the encyclical, *Mit brennender Sorge*.

On 24 August 1938 von Preysing became one of the founder members of the *Hilfswerk beim Bischöflichen Ordinariat Berlin* (Welfare Office of the Berlin Diocese Office) that gave aid to Catholics of Jewish origin among others. He was always a strong supporter of Jewish rights and helped many of the oppressed throughout the life of the Nazi government. He also vehemently protested against the Nazi euthanasia programme and sent letters to his priests encouraging them to speak out against Nazi policy at every opportunity.

In 1942 he issued his Pastoral Letter for Advent, which took human rights as its subject. The letter was smuggled out of Germany and found its way to England where the contents were broadcast on the German programme of the BBC World Service. Von Preysing's only comment when he heard about the broadcast was to say, 'That will make them build my gallows even higher'. Fortunately von Preysing had such a high profile and was respected by so many people that the Nazis did not dare to harm him. Had they known that he was in contact with some members of the Kreisau circle, who were planning a government after Nazism, and that he believed that there was a moral justification for the assassination of Hitler, perhaps they might have acted differently.

One of von Preysing's close confidantes was Catholic Priest Bernhard Lichtenberg, provost at St Hedwig's Cathedral in Berlin. A fierce opponent of the NSDAP, Lichtenberg became a member of both the *Friedensbund Deutscher Katholiken* (Peace Federation of German Catholics) and the *Arbeitsgemeinschaft der*

Konfessionen für den Frieden (Interdenominational Working Group for Peace). As an early detractor of Nazi policies he came under the scrutiny of the government almost as soon as they came to power. In 1933 his home was searched, but it was not until 23 October 1941, when he sent a strongly worded letter complaining about the murder of disabled people to the Reich Head of Medical Affairs, that he was arrested. He came to trial on 22 May 1942 in the Regional Court in Berlin and was sentenced to two years' imprisonment. He served his sentence at Berlin's Tegel prison. He was then sent to a transit camp in Wuhlheide before being taken to Dachau concentration camp. He was in poor health following his incarceration at Tegel and didn't survive the journey to Dachau. He died in Hof on the Saale River on 5 November 1943 just one month before his sixty-eighth birthday.

The Protestant movement embraced many different sects and within these sects the Nazi party had many supporters. The group called the *Deutsche Glaubensbewegung* (German Faith Movement) was formed in an effort to supersede the Protestant churches. Members of this movement accepted both the Nazi theories of Aryan superiority and their ideas of *Blut und Boden*. In 1934 Professor Ernst Bergmann issued the Twenty-Five Points of the German Religion, which included the following:

1. The Jewish Old Testament as well as parts of the New Testament are not suitable for the new Germany.
2. Christ was not Jewish but a Nordic martyr put to death by the Jews, a warrior whose death rescued the world from Jewish influence.
3. Adolf Hitler is the new Messiah sent to earth to save the world from the Jews.
4. The swastika succeeds the sword *[cross?]* as the symbol of German Christianity.
5. German land, German blood, German soul, German art – these are the sacred assets of German Christians.

It is hard to see how anyone could seriously consider the above as being anything other than utter drivel. The second point alone highlights the inconsistency of the 'doctrine'. If Christ's death rescued the world from Jewish influence, why did the Nazis find it necessary to persecute them? The entire document was complete nonsense and utterly at odds with any conventional view of Christianity. In spite of this it had its supporters, who became known as German Christians.

In May 1933 an election was called to vote for a Protestant Reich bishop. Hitler's choice for this position was an army chaplain called Ludwig Müller. At first he received support from a number of Protestant clergy, but it soon became clear that he was not an ideal candidate, being more politically than spiritually inclined, which was perhaps why he was the choice of the Führer. The clergy instead elected a respected churchman called Friedrich von Bodelschwingh. Hitler was furious and tried to exert pressure on von Bodelschwingh to adhere to Nazi doctrine. The bishop tried to remain independent and to rally support from the other church leaders to maintain the independence of his office, but to no avail. One month after being elected Reich Bishop von Bodelschwingh gave up and resigned.

In July another election was called. This time Hitler had his way and Ludwig Müller was voted into office with the massive backing of the Nazi party. German Christians were appointed to key positions within the new organization. It now seemed as if Hitler was succeeding in his aim to rid himself of traditional Christian religions in favour of the *Deutsche Glaubensbewegung* and of uniting the various splinter groups under one government-controlled bishop. This state of complete Church compliance with Nazi doctrine lasted for only a very short time.

Two months later, on 21 September, a forty-one-year-old clergy-man named Martin Niemöller became so concerned about what was happening in the Church that he wrote to all German pastors inviting them to join him in his newly formed *Pfarrenotbund* (Pastors' Emergency League). In his letter he said:

> We have called into being an 'Emergency Alliance' of pastors who have given one another their word in a written declaration that they will be bound in their preaching by the Holy Scripture and the Reformation confessions alone.

Over 7,000 pastors took up his invitation to join the *Pfarrenotbund* and, although those figures dropped over the next few years, they eventually stabilized at around 4,000. Included in those who joined the *Pfarrenotbund* were the Swiss-born theologian Karl Barth, who was a professor at the University of Bonn, and the German theologian Dietrich Bonhoeffer.

Martin Niemöller, who was born on 14 January 1892, had been a U-boat commander in the First World War and had been awarded the Pour le Mérite for his wartime service. When the war ended he studied theology and was ordained as a pastor in the Evangelical Church in 1924. He served in the Berlin parish of Dahlem from 1930 to 1937, which was regarded as one of the richest parishes in Germany. He had, at first, supported the Nazis. Being vehemently opposed to communism, he saw the NSDAP as an effective way of ensuring that the communists never came to power, but he began to change his mind when he realized that Hitler was as much of a threat to religion as was communism.

At first the Nazis had been glad to have Niemöller's support. He was paraded as being the perfect example of a German clergyman and hero, but this soon turned sour when Niemöller began to speak out against them and ultimately Hitler hated him for his bold stance against the dictates of the evil regime.

Niemöller's colleague, Karl Barth, wrote a scathing criticism of German Christian doctrine in which he stated that the source of their errors was that they maintained that in nationality, history and politics was a revelation that should be given equal weight with the Scriptures. This led many pastors to resign from the Church and annoyed Reich Bishop Müller so much that he issued a decree which became known as the 'Muzzling Decree', which forbade pastors from criticizing the German Christian church or from discussing anything to do with it. He insisted that the only thing they were allowed to speak of in their sermons was the Gospel.

Following this decree, Niemöller and 320 other elders and ministers of the Church gathered in Barmen in May 1934 to issue their own declaration, written by Karl Barth and called the *Declaration on the Correct Understanding of the Reformation Confessions in the Evangelical Church*. It set forth six articles of faith and dismissed the precepts of the church of the German Christians, declaring them to be false doctrine.

Following the meeting at Barmen, a new church, which became known as the *Bekenntniskirche* (Confessing Church), was set up to unify all the different Evangelical groups and to oppose Nazi values.

Because Ludwig Müller was having little effect in silencing the Church dissenters he was dismissed from his post as Reich bishop in July 1935. The position of Reich bishop was also set aside, making way for a new position, that of Minister for Ecclesiastical Affairs.

In spite of Nazi opposition, the Confessing Church flourished and continued its work of spreading the Gospel and attacking Nazi beliefs and persecution throughout the rest of the life of the Third Reich. Unfortunately not all of its most outspoken members fared so well.

Karl Barth, who had refused to take an oath of loyalty to the Führer that didn't include an additional clause addressing his religious beliefs, was deported in the autumn of 1934 and went back to Basle, his birthplace. Many pastors and other Church officials who had spoken out against the government were arrested and sent to concentration camps without trial.

Friedrich Weissler, a Church lawyer who had condemned the *Blut und Boden* doctrine and who had Jewish ancestry, was arrested and sent to Sachsenhausen concentration camp where, because he was regarded as being Jewish, he was badly treated and, ultimately, murdered.

Martin Niemöller remained at his parish of Dahlem in Berlin and continued preaching against the Nazi regime. On 27 June 1937 he said in his sermon that:

> No more are we ready to keep silent at man's behest when God commands us to speak. We must obey God rather than man!

The Gestapo arrested Niemöller four days later while he was entertaining a group of colleagues at his home. His house was ransacked and his wife and his colleagues placed under house arrest. Eventually everyone except Niemöller was freed. He was taken to Moabit prison in Berlin where he was held for eight months before coming to trial in March 1938, accused of attacks against the state. He was found guilty and sentenced to seven months' imprisonment, but on his release was immediately rearrested and sent to Sachsenhausen concentration camp on the direct orders of Hitler. Niemöller remained in Sachsenhausen until he was transferred to Dachau from where he was released by Allied troops at the end of the Second World War.

1. Adolf Hitler in August 1914 in the Odeonsplatz, Munich, listening to the declaration of war.

2. Hitler circa 1921.

3. A painting by Hitler of the Vienna Opera House. His early ambition was to be an artist.

4. Landsberg Prison, 1924. It was here that Hitler *(left)* dictated his book *Mein Kampf* to Rudolf Hess *(second from right)*.

5. The Reichstag fire of 27 February 1933. Although Dutchman Marinus van der
   Lubbe was convicted of starting the fire it was more likely to have been ordered by
   the Nazis themsleves.

6. Hitler's design for a 'people's car' (Volkswagen).

7. The benign face of Nazism. Hitler beginning the work on the building of an Autobahn.

8. Popular support for the Nazis.

9. 'One people, one
   state, one leader!'

Ein Volk, ein Reich, ein Führer!

HEAR THE VOICE OF

FREE ITALY AND GERMANY

MONSTER MASS MEETING

AT

EAGLES HALL, 273 Golden Gate Ave.

WEDNESDAY, JAN. 30, 1935

Speakers:

GIUSEPPE E. MODIGLIANI—Leader of Italian Social-Democracy. Foremost opponent of Facism—now in Exile, will speak on

WORKERS IN ITALY TODAY

GERHARD SEGER—Former member of the German Reichstag who escaped from a Hitler concentration camp, will speak on

WORKERS IN GERMANY TODAY

ADMISSION FREE. A collection will be taken for the victims of Fascism in both Italy and Germany.

Meeting Under the Auspices of
THE SAN FRANCISCO JOINT BOARD of the INTERNATIONAL LADIES' GARMENT WORKERS' UNION (A. F. of L.)
and
THE AMALGAMATED CLOTHING WORKERS OF AMERICA

This meeting is an undertaking of your Union. Be sure to come! Make it a success! Advertise it! Bring all your friends!

The I. L. G. W. U. is touring Signor Modigliani through the country in an effort to help the Labor Movement of the Fascist-dominated countries.

10. In 1945 many Germans claimed not to know about the concentration camps. This poster shows that Americans were told of their existence at least ten years earlier.

Jugend dient dem Führer

Alle 10jährigen zu uns

ALLE ZEHNJÄHRIGEN IN DIE HJ.

1. Posters encouraging girls to join the *Bund Deutscher Mädel* and boys the *Hitler Jugend*.

2. *Kristallnacht*, 9 November 1938. A synagogue burns.

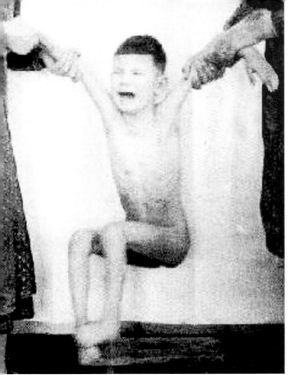

13. The Nazi euthanasia programme. A
young boy being starved to death.

14. Otto Wels, the leader of the SPD befo
it was banned by Hitler.

15. Communist party leader Ernst Thälmann
speaking out against the Nazis.

16. Resistance leader Robert Uhrig of the
Uhrig-Römer group

Anton Saefkow.

18. Red Orchestra members Harro Schulze-Boysen and his wife Libertas.

Arvid Harnack and his Amercian wife Mildred of the Red Orchestra.

20. Christianity 'Nazi style'. Members of the clergy giving the Nazi salute.

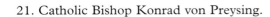

21. Catholic Bishop Konrad von Preysing.

22. Catholic priest Bernhard Lichtenberg who was provost at St Hedwig's Cathedral in Berlin.

Pastor Dietrich Bonhoeffer. He was executed in April 1945 in Flossenbürg concentration camp for his resistance work.

24. The spy in the SS – Kurt Gerstein.

The White Rose group. *Left to right:* Hans Scholl, Sophie Scholl and Christoph Probst.

26. White Rose member Alexander Schmorell.

27. Professor Kurt Huber of the White Rose group.

28. Falk Harnack, brother of Arvid Harnack. He was to form a link between Dietrich Bonhoeffer and Hans Scholl of the White Rose, but Scholl was arrested and executed before a meeting could be set up. Harnack was one of the very few members of the resistance to survive the Nazi era.

29. Karl Goerdeler, who would have become Chancellor of Germany if the attempt to overthrow Hitler had succeeded.

General Ludwig Beck who would have been Head of State in a post-Hitler government

Fabian von Schlabrendorff who placed the bomb, which failed to explode, on Hitler's aeroplane. He, too, survived the Nazi era.

31. Henning von Tresckow, Reich Police Minister elect. He made several unsuccessful attempts to assassinate Hitler and committed suicide after the failed plot on 20 July 1944.

33. *Abwehr* lawyer and Resistance member, Hans Dohnanyi, who, with his brother-in-law, Dietrich Bonhoeffer, managed to save a number of Jews in what became known as Operation Seven. He was executed in Flossenbürg concentration camp.

34. Admiral Wilhelm Canaris, chief of the *Abwehr* and supporter of the Resistance movement. He was executed for his resistance to Hitler.

35. Klaus von Stauffenberg, who planted the bomb at the Wolf's Lair on 20 July 1944. He was shot dead the same evening in Berlin.

36. Hitler and some of his wounded colleagues following the assassination attempt.

37. The guillotine at Plötzensee prison at which so many members of the Resistance lost their lives. In the twelve years of the Nazi regime, 2,891 executions took place in the prison.

38. A partially burnt body in a crematorium oven in Buchenwald concentration camp.

39. The execution chamber at Plötzensee prison. Note the meat hooks from which several members of the Resistance were hanged.

40. German citizens made to visit a camp by Allied soldiers at the end of the Second World War.

41. Nazi supporters, the Duke and Duchess of Windsor. It is believed that Hitler had decided to reinstate the Duke as King following a Nazi takeover of Great Britain.

42. Joseph Kennedy, American Ambassador to Great Britain and supporter of Hitler. He believed that the Germans were the natural leaders of Europe.

Although he had done more than most to oppose the Nazi regime, Niemöller always felt a sense of guilt at what the German nation had done and in 1946 at a conference in Geneva he made a speech in which he admitted that Germany had committed war crimes. He often spoke of the atrocities of Nazi Germany and was particularly hard on himself when he said:

> First they came for the socialists and I did not speak out because I was not a socialist. Then they came for the trade unionists and I did not speak out because I was not a trade unionist. Then they came for the Jews and I did not speak out because I was not a Jew. Then they came for the Catholics, and I did not speak out, because I was a Protestant. Then they came for me and there was no one left to speak for me.

In spite of all that he had suffered Niemöller went on to live a full and active life until his death, at the age of ninety-two, in 1984.

Dietrich Bonhoeffer, another of the early members of the Confessing Church, had, like Pastor Niemöller, strong convictions, but his opposition to the Nazi movement manifested itself in ways very different from those of Niemöller.

Born in Breslau on 4 February 1906, Bonhoeffer was one of the eight children of Paula Bonhoeffer and her husband, Karl, an eminent German psychiatrist. Dietrich decided at an early age that he wanted a life in the Church and at the age of seventeen went to Tübingen to study theology from where he went on to further his studies in Berlin. In 1930 he went abroad and enrolled at the Union Theological Seminary in New York where he stayed for a year. One of his closest friends at the Union Seminary was a black American named Frank Fisher, from whom he learnt what it was like to live as a victim of racism.

He returned to Berlin to become a lecturer at the theological faculty of the university, but by the autumn of 1933 had become thoroughly disillusioned with the Nazi government and its manipulation of the Church. Feeling that he could no longer be a part of an organization that was so much under the control of the Nazis, he again decided to go abroad and took up a post as a Lutheran pastor in London, serving both in the East End and in the south

London suburb of Sydenham, where he remained until 1935. During his time in London he became a close friend of George Bell, the Bishop of Chichester.

Returning once more to Berlin, Bonhoeffer accepted a position teaching at a Church seminary in Finkenwalde, north-east of Berlin, near to the city of Stettin (now Szczecin in Poland). He was in Finkenwalde when the Nuremberg Laws were enacted in September 1935. Answering the call of some good friends soon after, he went to the Berlin suburb of Steglitz where Church leaders were holding a conference.

Church Superintendent Martin Albertz tried to put on the conference agenda a statement made by a Berlin deaconess, Marga Meusel, about the attitude of the Church to the treatment of Jews by the Nazis. Most Church leaders, with the exception of a small group of dissidents, were unwilling to discuss the plight of the Jews. Some Church leaders were so opposed to Meusel's statement that they threatened to leave the conference altogether if it were discussed. They further thought it a good idea to support the Nazis in their anti-Semitic activities.

Bonhoeffer, like Meusel, was disgusted by their attitude. He returned to Finkenwalde determined both to do more to help the Jews and to rid his country of the evil influence of the Nazis.

For the next two years Bonhoeffer continued his teaching at the seminary in Finkenwalde. Then in August 1937 the government delared the education of Confessing Church students to be illegal and the seminary was closed the following month. For some time Bonhoeffer travelled throughout the region keeping an eye on his former students and encouraging them in their vocations, but many of them were arrested and those that were still free were working illegally. Because of his vociferous opposition, Bonhoeffer was becoming known to the authorities and, although he tried to stay out of the limelight, by August 1938 the Gestapo had banned him from going to Berlin.

Following the atrocities of *Kristallnacht* the international religious community could no longer ignore what was happening to the Jews in Germany. Several organizations were set up to enable Jews to leave and cooperated with groups within Germany, one of which was led by Confessing Church Pastor Heinrich Grüber, who eventually assisted over 2,000 Jews to leave the country.

Bonhoeffer also decided to leave. He was offered a post at the Union Seminary in New York and left in June 1939 to take up his new position. Almost as soon as he arrived in America he realized he had made a mistake. Writing to Professor Reinhold Niebuhr at the seminary, Bonhoeffer said:

> I have come to the conclusion that I made a mistake in coming to America. . . . I shall have no right to take part in the restoration of Christian life in Germany after the war unless I share the trials of this time with my people.

In July he returned to Germany to begin his active resistance.

One of Bonhoeffer's sisters, Christel, was married to Hans von Dohnanyi, a lawyer who worked for Admiral Wilhelm Canaris as a special director in the *Abwehr* (Counter Intelligence). Although Canaris was a favourite of Hitler he was secretly opposed to the Nazi regime and worked with von Dohnanyi and others to bring about its downfall. Through his brother-in-law Bonhoeffer was able to travel abroad during the war to further his own resistance work. In October 1940 he became an agent for the *Abwehr*, and, while travelling supposedly on official business, managed to contact many of his friends overseas to enlist their help.

Hearing in May 1942 that George Bell, Bishop of Chichester, was going to be in Sweden, Bonhoeffer and another clergyman, Hans Schönfeld, decided, independently of each other, to go to Sweden and enlist Bell's help in their struggle against Nazism. Bonhoeffer was of the opinion that Hitler must be assassinated, while Schönfeld simply wanted to know if the Allies would look more favourably on the German nation should it succeed in freeing itself from Nazi tyranny. George Bell made a report, which, on his return to England, he took to Foreign Secretary Anthony Eden at the Foreign Office in London. In a letter he wrote to Bell dated 17 July 1942 Eden said:

> When you visited me on 30 June you were kind enough to let me have a memorandum on your talk with two German pastors whom you had met in Stockholm at the end of May, together with a report on a statement made by one of the pastors.

These interesting documents have, by now, been carefully

examined. Without challenging the honest conviction of your informers in the least, I have no doubt that it would be contrary to the interest of our nation to provide them with any answer whatever. I know well that this decision will be some-what disappointing to you. But in view of the delicate circumstances connected with it, I cannot do other than ask you to accept it, something that you will surely understand.

In his excellent book *Plotting Hitler's Death* Joachim Fest has recorded:

> When Bell approached the British Foreign Office again, Eden noted in the margin of his reply, 'I see no reason whatsoever to encourage this pestilent priest!'

This arrogant, self-righteous comment came from the man who would later become British Prime Minister. It is sad to note that while there was not a very large number of Germans who were willing to risk everything to rid their country of the scourge of Nazism, those that did were treated with contempt by the very people who could have made a difference. Just to know that they were not alone could have prompted many more Germans to rebel against their leaders and, at the very least, it would have boosted the morale of those who were already engaged in the dangerous business of resistance against the state.

Bonhoeffer, although discouraged, refused to give up his resistance work and became involved in a plan to help Jews leave the country. Several times in the past the *Abwehr* had used Jews as agents, the theory being that no one would suspect a Jew of working for the Nazis. Using this same theory, Canaris and von Dohnanyi 'employed' fourteen people, most of whom were Jews, as agents and, in an exercise that came to be known as Operation Seven, managed to get them out of Germany and into Switzerland. Bonhoeffer used his many connections to obtain visas and sponsor-ship of the refugees. It was a dangerous plan for all those involved. The fourteen 'agents' were Mr and Mrs Julius Fliess and their daughter, Dorothee, Mr and Mrs Friedrich Wilhelm Arnold, their son and two of their daughters, Ilse Rennefeld and her husband, neither of whom was Jewish, Mrs Anne-Marie Kunzen and her two daughters, who were friends of Admiral Canaris' wife, and Mrs

Charlotte Friedenthal, who was a convert from Judaism and was included at the insistence of Pastor Bonhoeffer.

Sadly this act of charity was to bring about the downfall of both Bonhoeffer and his brother-in-law, Hans von Dohnanyi. While they planned another trip to enable more Jews to leave the country, the Gestapo were checking records to find out why large amounts of money were being sent from the *Abwehr* offices to Switzerland. At first they didn't realize that the money was to enable the Jewish refugees to begin a new life and they thought that von Dohnanyi had been stealing it for his own purposes. They soon discovered its true use, however, and von Dohnanyi and Bonhoeffer were both arrested on 5 April 1943.

Charged with subversion of the armed forces they were imprisoned in Tegel in Berlin, where they remained until October 1944. Bonhoeffer was then removed to the dreaded Gestapo prison cells in Prinz Albrecht Strasse. In February 1945, in the dying days of the Nazi regime, Dietrich Bonhoeffer was sent to Buchenwald concentration camp and from there on to Flossenbürg concentration camp where, on 9 April, he was executed. A few days later his brother-in-law, Hans von Dohnanyi, was also executed.

Dietrich Bonhoeffer came to be regarded as one of the most courageous opponents of the Nazis and a shining example of an honourable man of principle.

British Prime Minister Tony Blair, himself a committed Christian, when asked which German figure, past or present, he most admired is said to have replied, 'Dietrich Bonhoeffer, the German pastor who spoke out against the Nazis and died in a concentration camp in April 1945.'

Others have not been so forthcoming in their praise. The Israeli government, who set up the Yad Vashem memorial in which they honour non-Jews who have risked their own lives to save those of Jews, have consistently refused to honour Dietrich Bonhoeffer, believing that he opposed the Nazis because of their attitudes to other aspects of German life and not because of their anti-Semitism. The fact that he did save Jews at the risk of his own safety and that he was ultimately arrested and executed as a direct result of this has not convinced the Yad Vashem authorities. Nor has the testimony of Dorothee Fliess, one of the Jews that he saved.

The following illustrates their attitude and is taken from an article by Marilyn Henry, entitled, *Who, exactly, is a Righteous Gentile?* published in the *Jerusalem Post* on Wednesday, 29 April 1998:

> The issue, said the director of Yad Vashem's Department for the Righteous Among the Nations, Mordechai Paldiel, is not whether Bonhoeffer deserves our admiration for his courageous anti-Nazi stand, which eventually doomed him – he is a martyr in the struggle against Nazism. Our program of Righteous Among the Nations, however, is geared to persons who specifically helped Jews, and this aspect has not been established with regard to Dietrich Bonhoeffer.
>
> Yad Vashem's decision on Bonhoeffer, said Paldiel, is a question of principle and sticking to the main outline of the program. This is not about the good guys vs. the bad guys. He's one of the good guys. But, he added, we wish to underline that the Righteous program was not designed by the Israeli parliament to cover all those who died as martyrs in the anti-Nazi struggle, but to honor non-Jews who specifically addressed themselves to the Jewish issue and risked their lives in the attempt to aid Jews.
>
> Yad Vashem remains prepared to re-examine the Bonhoeffer case, he said. We are still looking for that piece of evidence that will link him directly to the rescue of Jews.

One wonders exactly what would convince Mordecai Paldiel. Perhaps he thinks that twelve Jews were not enough to warrant a mention. Yad Vashem has recognized Heinrich Grüber, the Confessing Church pastor who helped to save 2,000 Jews, but has also withheld recognition of the sacrifice of Hans von Dohnanyi. Of him Mordecai Paldiel has said:

> With all our respect and admiration, the decision was that he had not risked his life in the operation, because he had had the full knowledge and consent of the organization, of Canaris. Von Dohnanyi was executed, but this had nothing to do with this operation.

Does he really think that the knowledge and consent of Admiral Wilhelm Canaris, a man who was also convicted and executed as a traitor to his country, was sufficient protection for von Dohnanyi?

*   *   *

Not all resistance to the Nazi regime came from pastors free to preach to their congregations. Pastor Paul Schneider was known as the Preacher of Buchenwald. He was born in 1897, the second child of Gustav Adolf Schneider, a Calvinist minister. He served with the army during the First World War where he sustained a serious stomach injury. He had intended to become a doctor but during the course of the war he changed his mind and decided to make the church his life. He completed his theological training at a college in Soest, a Westphalian town to the north-east of the industrial city of Essen, and was ordained in 1925. He became assistant pastor in Essen-Altstadt but soon afterwards his father died and Paul succeeded him as pastor of Hochelheim. All went well for Schneider until the Nazis came to power. He was outspoken in his condemnation of them and their policies and, although his congregation seemed to support him, he felt that he was not supported by his superiors within the Church and so left to accept a position in the Rhineland town of Dickenschied in 1934. Here he became an extremely popular pastor, loved and respected by his congregation.

Soon after his arrival in Dickenschied he conducted the funeral of a young man and had cause to reprimand a Nazi who came to the funeral and declared that he would enrol the dead man in the Storm Troops of heaven. Following this reprimand he was arrested and imprisoned for a week. He was only released after a great outcry from his parishioners. He found himself in trouble with the authorities many times over the next three years and on 31 July 1937 he was arrested and sent to prison in Koblenz. He used the time of this imprisonment to study the bible and to learn passages by heart. Upon his release he was taken to Wiesbaden and told that he was no longer allowed to preach in the Rhineland. His first action after his arrival in Wiesbaden was to go to the railway station and buy a ticket back to Dickenschied, where he preached to his parishioners the next morning. Later that day he was again arrested and imprisoned. He was never to preach in his church again.

In November 1937 Paul Schneider was taken to Buchenwald concentration camp. There he was told that he must salute the Nazi flag and when he refused he was sentenced to twenty-five lashes. He suffered this and subsequent tortures bravely. Whenever he was able, he shouted encouragement to his fellow prisoners and quoted passages from the bible to them, thus earning himself the title of Preacher of Buchenwald. He was put into solitary confinement and told that if he would only promise to stay away from his congregation in Dickenschied he would be released. He steadfastly refused to do so and continued shouting out the scriptures from his isolated cell. The authorities at Buchenwald continued torturing him throughout 1938 and into the early summer of 1939. In July 1939 Pastor Paul Schneider died. His wife, Margarethe, received the following telegram, informing her of his death:

> Paul Schneider, born 29th August, 1897, died today. If it is wished to bury at own cost, contact within 24 hours, Registrar of deaths, Weimar. Otherwise cremation. Camp Commandant, Buchenwald.

Margarethe brought her husband's body home to Dickenschied where he was buried. The minister who conducted his funeral said of him, 'He is delivered, his faith has become sight, he has gone home.'

The actions of the Seventh Day Adventists sadly do not stand up to scrutiny during the Nazi regime. This religious group, which came into being in America in 1863, did not reach Europe until 1874. In 1888 the church established itself in Germany under the leadership of L.R. Conradi, who, the following year, set up the German headquarters of the Adventist Church in the north German city of Hamburg.

In early conflicts the Adventists had been conscientious objectors, serving in medical and other non-combatant units. By the time of the First World War most of the German Adventists had compromised their principles and decided that it was acceptable to serve in a combatant role. Those who did not broke away from the mainstream church and called themselves the Seventh Day Adventist Reform Movement.

When Hitler came to power in 1933 the Seventh Day Adventists welcomed him. He at first seemed to embrace their own principles. He did not smoke or drink alcohol, tea or coffee, nor did he eat meat. The Adventists believed that he was in favour of religious freedom and, even when it became clear that he was not, they excused him by saying that it was the policy of the Nazis and not of Hitler himself. When many of the small Christian sects were banned and pressure was put upon all Christians to belong to the State church, Adventists declared themselves to be in agreement with Nazi policies of sterilization and race and were allowed to continue functioning. They also decided to work on the Sabbath, in direct defiance of their principles; the rationale being that if they did not do so they would have been imprisoned. It was a strange logic that allowed them to function almost unhindered throughout the Nazi regime.

Although most Adventist leaders within Germany were quite happy to abandon their beliefs for the sake of convenience, the General Conference of the church overseas criticized them heavily for their betrayal of the most fundamental of their principles and for bringing the name of the church as a whole into disrepute.

I do not mean to suggest that there were not individual Adventists who went against the dictates of their leaders and chose instead to obey their consciences. There were undoubtedly those who held true to their beliefs. Their self-seeking leadership betrayed them also.

Another sect that failed dismally to stand up to the atrocities of the Nazi regime was the Church of Jesus Christ of Latter Day Saints, more commonly known as Mormons. Like the Seventh Day Adventists, Mormons also accepted Nazism almost without question.

In certain respects there were Nazi beliefs that would seem, at first sight, to agree entirely with Mormon doctrine. Mormons did not, and still do not, drink alcohol, tea or coffee, nor do they smoke. All worthy male members of the Church of Jesus Christ of Latter Day Saints were entitled to hold the priesthood, all, that is, except black Church members. Church leadership will tell you that it is because it was decreed so by God because of the 'Curse of Cain'. This curse was because Cain killed his brother Abel. The Lord decreed that Cain and his descendants should wander the earth and would be marked to show that they were descendants of Cain. This mark took the form of a black skin. Instead of Cain, the elder brother, and his descendants receiving their birthright of the priesthood before Abel's descendants, they would have to wait until after all of Abel's descendants had been given it because of Cain's crime. This, of course, does not mean that Mormons regarded all black people as being guilty of Cain's sin but it did, nonetheless, prohibit black men from holding the priesthood of the Church until 1 June 1978 when the then Church president, Spencer W. Kimball, received a revelation that all men should be given the priesthood regardless of race or colour. This, however, was thirty-three years *after* the fall of the Nazis.

Perhaps the other most likely reason that the Mormons accepted the Nazis, can be explained by their Twelfth Article of Faith, which says, 'We believe in being subject to kings, presidents, rulers, and magistrates, in obeying, honouring, and sustaining the law,' and by a reference in the Mormon book, Doctrine and Covenants, section 58, verse 21, which states: 'Let no man break the laws of the land, for he that keepeth the laws of God hath no need to break the laws of the land.'

Perhaps, most damning of all when considering whether or not to obey Nazi laws were numbers 5 and 8 of the *Declarations of Belief Regarding Governments and Laws in General* which were issued by the first Prophet of the Church, Joseph Smith, and were adopted by a unanimous vote at a general assembly of the Church on 17 August 1835 in Kirtland, Ohio, USA:

> 5. We believe that all men are bound to sustain and uphold the respective governments in which they reside, while protected in their inherent and inalienable rights by the laws of such governments; and that sedition and rebellion are unbecoming every citizen thus protected and should be punished accordingly; and that all governments have a right to enact such laws as in their own judgements are best calculated to secure the public interest; at the same time, however, holding sacred the freedom of conscience.
>
> 8. We believe that the commission of crime should be punished according to the nature of the offence; that murder, treason, robbery, theft, and the breach of the general peace, in all respects, should be punished according to their criminality and their tendency to evil among men, by the laws of that government in which the offence is committed; and for the public peace and tranquillity all men should step forward and use their ability in bringing offenders against good laws to punishment.

Had more Mormons wished to follow their consciences they could have paid heed to declaration 4 of the same document, which stated that:

> 4. We believe that religion is instituted of God; and that men are amenable to Him, and to Him only, for the exercise of it, unless their religious opinions prompt them to infringe upon the rights and liberties of others; but we do not believe that human law has a right to interfere in prescribing rules of worship to bind the consciences of men, nor dictate forms for public or private devotion; that the civil magistrate should restrain crime, but never control conscience; should punish guilt, but never suppress the freedom of the soul.

Since the Nazis had made it a law that their dictates must be obeyed and since they would allow no dissention among the population, it could be said that, in following one's conscience, the laws of the land were being broken, which was against the teachings of the Prophet Joseph Smith. These are, of course, very flimsy excuses for accepting an evil doctrine and embracing it wholeheartedly. In later years the Church has tried to distance itself somewhat from the acceptance of these Nazi beliefs. In his book *Mormon Doctrine* Church member Bruce R. McConkie wrote in 1966:

> In the ultimate sense Satan is the father of all persecution. He uses it in an attempt to deny men their agency *[free will]*. Obviously he works through mortal persons who hearken to his enticements and who bow to his decrees. From earliest times, individuals, organizations, governments and churches have become instruments in his hands to carry on projects of persecution. In modern times Hitler chose to persecute the Jewish people and Stalin chose to heap onerous burdens upon whole nations of non-communistic peoples. Both received their inspiration from beneath.

Although there undoubtedly were Mormons who did their best to resist the government of Nazi Germany, I have been able to find only one documented example of Mormons doing anything at all to defy the Nazis. These exceptions were Helmuth Huebener and his friends, Karl-Heinz Schnibbe and Rudi Wobbe. Huebener was an administrative apprentice in Hamburg and a member of the local Mormon chapel. However, his resistance to Hitler seems to have been prompted more by outrage at the regime's policies and lies than by any religious beliefs. He used to listen to banned radio broadcasts from the BBC and produced flyers which he and his friends, Schnibbe and Wobbe, distributed to public buildings, phone boxes and letter boxes in the areas in which they lived. Gerhard Düwer, another administrative apprentice, joined them in their dangerous work. The flyers highlighted the difference in reports of the German authorities with those of the Allies and, perhaps more the result of youthful high spirits than political conviction, also made fun of Josef Goebbels in verse.

Huebener and his friends only managed to produce and distribute their leaflets for a few months between the summer of 1941 and the beginning of 1942. In February 1942 Huebener decided to try to expand his resistance and was caught by one of his work supervisors trying to get a French-speaking colleague to translate his flyers into French to be distributed among the foreign workers. He and his three friends were arrested and imprisoned in Berlin where, on 11 August 1942, having been tried by the infamous People's Court, they were found guilty of treason. Schnibbe, Wobbe and Düwer were sentenced to prison terms of between four and ten years. Helmuth Huebener was sentenced to death. On 27 October 1942 he was beheaded at the prison of Plötzensee in Berlin. He was just seventeen years old and one of the youngest resisters to be executed.

The Christians who did take heed of the biblical warnings in St Matthew's gospel were not always from the largest or the strongest church groups.

The Quakers or Religious Society of Friends' official policy was to condemn the Nazis and their doctrine and to assist anyone who sought help as a result of mistreatment by the government. Following the *Kristallnacht* atrocities the Quakers raised funds to help Jews leave Germany and settle in other countries. They also rescued an estimated 10,000 German and Austrian Jewish children by sending them to England where sympathetic families looked them after until they could be reclaimed by their parents when the Nazi regime had fallen.

There are countless stories of help provided by individual

Quakers, often at great risk to themselves, to Jews and other groups who had fallen foul of the Nazi regime. Many of these good people ended their days in Nazi concentration camps, but they had been true to themselves and their principles and didn't seem to mind that they had suffered for them.

The only other group of people who seem to have been able to endure the horrors of Nazi Germany and emerge with their collective conscience intact were the Jehovah's Witnesses.

Established in Germany in 1897 the Jehovah's Witnesses were a religious group that had been founded in America by Charles Taze Russell. The group, at first called the International Bible Students Association, began in Pittsburgh in 1872. Seven years later Russell started a magazine, which became the journal of the association and was called *The Watchtower*.

There had been opposition to the Jehovah's Witnesses or *Bibelforscher,* as they were known in Germany before the Nazis came to power. In 1921 an article in a church newspaper accused them of being linked with the Jews in subversive political movements. Nine years later they were again accused of forming links with Jewish organizations to start a revolutionary movement. Another Jehovah's Witness magazine *The Golden Age* countered this accusation in an article on 15 April 1930, which said:

> We have no reason to regard this false accusation as an insult—as we are convinced that the Jew is at least as valuable a person as a nominal Christian; but we reject the above untruth of the church tabloid because it is aimed at deprecating our work, as if it were being done not for the sake of the Gospel but for the Jews.

This would seem to mean that they regarded Jews as being as valuable as anyone else who was not of their faith which was certainly a lot better than many of the other religious groups' official policies.

On 24 April 1933 the Nazis closed the *Watchtower* office in Magdeburg, but, through the influence of the American State Department, property seized from the Witnesses was returned and their office was reopened.

Joseph F. Rutherford, president of the Watchtower Society, was anxious to let Hitler and his government know that the Jehovah's Witnesses were not a threat to their administration and so a conference was hastily arranged on 25 June 1933 at the Wilmersdorfer Tennishallen in Berlin to put forward the official policy of the church. Rutherford came over to Berlin from America to lend support at the conference. Although only 5,000 Witnesses were expected to attend, over 7,000 actually turned up. Conference delegates put forward a motion setting out their collective view, which was adopted and called the Declaration of Facts. It complained about the restriction that had been placed on the work of the Witnesses and sought to reassure the government that they were only trying to spread the word of God by declaring that 'Our organization is not political in any sense. We only insist on teaching the Word of Jehovah God to the people.'

It further stated that:

> We are wrongfully charged before the ruling powers of this government . . . We do respectfully ask the rulers of the nation and the people to give a fair and impartial consideration to the statement of facts here made.
>
> We have no fight with any persons or religious teachers, but we must call attention to the fact that it is generally those who claim to represent God and Christ Jesus who are in fact our persecutors and who misrepresent us before the governments.

The Declaration of Facts did nothing to appease Hitler and Nazi persecution of the Witnesses began in earnest. Because of their support for the Jews and the fact that they refused to give the Nazi salute or use the Nazi greeting of 'Heil Hitler!' Adolf Hitler spoke disparagingly of Jehovah's Witnesses:

> These so-called 'Earnest Bible Students' are trouble-makers; they disturb the harmonious life amongst the Germans; I consider them quacks; I do not tolerate that the German Catholics be besmirched in such a manner by this American 'Judge' Rutherford; I dissolve the 'Earnest Bible Students' in Germany; their property I dedicate to the people's welfare; I will have all their literature confiscated.

On 24 June 1933, one day before the conference in Berlin, the Nazis had banned the Jehovah's Witness movement in Germany, but the news had not reached many of them and did not do so until several days later.

At the end of the conference the delegates distributed over 2 million copies of the Declaration of Facts. Since many of the Witnesses were not aware that they were promoting the views of a banned organization they did not realize that what they were doing was very dangerous.

The arrests and imprisonment began almost immediately. Just as the Jews were forced to wear armbands with a yellow Star of David, so the Jehovah's Witnesses who were sent to concentration camps had to wear purple triangles. They were told that if they would only renounce their religion they would be set free. They were given a document to sign. The following is a translation, which very few of them did sign, in spite of fierce interrogations and brutal treatment:

DECLARATION RENOUNCING BELIEFS

Concentration camp. . . . .

Department II

DECLARATION

I, ...

Born on . . . .

In . . . .

herewith make the following declaration:

1. I have come to know that the International Bible Students Association is proclaiming erroneous teachings and under the cloak of religion follows hostile purposes against the State.

2. I therefore left the organization entirely and made myself absolutely free from the teachings of this sect.

3. I herewith give assurance that I will never again take any part in the activity of the International Bible Students Association. Any persons approaching me with the teaching of the Bible Students, or who in any manner reveal their connections with them, I will denounce immediately. All literature from the Bible Students that should be sent to my address I will at once deliver to the nearest police station.

4. I will in the future esteem the laws of the State, especially

in the event of war will I, with weapon in hand, defend the fatherland, and join in every way the community of the people.

5. I have been informed that I will at once be taken again into protective custody if I should act against the declaration given today.

. . . . Dated

. . . . Signature

Rudolf Franz Ferdinand Hoess was commandant of Sachsenhausen concentration camp between 1938 and May 1940 when he was transferred to Auschwitz. During his time at Sachsenhausen he presided over many executions, including those of Jehovah's Witnesses, whose fellow members were sometimes made to watch their friends die. He said of the Witnesses:

> These Jehovah's Witnesses became even more fanatical in their faith as a result of the martyrdom of their comrades. Several of them who had already signed a declaration that they would cease to proselytise, a declaration which helped them to obtain their freedom, now withdrew it, since they were anxious to suffer even more for Jehovah.

Many of the prisoners who knew Witnesses in the camps were impressed with their behaviour. They were usually cheerful, helpful and steadfast in their belief that by opposing the Nazi government and holding true to their religious convictions they were serving God.

There were many instances of Witnesses helping other prisoners, Jews and Gentiles alike, and some have described them as being 'the most astonishing groups in the concentration camps'. Although the Nazis appeared to be worried by their inability to break the spirits of this group they also valued them as workers and Witnesses were given positions of trust, even being allowed to work outside of the concentration camps because they had given their word that they would not escape.

By the time that the Nazi era had come to an end over 10,000 Jehovah's Witnesses had been imprisoned. Two thousand had suffered the brutality of the concentration camps and it is believed that around 1,200 had died for their beliefs, 250 having been executed. Although these figures are usually quoted as being correct, since the fall of the Nazis there have been reports that they have been greatly exaggerated and that no more than 635 Jehovah's Witnesses died. I have been unable to ascertain which figure is correct, but I wonder whether it really matters how many Witnesses died for their faith; every single death was a tragedy. Whether it was 635 or 1,200, each of those people died for what they believed in and went to their graves, such as they were, knowing that they had not compromised their faith or their integrity and that, surely, is what counts.

Chapter Eight

The Lone Assassin

Of the many attempts on the life of Adolf Hitler that were made during his twelve years in office those that came the closest to succeeding took place just before and during the Second World War.

In his first year as Chancellor there were said to be as many as one attempt every week to rid the country of the man who would ultimately bring shame to the German people, but these were often 'spur of the moment' attempts or badly planned and executed.

The first serious lone attempt to assassinate Hitler came in November 1939 on the anniversary of the abortive Munich *putsch* of 1923. It was usual for Hitler to lead a parade through the streets of Munich, recreating the march made on 9 November 1923 to the headquarters of Bavarian army commander, Otto von Lossow. The parade would then go on to the *Bürgerbräukeller* where Hitler would make a lengthy speech, usually lasting about ninety minutes, and then he and his cronies would reminisce about the old days and their colleagues who had given their lives in the attempted *putsch*. The event lasted several hours and always followed the same procedure. On 8 November 1939, however, the 'memorial day' turned out to be quite different from those of previous years.

Johann Georg Elser was born on 4 January 1903 in Hermaringen. After completing his schooling he trained to be a cabinet-maker, but by 1930 was unemployed, like so many of his fellow Germans. Although the rise of the NSDAP brought promises of better conditions for the workers, Elser was unimpressed and thought that conditions had, in fact, deteriorated after the Nazis came to power. By 1938 he believed that the policy of *Lebensraum* would inevitably lead to war and he decided that the only way to stop this would be to assassinate Hitler and rid the country of the Nazis.

Elser decided to make his assassination attempt on 8 November 1939 at the *Bürgerbräukeller* while Hitler was making his usual speech. He began going there on a regular basis to see how his task might be accomplished and decided that a bomb, placed by one of the pillars that supported the ceiling, would be the best way to ensure Hitler's demise.

Some weeks before the 'memorial day' march Elser hid in the *Bürgerbräukeller* when it closed so that he could work on his plan. As soon as everyone left the building he emerged from his hiding place and removed a wooden panel from the base of the pillar he had chosen. He then began gouging out a space in the pillar so that he could place a bomb there. Night after night he continued his secret work, replacing the panel before the staff arrived each day and then hiding again until it was safe to emerge and drift out of the beer cellar while there were plenty of people around. It was painstaking work and conducted in very difficult conditions. Because he needed the space to be near to the bottom of the pillar in order to do the most damage, he had to work crouched on his knees on the ground. His knees became very grazed and seemed to be permanently covered in sores and scabs.

During the time that he was away from the *Bürgerbräukeller* Elser perfected his bomb-making skills. He not only had to construct a device that would explode, he also had to ensure that it would work on a timer and that it could be remotely detonated in case of any problems with the timer. Eventually, after much experimenting, he was satisfied that everything was in order and ready for the 'memorial day' speech.

The week before the speech was due to be given Elser began to install the bomb in the space he had hollowed out of the pillar. His work was completed on 5 November and then all he had to do was to go into the *Bürgerbräukeller* on the evening of 8 November and set the timer. This he did with no problems and immediately left Munich and travelled to the Swiss border to make his escape.

The parade took place through the streets of Munich, to the headquarters of the former Bavarian army commander and then on

to the *Bürgerbräukeller*. Up to this point everything was going according to the plan of previous years. At around 8.30 p.m. Hitler would stand to tumultuous applause and begin his speech. He rarely sat down again before 10.00 p.m. This evening, however, he started to speak at 8.00 p.m. and finished at 9.07 p.m. His speech was almost half an hour shorter than normal and he left immediately after he finished speaking. The gathered crowds were told that he couldn't stay to socialize with them, as he had to go to Berlin that same night. Minutes after he left, at 9.20 p.m., a huge explosion rocked the *Bürgerbräukeller*. The pillar in which the bomb had been placed collapsed, causing the ceiling to cave in. Six people died instantly, another died as he was being rushed to hospital and sixty-three others were badly injured.

Georg Elser, meanwhile, had arrived at the border town of Constance and attempted to cross into Switzerland. His greatest mistake was, perhaps, to try to get into Switzerland illegally, for he was caught in the attempt and placed under arrest while the authorities investigated the reason for his hurried flight from Germany. While he was still in custody, news reached the border officials of the assassination attempt and, since he had been carrying a postcard showing the *Bürgerbräukeller* with a cross marked on the pillar in which the bomb had been placed, they immediately decided that they had found the culprit and returned Elser at once to the Gestapo in Munich.

At first he denied any knowledge of the event but when the injuries to his knees were discovered and certain members of the staff at the *Bürgerbräukeller* told of having seen Elser hanging around the place on numerous occasions, he changed his story and confessed to having placed the bomb. He was sent to Sachsenhausen concentration camp where he was placed in solitary confinement for much of the time. Curiously he was given special privileges while in the camp and he remained there for the next five years. At the end of 1944 he was transferred to Dachau where, on 9 April 1945, he was executed.

So ended the first serious attempt on the life of Adolf Hitler. But was it really an assassination attempt at all or had it been an elaborate ruse, orchestrated by the Nazis themselves to implicate the British Secret Service?

The day after the bomb explosion the *Völkischer Beobachter,* the

Nazi newspaper, printed an article about the event in which it blamed the British Secret Service and Prime Minister Neville Chamberlain.

For several weeks prior to the assassination attempt the small group of German army officers led by Chief of the General Staff, General Franz Halder, and his superior officer, Commander-in-Chief of the Army, Field Marshal Walther von Brauchitsch, had been planning the overthrow of Hitler and his government. At best it was a very half-hearted attempt brought about mainly by their irritation at the interference of Hitler in military matters and because they had been told by the Führer that he was planning an attack on the neutral countries of Luxembourg, Belgium and Holland. Von Brauchitsch in particular was torn between his dislike for Nazi policies and his natural desire as a career military officer to obey orders. Halder was only marginally more decisive in his resolve to overthrow Hitler. Although both tried, without success, to dissuade Hitler from attacking the neutral countries they finally decided that they would begin their attempt once they had been given a final date for the attack. However, when the order came, both by telephone and in writing, to attack on 12 November they still did nothing, and, because there was bad weather and Hitler kept changing the date for the attack, they felt justified in doing nothing.

Only Colonel Hans Oster, Chief of Staff of the *Abwehr*, had the presence of mind to do anything at all and he contacted the Dutch and Belgian embassies in Berlin and told them to expect a German attack on their countries.

On 7 November a joint declaration was made by King Leopold of Belgium and Queen Wilhelmina of Holland in which they offered to mediate a peace before the war in the west of Europe became too violent. The following day the German ambassador to Belgium sent a message to Berlin informing the authorities that King Leopold had told Queen Wilhelmina that he had discovered evidence that the German army was about to attack. This confirmed to the Nazis that there was either a traitor or a group of traitors in their midst, passing information to the then neutral countries and, perhaps, to Britain.

Because they had suspected that there were enemies of the state working alongside the British, Heinrich Himmler had ordered one of his most promising SS officers, Walter Schellenberg, to go to Holland and try to find out which British secret agents were working there and what they were doing. In this way he hoped that the British would, unsuspectingly, lead him to the German traitors. Calling himself Major Schaemmel, Schellenberg had gone to Holland where he had made contact with two British agents, Captain S. Payne Best and Major R. H. Stevens. He told them that he was anti-Nazi and that there were a number of high-ranking German military leaders who were anxious to depose Hitler and end the war as soon as possible. He said that what they wanted was a reassurance from the British government that they would look favourably upon a new German government after Hitler. The British were curious and felt that it was in their interest to explore further the possibilities of cooperating with such a group of Germans and so they provided a radio so that 'Major Schaemmel' could keep in touch with their two agents in Holland. Several contacts were made and meetings were arranged. Then, just hours after the assassination attempt in Munich, Himmler once again ordered Schellenberg to go to Holland and meet with the British agents, but this time he wanted Schellenberg to kidnap them and bring them back to Germany. SS *Sturmbannführer* Alfred Naujocks, who had made the attack on the Gleiwitz radio station that signalled the invasion of Poland and the start of the Second World War, assisted him in this task.

While Schellenberg waited at a café for his British contacts, Naujocks apprehended them as they parked their car. With them was a Dutch officer, Lieutenant Klop, who was wounded in the struggle and died a few days after being kidnapped. On 21 November Heinrich Himmler made an announcement telling the public that British Intelligence had been behind the bomb plot and assassination attempt on Hitler and that the person who had actually placed the bomb was a German Communist named Georg Elser. In this way the Nazis managed to convince the German people that a war against Britain was justified; they had, after all, tried to kill the beloved Führer, the Communists were again implicated because it was said that Elser was a Communist and, a few months later, Hitler had the excuse he needed to invade Holland as the British agents had been in collusion with the Dutch.

Captain S. Payne Best and Major R. H. Stevens were sent to Sachsenhausen concentration camp where they remained until, with the approach of Russian troops towards the end of the war, they were transferred to Dachau. The Americans eventually freed them in 1945.

While he was in the camp. Payne Best met Georg Elser for the first time. Elser spent some time talking to him about what had happened on 8 November and how he came to be involved with the assassination attempt in the first place. He said that in the summer of 1939 he had been arrested and sent to Dachau concentration camp because he was a Communist. While he was there he was approached by two men who spoke to him in the office of the camp commandant. They told him that it was possible that there were certain people close to Hitler who were traitors to the Nazi cause and had to be disposed of. They proposed to blow up the *Bürgerbräukeller* just after Hitler had left the building on the night of 8 November so that these traitors would be eliminated. They asked Elser if he would cooperate with them and plant the bomb. In return for this they promised him good treatment while he remained in Dachau and then a large sum of money and assistance to go into exile in Switzerland. Elser told Best that he had agreed to their request and that they had taken him to the *Bürgerbräukeller* in early November to enable him to plant the bomb, which he had constructed while still a prisoner in Dachau. Following the explosion they had taken him to the Swiss frontier where they gave him money and a postcard of the beer cellar with the pillar containing the bomb marked with a cross. As he prepared to cross into Switzerland the two men disappeared and the Gestapo arrested him. They took him back to Munich and then on to the Sachsenhausen concentration camp near Berlin. He was told that he must remember the names of Payne Best and Stevens so that when they all came to trial he could declare them to be the ringleaders of the plot. There never was a trial and it is here that the two stories once again become one.

Elser was given special treatment while at Sachsenhausen, it was said on the orders of Hitler himself. When he was transferred to Dachau he was known as Eller. After the transfer Elser told the same story to Pastor Martin Niemöller who believed what he said about the conspiracy but Walter Schellenberg, who had worked so hard to try to implicate the British, believed, perhaps understandably in view of his own position, that the assassination attempt was the act of a lone man.

In the following years there was much speculation and discussion about which of the two stories was true. The assassination attempt quite clearly had nothing to do with the British agents or with Neville Chamberlain, but there was much talk about whether or not it was a Nazi plot to promote Hitler. Whichever story was true, Elser was doomed from the start, as in either case he really had no chance of escape. Many people were convinced that he had worked alone and that the Nazis were in no way implicated. That may have been likely, although it is curious that Elser should himself promote the story of the Nazi conspiracy, especially since he told it to one of the very people he was supposed to blame at the non-existent trial. There are many others who believe that it was the work of the Nazis and that Elser was a scapegoat in much the same way that Marinus van der Lubbe had been following the *Reichstag* fire.

What strikes me as being particularly curious is that the Nazis, who were guilty of some of the most horrific crimes of modern times, should have felt it necessary to go to the trouble of pretending that this assassination attempt was the work of others. Although it would have seemed to have given them the right to attack Holland and to perpetuate the fight against Great Britain, their reasons were so flimsy that they were unlikely to have been believed by anyone outside Germany, and those within the country either wholeheartedly supported the Nazis or were too frightened to do anything about them.

The fact that Elser received special treatment while in Sachsenhausen on the orders of Hitler, including extra food and cigarettes, does lend credence to the conspiracy theory. Why give these special privileges to someone who has just tried to kill you? If there was a conspiracy it would also have been likely that Elser would have been killed to stop him talking about it, especially when it became clear that the Germans were going to lose the war.

Although the Nazis claimed that Elser had been killed in an Allied bombing raid on 15 April 1945 this would not appear to be true. Dr Johannes Neuhäusler, who was also a prisoner in Dachau, has claimed that a letter was sent to the camp commandant on 5 April 1945 from the 'Chief of the Security Police and of the Security

Service'. Dr Neuhäusler says that this letter, described as containing State Secrets, was stolen from an SS guard by Captain Payne Best and detailed the following treatment to be given to Georg Elser, or Eller, as he was known in Dachau:

> Also in the case of our special prisoner 'Eller' a conference was held by the highest authorities. The following instructions were issued:
>
> On the occasion of one of the next air raids on Munich or in the vicinity of Dachau, 'Eller' is to be presumed fatally injured.
>
> For this reason I ask you to liquidate 'Eller' in an absolutely secret manner after such an occurrence in the camp. I ask you to see to it carefully that only very few persons who are to be bound to secrecy know of it. The notice of the execution to me would then read:
>
> 'On . . . , as a result of the terror attack on . . . ., the prisoner 'Eller' was among those fatally injured.
>
> Having taken notice of this letter and carried out the instructions mentioned therein, I ask you to destroy it.

The signature at the bottom of this damning letter was illegible but the contents would seem to explain the death of Georg Elser.

There has never been a conclusive answer to the question of whether Georg Elser's assassination attempt was motivated by conviction or by money. With no one left to give a definitive answer it will probably always remain a mystery.

Chapter Nine

The Spy in the SS

With the exception of his great-grandfather, most of Kurt Gerstein's family had been in the service of the judiciary. His great-grandfather was considered to be the black sheep of the family, a role that perhaps Kurt inherited from him.

Kurt, born on 11 August 1905 in Münster, was the sixth of Judge Ludwig Gerstein's seven children. His brother Karl described him as being the 'most difficult' of his siblings. A solitary child, Kurt did not relate well to his brothers and sisters or to other members of his family. Brought up by his father in the German traditions of obedience and hard work, he defied his father and took delight in being rebellious and disobedient. He regarded both his parents as cold and remote and felt particularly neglected by his mother.

At school his behaviour was no better. Although he was intelligent and attended three different grammar schools as a result of his father being moved from Saarbrücken to Halberstadt and then on to Neurippin, he was lazy and totally unconcerned about his teachers' unfavourable opinions of him. He found it amusing to be regarded in such a bad light and no amount of chastising could make him change his ways. He 'thumbed his nose' at authority and took absolutely no notice of the bad reports he was always receiving. In spite of this attitude he worked sufficiently well to be able to graduate from his grammar school and attend university.

He was accepted at the University of Marburg in 1925 and became a member of a student association, the Teutonia, which his father had encouraged him to join. Although he obeyed him in this one request, he was only ever an associate member and he objected to the rituals of the association and saw its members as being empty-headed and without a purpose in life.

While he was at university Kurt became interested in religion, something not taught to him by his parents, and he joined several Christian organizations. Even after he left university in 1931 to become a mining engineer he stayed loyal to his Christian youth groups, being a member of the Federation of German Bible Circles until Hitler banned it in 1934.

At first Kurt Gerstein was in favour of the Nazi regime and he approved of German nationalism. On 2 May 1933 he joined the NSDAP, but soon discovered that his beliefs and those of the party were at odds, particularly on religious grounds. He found himself in trouble with fellow members of the party. Attending a play, *Wittekind* by Edmund Kiss, early in 1935, he suddenly stood up in the middle of the action and shouted, 'This is unheard of! We shall not allow our faith to be publicly mocked without protest!'

For his troubles he received a black eye, a cut mouth and some broken teeth. Eighteen months later he was arrested and imprisoned for attaching anti-Nazi literature to official Miners' Association letters. A search of his house produced a large number of similar leaflets ready for posting. This led to him being excluded from the NSDAP.

Released from prison after only six weeks, Gerstein lost his job in the mines and was unable to find further employment. For a time he played around with the idea of devoting his life to religion but then decided to go to the Protestant Missions Institute to study medicine.

On 31 August 1937, at the age of thirty-two, Gerstein married his long-time fiancée, Elfriede Bensch. Not content to settle down to domestic life, Gerstein continued his anti-Nazi work and, nearly a year later, was again arrested. He was sent to a concentration camp where he remained for nearly a year, totally losing his membership of the NSDAP as a further punishment. Although he tried to rejoin he was not allowed to do so.

During a conversation with the Bishop of Stuttgart, Gerstein was told about the euthanasia centres at Hadamar and Grafeneck. What he heard sickened him, and his agitation at the things that were taking place at these institutions was heightened when his own sister-in-law, Bertha Ebeling, died at Hadamar. Gerstein decided that he had to try to find out exactly what was being allowed to happen and, with this in mind, he joined the *Waffen* SS. Although this elite order was only open to party members no one questioned him and it was assumed that he did belong to the party.

Gerstein went to work in the hygiene section of the medical department of the SS where he designed a water filter for German troops. It was to be the key to his success at remaining within the organization.

In November 1941 he was spotted in uniform by someone who knew he had been thrown out of the party, but, in spite of this person informing on him, his superiors were so pleased with his work that they allowed him to stay on.

In January the following year Gerstein was promoted, becoming head of the Technical Disinfection Department where he worked with poisonous substances including the highly toxic gas, Zyklon B, the commercial form of hydrocyanic acid.

When the Nazis first started to order the mass killing of Jews, gypsies, political dissidents and other 'enemies of the state', they had gas chambers made that used carbon monoxide to kill their victims. It was a slow process and, although they didn't care at all about the suffering of the people, they did find it irritating and in-efficient to have to take so long over disposing of what they regarded as vermin. Adolf Hitler made it clear what his view of these people was when he said:

> Nature is cruel; therefore we are also entitled to be cruel. When I send the flower of German youth into the steel hail of the next war without feeling the slightest regret over the precious German blood that is being spilled, should I not also have the right to eliminate millions of an inferior race that multiplies like vermin?

It was believed that efficiency in killing these people could be increased by the use of Zyklon B in the gas chambers and Kurt Gerstein found himself ordered to the camps of Majdanek, Belzec and Treblinka in Poland to observe the present methods with a view to seeing how the system could be improved.

At Belzec he had to witness the killing of an entire trainload of Jews. When the train arrived many were already dead, having been packed into the train with no room to move or lie down. The survivors were told that they were being sent to the bathhouse to be disinfected. They were assured that they would come to no harm and that they should breathe deeply to ensure that infectious diseases were prevented.

The people were herded naked into the gas chamber. Families still clung together, children holding their parents' hands, husbands putting protective arms around their wives. The doors were slammed shut and the diesel pumping engine was started. Almost immediately it broke down. Gerstein, as an observer to these atrocities, was making notes, trying to look unconcerned when in reality he was filled with a horror he found hard to control. The minutes passed while engineers were brought in to mend the faulty engine. From inside the gas chamber the sound of crying could be heard. Periodically an SS officer peered through the glass window in the door of the chamber to see what was happening inside. He reported that they were wailing like they did in the synagogue. This officer seemed to feel no sorrow or pity for the wretched souls squashed inside the small chamber, bodies pressed so tightly together that there was no room to turn or shift their weight from one leg to the other; no room for a mother to bend to comfort the small child clinging to her legs. Eventually, after being trapped for more than two hours, the diesel engine croaked into life, but it took another thirty minutes of pumping the deadly carbon monoxide into the chamber before everyone inside was dead. When the doors were finally opened, Gerstein observed that 'One could tell families even in death. They were still holding hands, stiffened in death so that it was difficult to tear them apart to clear the chamber for the next load.'

The sickening spectacle was still not over for Gerstein, who was then shown how the bodies were processed:

With gold to the left – without gold to the right. . . . Dentists hammered out gold teeth, bridges and crowns. In the midst of them stood Captain Wirth. He was in his element and, showing me a large can full of teeth, he said, 'See for yourself the weight of that gold! It's only from yesterday and the day before. You can't imagine what we find every day – dollars, diamonds, gold. You'll see for yourself!'

While travelling back by train to Germany Gerstein found himself sharing a compartment with Baron Göran von Otter, Secretary to the Swedish Legation in Berlin. They struck up a conversation and von Otter could see that Gerstein was distressed. He recalled later:

> There were beads of sweat on his forehead. There were tears in his eyes and his voice was hoarse when he said at once, 'I saw something awful yesterday. Can I come and see you at the Legation?'

Von Otter asked if Gerstein was referring to the Jews and when he nodded, suggested that they should speak immediately. Gerstein then began a rambling account of what he had seen. He was distraught and kept going over everything. Von Otter listened patiently to what he had to say and later described that evening on the train:

> We stood there together all night, some six hours or maybe eight, and again and again Gerstein kept on recalling what he had seen. He sobbed and hid his face in his hands. From the very beginning as Gerstein described the atrocities, weeping and broken-hearted, I had no doubt as to the sincerity of his humanitarian intentions.

Gerstein begged von Otter to pass what he had told him on to the Allies so that they might do something to stop the killing. Von Otter promised that he would and when he arrived back at his Legation in Berlin he made a full report that he passed to his superiors. The incredulous Swedes did not believe a word that von Otter had written. Von Otter bumped into Gerstein several months later:

> Some months after the journey in question, Gerstein suddenly found himself face to face with me as I was coming out of the Swedish Embassy in Berlin. He seemed utterly desperate and could scarcely articulate a sentence. He looked as though his nerves were absolutely spent. He asked me what had happened about the plans we had discussed in the train. When I informed him of the steps I had taken to back up my report, I had a feeling that I had brought him comfort and that my statements had given him new hope.

Time and time again Gerstein passed on each new piece of information about what he had witnessed to the Swedes and each time nothing was done. He went further afield and spoke to other foreign diplomats and to Church figures. An increasingly depressed Gerstein continued to try to spread the word about what was happening to whoever he thought might be able to help but nothing was ever done. Memories of what he had seen haunted his waking hours and destroyed his sleep. If only something had been done to stop the killing it would have been worth it but to have witnessed the horror for nothing was unbearable. In a report made by him he recalled the steps he had taken to try to make his knowledge of what was happening public:

> My attempt to report all this to the head of the Legation of the Holy See had no great success. I was asked if I was a soldier. Then I was denied any kind of interview and was requested to leave the legation forthwith.
>
> I relate this to show how difficult it was, even for a German who was a bitter enemy of the Nazis, to succeed in discrediting this criminal government. . . .
>
> I continued to inform hundreds of people of these horrible massacres. Among them were the Niemöller family; Dr Hochstrasser, the press attaché at the Swiss legation in Berlin; Dr Winter, the coadjutor of the Catholic Bishop of Berlin – so that he could transmit my information to the Bishop and to the Pope; Dr Dibelius, and many others. In this way thousands of people were informed by me.

Gerstein was taking enormous risks in trying to get his information through to the outside world. Seeing that it was having no effect, he also tried to stop the killings by declaring cans of Zyklon B to be unstable and insisting on them being buried to prevent a disaster. It was a valiant attempt, but the amount of the chemical he destroyed was merely a drop in the ocean compared with the amount being produced. For every can that he destroyed, another could be ordered from the manufacturer, Degesch, the *Deutsche Gesellschaft für Schädlingsbekämpfung* (German Pest Control Company).

Never one readily to accept the restrictions of authority, Gerstein was completely careless of his own safety. He listened to banned wireless broadcasts from the BBC, playing them openly and very loudly and not seeming to care who was also listening. Nothing seemed to give him comfort from the desperation he felt at being unable to stop the carnage. The one person who might have been able to give him some solace was his wife, Elfriede, but, because he was so frightened for her safety and for that of their three children, he told her very little when he visited her at their home in Tübingen.

Every minute Gerstein expected to be betrayed and arrested, but the war went on and no one came for him. In June 1944 the Allies landed on the beaches of Normandy and began their push through France towards Germany.

In March 1945 Gerstein visited his wife in Tübingen for what was to be the last time. He now had hope that he might be able to survive and tell his story directly to the Allies. On 22 April 1945 he surrendered to French forces in the town of Reutlingen, to the south of Stuttgart. The French sent him westwards to Rottweil where he was housed in the Hotel Mohren. He was required to check in with the French forces every day, but otherwise was free to do as he pleased. He spent the time compiling reports about what he had seen at the death camps, writing his story in both German and French.

At the beginning of May he met two Allied servicemen, British Major D.C. Evans and American John W. Haught. He gave them his French report along with some invoices for Zyklon B, a letter written to him by Degesch and a list of his anti-Nazi friends and acquaintances.

The following is the report that the two Allied officers made, as quoted in Saul Friedländer's book, *Counterfeit Nazi*:

> We were approached in a requisitioned hotel in Rottweil by a man who identified himself as Kurt Gerstein. He told us that we were the first British and American personnel he had seen and that he wanted to speak to us regarding what he knew about German concentration camps. He informed us that he was a personal friend of Pastor Niemöller and that, working for him as a secret agent, he had obtained a post of responsibility in the Nazi Party. In this capacity, he had been present at meetings which dealt with the fate of prisoners in the

114

concentration camps. When he was asked whether he was familiar with the use of gas chambers for killing prisoners, he replied that as an engineer he had often been called upon to advise on the workings of these installations. He said that the two gases used were hydrocyanic acid and the exhaust gas of internal combustion engines. He was unable to give any details of the concentration used, but he said that with HCN death was almost instantaneous, while in the case of exhaust gas it took fifteen to twenty minutes.

Dr Gerstein fled from the Nazis only three weeks ago. He is evidently still affected by his experiences and has difficulty in talking about them. But he is anxious that the guilty parties be brought to trial for their crimes and states that he is prepared to act as a witness. He hopes that the information he has supplied will be transmitted as quickly as possible to the competent authorities in London. He handed over to the signatories a note in English, a seven-page typewritten report and some invoices from the firm of Degesch for the supply of 'Zyklon B' [hydrocyanic acid] to concentration camps. He also showed us, as evidence of his past activities, a religious pamphlet written by him in 1938.

There is reason to consider whether Dr Gerstein should not be protected against the local Nazis.

Gerstein also told the two officers that he had tried to give his report in French to the French authorities to whom he had surrendered, but that they were not interested in receiving it.

At the end of May Gerstein was transferred to the town of Constance and then in June he was taken to Paris in the custody of the *Sûreté*.

On 5 July 1945 Gerstein was put into the *Cherche-Midi* military prison where he was held by the French as a war criminal. Conditions in the prison were disgusting, the cells were full of lice, it was cold and dark and the food was terrible. Twenty days after being arrested as a war criminal, Kurt Gerstein's body was found hanging in his cell. He appeared to have torn a strip from his thin blanket and committed suicide. It was never discovered whether this was a result of the conditions he had to suffer or whether he found it impossible to endure being regarded as a war criminal after all the risks he had taken to inform the Allies of what the Nazis were doing.

Gerstein's body was buried in the Thiais cemetery in Paris by the French authorities who couldn't even be bothered to record his name correctly. He was listed as 'Gastein'. The cemetery still exists, it was the burial place for the former Albanian King, Zog I, who died in 1961 and it has a memorial to the victims of the 1974 Turkish Airlines crash, but the section in which Gerstein was buried has been flattened and no record remains of the exact location of his grave.

In August 1950 Gerstein's name was put before the Denazification Court in Tübingen. The result of the court's findings would have depressed Gerstein had he still been alive and would certainly seem to have done him a great injustice, considering the great efforts he went to to pass on his information about the Nazi death machine. Part of the court's findings are noted here:

> After his experiences in the Belzec camp, he might have been expected to resist, with all the strength at his command, being made the tool of an organized mass murder. The court is of the opinion that the accused did not exhaust all the possibilities open to him and that he could have found other ways and means of holding aloof from the operation. It is incomprehensible and inexcusable that, as a convinced Christian who in earlier years had repeatedly shown such an upright and courageous bearing in the face of National Socialist actions, he allowed himself to be used, in a decisive manner a year later, as an agent passing orders to the Degesch Company. After all his previous experience, it must have been absolutely clear to him that he, as an individual, was in no position to prevent these extermination measures or, by rendering useless trifling quantities of the prussic acid supplied, to save the lives of even some of the persons concerned.
>
> Accordingly, taking into account the extenuating circumstances noted . . . the court has not included the accused among the main criminals but has placed him among the 'tainted'.

The Premier of Baden-Württemberg overturned this verdict on 20 January 1965.

Perhaps the most fitting epitaph for Kurt Gerstein were the words spoken by his friend, the Confessing Church Pastor, Martin Niemöller who said, 'He was a very special kind of saint, but perfectly pure and of irreproachable rectitude. He was prepared to sacrifice, and indeed did sacrifice, his honour, his family and his life.'

Chapter Ten

The White Rose

On 22 February 1943 Roland Freisler, head of the *Volksgericht*, or People's Court, officiated at the trial of three young students – Hans Scholl, his sister Sophie, and their friend Christoph Probst.

The Scholls, students at the University of Munich, had been arrested on 18 February and had been taken to the prison at Wittelsbach Palace. They had been caught at the university by a caretaker, Jakob Schmid, distributing leaflets denouncing the Nazi regime. Christoph Probst was arrested the following day. He had written the draft of a new leaflet, which he had given to Hans Scholl for him to check. Although Hans swore that it had been given to him by a complete stranger, the writing matched that of Christoph and Hans was unable to stop his friend's arrest.

Following interrogation, they were charged with treason on 21 February. Although usually conducting his grisly work in Berlin, Freisler came to Munich for the trial, which aroused much interest both at home and abroad.

Although the three friends had been allocated a defence lawyer there had been no time to prepare a proper defence and they were all aware that it would have been in vain anyway. In an effort to spare other members of what they called the White Rose group, who had worked alongside them in their endeavours to educate the community about the evils of Nazism, the brother and sister both confessed to their guilt and tried to impress upon their interrogators that they had worked alone. They particularly wanted to spare Christoph Probst who, although only twenty-three years old, was married and the father of three small children, Micha, Vincent and

Katharina. Christoph's wife, Herta, had given birth to Katharina a few days before her husband's trial and Christoph had been on his way to see them both when he was arrested. He never met his only daughter, nor did he ever see his wife again.

Christoph was born on 6 November 1919, the son of a wealthy father, Hermann Probst. He had one sister, Angelika, whom he adored. When the children were still young their parents divorced and both remarried; their stepmother was Jewish. Because of the divorce both children were sent to boarding school and had very little home life at all after that. That was probably the reason that Christoph married so young and had children at an early age; they were the family he had never really had.

In spite of the divorce both Christoph and Angelika were fond of both sets of parents. When in 1936 their father committed suicide in a fit of depression, it was Christoph who comforted his stepmother. He knew that she was in a dangerous position, being Jewish, but never tried to distance himself from her and when he and Herta married they lived with her in Zell bei Ruhpolding for a time.

Following their arrest it soon became clear to Hans, Sophie and Christoph that they were unlikely to survive. Sophie is said to have told the defence lawyer that, if her brother was sentenced to death, then she also must suffer the same fate. Although none of them wanted to be martyrs, they were aware that if they were found guilty and sentenced to death they would gain great publicity for their cause.

The trial lasted only three and a half hours. It was, so far as the state was concerned, an open and shut case. At the end of the trial Freisler pronounced the sentence of death for all three defendants. Each of them was given a chance to speak briefly. Sophie chose to say nothing; Christoph asked that his life be spared for the sake of his three children; Hans asked nothing for himself but requested that Christoph's life be saved. Freisler cut him short, declaring that if he had nothing to say in his own defence he should just keep quiet. The Scholls' parents and young brother had hurried to Munich when they heard of the arrests of Hans and Sophie and were met by one of their friends in the White Rose. They arrived at the court while the trial was taking place and heard the verdict. They at once began to think about how they might plan an appeal, but it was not to be. The students were taken directly to Stadelheim prison where the sentence was to be carried out.

Late that afternoon Hans and Sophie's parents were allowed to visit their children in prison. They found them to be calm and in control of themselves. Each was relieved and pleased that they had managed to take the blame for their actions on themselves and had not betrayed any of their friends. Sophie is said to have told her mother that it didn't matter that she would die early. Everyone had to die at some time and the few years that she had lost of her life would not make much difference at all. She accepted a sweet, remarking that she had not had time for lunch that day, and was then led away.

Christoph Probst asked to see a priest and that afternoon was baptized into the Catholic Church. Soon afterwards the prison guards, unusually, allowed the three friends a few moments alone together before informing them that the sentence was to be carried out immediately. All three young people were beheaded that evening.

Herta Probst, still in hospital after the birth of her daughter, did not learn about her husband's trial and death sentence until after his execution.

On the evening of 22 February an article appeared in a Munich newspaper, the *Münchener Neueste Nachrichten*, giving details of the court case. It stated that:

> On 22 February 1943 the People's Court, convened in the Court of Assizes Chamber of the Palace of Justice, sentenced to death (together with loss of the rights and privileges of citizenship) the following persons: Hans Scholl, aged 24, and Sophie Scholl, aged 21, both of Munich, and Christoph Probst, aged 23, of Aldrans bei Innsbruck, for their preparations to commit treason and their aid to the enemy. The sentence was carried out on the same day.
>
> Typical outsiders, the condemned persons shamelessly committed offences against the armed security of the nation and the will to fight of the German people by defacing houses with slogans attacking the state and by distributing treasonous leaflets. At this time of heroic struggle on the part of the

German people, these despicable criminals deserve a speedy and dishonourable death.

Robert Scholl met his wife, Magdalena, during the Great War. He was a medical orderly and she a nursing sister. They married and settled in the small town of Forchtenberg, near Heilbronn in south-west Germany, where Robert became the mayor. He was a big man with definite opinions that he was not afraid to express. Magdalena, in contrast to her outgoing husband, was quiet and sensitive. It was she who provided the calming influence in the Scholl household.

The couple had five children, Inge, Hans, born on 22 September 1918, Elisabeth, Sophie, born on 9 May 1921, and Werner, who were all encouraged to think for themselves and to act on their own convictions rather than follow the lead of the majority. They had happy childhoods in the sleepy little town of Forchtenberg. Their father, the Mayor, had plans for the town and succeeded in bringing the railway into the little backwater and opening it up to the outside world. This forward-thinking attitude did not suit all the residents of the town and, in 1930, they voted for another mayor. Robert and Magdalena decided to move and finally settled in the city of Ulm where Robert rented a large apartment and became a tax consultant.

When Hitler came to power in 1933 the Scholl children were enthusiastic supporters and anxious to join the *Hitler Jugend* or the *Bund Deutscher Mädel*. Their parents were much less impressed with Nazism than their children, but did not try to discourage them from their chosen pursuits; rather they encouraged discussion of the way German life was being led, so that the children could decide for themselves the merits of Hitler and his party.

For a time Hans in particular had a very difficult relationship with his father and the two barely spoke to each other. Then gradually he began to see things that made him question the importance of the Hitler Youth.

Although he had been made a *Fähnleinführer* (Squad Leader) of a unit of approximately 150 boys, the position gave Hans less, rather than more, freedom, as he had to hold fast to Nazi party ideals and ensure that the boys in his charge did the same. At first Hans had not taken the strictness of the Hitler Youth too seriously.

While he enjoyed the meetings and the outdoor pursuits, he also had a fondness for playing his guitar and singing folksongs, both German and those of other lands. He continued to enjoy this harmless pastime along with the boys under his command, perhaps not really understanding the way in which his actions would be interpreted. Boys of the Hitler Youth had to adhere to the strict discipline of the movement. They were only allowed to sing songs that were approved by their youth leadership and that did not include foreign folksongs. It did include, however, an unofficial but, nonetheless acceptable, little number entitled '*Wenn das Judenblut vom Messer spritzt*' (When Jewish blood spurts from the knife) whose words told of a better life when Jewish blood had been spilt.

This type of song was not popular with Hans Scholl. He had no hatred of Jews and had not been brought up to condemn them, no matter what the Hitler Youth policy was on the subject. The Scholl family had friends from many different backgrounds and the children had been taught by their parents to accept people for what they were as individuals, not for their race or religion.

In spite of the doubts that were beginning to creep in, when Hans was selected to carry the banner of the Ulm section of the Hitler Youth at the party rally in Nuremberg in 1936, he did so willingly. Hitler addressed the boys himself, whipping them up into a frenzy. They shouted and cheered him for several minutes and, as their enthusiasm for him increased, that of Hans Scholl decreased correspondingly. He found it hard to explain even to himself what was happening to him, but he suddenly seemed able to recognize that the enthusiasm shown at the rally was more the result of brainwashing than of real conviction. How could young boys have objective views of the Nazi regime when they were not even allowed to consider anything that opposed it?

When, soon after he returned from Nuremberg, Hans's squad decided that they would like to have their own individual banner he decided to help them produce one although he knew that it was not allowed to do so. When the banner was finished and the boys wanted to parade through the streets of Ulm to show it off, they were stopped by one of the Hitler Youth leaders, who demanded that they give him the banner. The boy carrying it stood confused for a moment and, seeing his indecision, the leader snatched it away. Immediately Hans sprang forward and hit him before he had the chance to attack the young boy. He was stripped of his position within the movement with immediate effect. Rather than feel upset, Hans discovered that he felt relieved no longer to be part of an organization with such narrow views and disregard for the feelings of its members.

From the moment of his awakening to the evils of the Nazi regime, Hans and his father Robert once again established a close relationship. The more he questioned the actions of the government the more convinced he became that the Nazi party was not the benevolent organization he had supposed it to be. This discovery was, perhaps, easier for Sophie to understand than it had been for Hans. Although she had looked forward to joining the League of German Girls and enjoyed some of its activities, a large part of what was taught to the girls was the importance of becoming a good wife and mother. Girls were supposed to be content being house-wives and were not encouraged to have any personal ambitions or thoughts of a career other than as someone who looked after the needs of a good party-member husband and regularly produced children for the Fatherland and the Führer. This was not a role that appealed to Sophie. Although she was not against the idea of a husband and family, she had a good brain and wanted to make use of it before devoting herself to housework. She also struggled with the stereotypical image of the German 'Hausfrau' wearing a tra-ditional dirndl and plaiting her hair. Sophie had a close-cropped haircut, which would have looked quite at home in the world of twenty-first century Germany.

Like her brother, Sophie saw no reason to abandon the things that gave her pleasure simply because they were not on the list of authorized League activities. She once told a horrified leader that one of her favourite authors was the Jewish writer Heinrich Heine. 'Whoever does not know Heine, does not know German literature,' she is said to have declared.

She also had problems with Nazi racial ideas. Her friend, Luise, was blonde; she, herself, was dark, and yet it was she who was allowed to belong to the League of German Girls, not Luise. The reason, of course, was that, despite her 'Aryan' looks, Luise was Jewish. To Sophie this seemed to be completely illogical and she began to question it and other aspects of Nazi doctrine. She found the Nazi party wanting in most respects.

In the end virtually the only thing that the Scholl children could find in favour of Hitler and the Nazis was that, under the regime, unemployment had fallen. However, even this advantage disappeared when they discussed it with their father. He agreed that unemployment had fallen, but asked them to consider what it was that had brought this about. He cited, as an example, the extra building work to construct camps to house political opponents and, when they considered this, they decided that it might have been better had the unemployment figures stayed as they were.

In 1937 Hans Scholl joined the German Boys' Club of November 1. This was an organization set up by Eberhard Koebel and was usually known as d.j.1.11. It was an organization of likeminded intellectual young men and operated without the permission of the government, promoting freedom of thought and culture. Its founder had been arrested by the Nazis as early as 1934 and had eventually gone into exile, but d.j.1.11 flourished in spite of this and Koebel managed to keep in touch from beyond Germany. For Hans, membership of this group was his first act of resistance against the regime he had rapidly come to despise.

Soon after joining d.j.1.11 Hans became eligible to serve in the *Reichsarbeitdienst* (National Labour Service). The required period of service was six months, after which he was conscripted into military service. While Hans was serving with the *Reichsarbeitdienst*, helping to build roads, the Gestapo decided to make a final effort to eliminate all youth organizations with the exception of the Hitler Youth. He had hardly started on his military service when officers of the Gestapo arrived at his barracks and arrested him for membership of an illegal organization. He was taken to prison in Stuttgart.

Hoping to discover more about his illegal activities the Gestapo then raided the family home in Ulm. They arrested Inge, Sophie and Werner. Their mother grabbed her shopping basket when the Gestapo broke into their home and quickly went to her children's rooms and put everything she could find that she thought might be incriminating into her basket. Then she calmly announced to the Gestapo officers that she could not stay and watch them search her home, as she had to get to the shops.

Sophie was released from prison that afternoon, but Inge and Werner spent a week in custody and Hans was detained for a month before being released following an appeal from his cavalry officer at the barracks.

With the start of the Second World War Hans's military service was extended and he became a medical orderly, sent to France during the German invasion of its neighbour. Since he had qualified to attend university he spent alternating periods at Munich University, where he had enrolled to study medicine, and attending to the wounds of German soldiers in France.

Sophie, too, had managed to pass the exams needed for a place at university, in spite of the obstacles put in her way both by her teachers, who thought that she was not enthusiastic enough about Hitler, and by the authorities themselves who, adhering to the policy of making German girls into good housewives, had only allocated ten per cent of all university places to women. First of all, however, she too had to serve in the *Reichsarbeitdienst.*

Hoping to be able to avoid the manual labour that was the normal form of service, Sophie applied to join the Fröbel Institute in Ulm to train as a kindergarten teacher. She was accepted and began her studies, which she enjoyed. They, however, did not prevent her being called for manual labour at the end of her period of study and she had to endure some months working hard on the land in the company of girls with whom she had nothing in common and being supervised by uncouth, bullying Nazi women.

At the end of her labour service Sophie received another blow to her plans to attend Munich University in the form of call up orders from the War Assistance Programme. She found that she was expected to serve a further six months as a teacher in a kindergarten that was attached to the munitions works in Blumberg. Blumberg was an ugly industrial place and Sophie hated it, but somehow she endured it until May 1942 when she was able to leave to enrol at Munich University to study biology and philosophy.

Just before she left Blumberg Sophie heard that her father had been arrested. He had, apparently, been in a temper one day and had called Hitler the 'scourge of humanity'. One of the women who worked for him had heard this unguarded remark and had thought it her duty to report it to the Gestapo. Robert Scholl was arrested but released almost immediately as he had a complicated project in hand for the finance department of the local council. He was not, however, exonerated and had to live with the threat of an upcoming trial when his work project was complete.

Once she arrived in Munich Sophie spent much of her free time with her brother Hans and his friends. They all had things in common – a love of literature and art, a fondness for the outdoors and nature and, perhaps most importantly, a hatred for the Nazi regime.

Alexander Schmorell, Shurik to his family and friends, was born in Orenburg in Russia on 6 September 1917 and was baptized into the Russian Orthodox Church. He was the son of a German doctor and his Russian wife. He spent his first few years in Russia, but his mother died when he was less than five years old and, soon after, his father took him to Germany. They settled in Munich along with Alexander's Russian nanny with whom he spoke only Russian.

Alexander met Christoph Probst when they attended the same high school and they became firm friends. Their friendship was to last for the remainder of their short lives. Both young men had ambitions to become doctors and they enrolled to study medicine at Munich University, where they met Hans Scholl. Following his obligatory service with the *Reichsarbeitdienst* Alexander was conscripted into the army. He was with the German troops that marched into Austria in 1938 and later into Czechoslovakia. When asked to swear the oath of allegiance to Hitler, Alexander refused and asked to be discharged from the army, which he loathed. The request was, of course, refused and Alexander had to continue with his army service, interspersed with his medical studies at Munich University.

Alexander's father had a house on the *Benediktenwandstrasse* in the Munich district of Harlaching, where Alexander would meet his friends to discuss philosophy, history, art and literature. Later on their talk was of politics and the way the German nation was being led. They were all of one mind about the corruption and evil of the Nazi regime.

When, in the middle of 1942, Alexander was ordered to the Russian front as a medical orderly, his friends Christoph Probst and Hans Scholl accompanied him. For Alexander it was a time of mixed emotions. He was delighted to be back in the land of his birth, but the circumstances of his visit troubled him greatly. He

126

and his friends were appalled by the way in which the ordinary Russian citizens had to live and by the way they were treated. They also witnessed the treatment meted out to the Jews, including some executions, which horrified them. With them in Russia was another friend, German student Willi Graf, who had also been conscripted to serve as a medical orderly.

Willi Graf was born in Kuchenheim near Euskirchen on 2 January 1918, the son of a wine merchant. In 1922 the family moved to Saarbrücken where Willi and his two sisters grew up. He was sent to the *Humanistische Ludwigsgymnasium* in Saarbrücken, a grammar school that concentrated on classical studies, from where he graduated in 1937. In spite of it being compulsory to join the Hitler Youth, Willi managed to avoid membership and instead spent his teen years as a member of several different youth groups including the Catholic organizations *Neudeutschland* (New Germany) and the *Graue Orden* (Grey Order), which convinced him that Christianity and Nazism were diametrically opposed. In January 1938 Willi was arrested, accused of subversive youth activities. He was held in custody for only three weeks before being released as the result of a general amnesty in honour of the *Anschluss*; the union of Germany and Austria.

Following his six months' compulsory service with the *Reichsarbeitdienst* Willi enrolled at the University of Bonn to study medicine. He was then conscripted into the army in January 1940 and sent to France as a medical orderly. He served in Yugoslavia in March and April 1941 and the following month was sent to the Eastern Front where he remained until April 1942. He was then allowed to pick up his studies again and was allocated to the Second Students' Company in Munich where he studied at the university. In June he met and became friends with Christoph Probst, Alexander Schmorell, Hans and Sophie Scholl and Jürgen Wittenstein. Their studies continued for only another month before they were all uprooted again and the young men were sent to the Russian front as part of Operation Barbarossa, where they remained until the autumn.

By the time they went to Russia Hans Scholl and Alexander Schmorell had already written and distributed the first two of their White Rose leaflets (see appendix 3). On their return Willi Graf decided that he wanted to join the group in its resistance activities.

127

He painted anti-Nazi slogans on the walls of public buildings and helped to produce and distribute more of the leaflets.

During the winter break from university Willi packed a bag full of leaflets and a duplicating machine and left Munich to visit his old friends from the University of Bonn and school friends in Saarbrücken. He also went to Cologne, Ulm and Freiburg to try to involve some of his friends from his various youth organizations in the flourishing resistance movement. He managed to recruit only four – Heinz and Willi Bollinger, Helmut Bauer and Rudi Alt.

Jürgen Wittenstein, who also went as a medical orderly to Russia during Operation Barbarossa, became an early member of the White Rose group, editing the third and fourth of the leaflets. It was he who met Mr and Mrs Scholl and their son, Werner, when they arrived in Munich on the day of Hans and Sophie's trial in February 1942 and accompanied them to the court. He, like Willi Graf, travelled in his spare time, taking leaflets to Berlin in order to distribute them there and hopefully recruit members in the capital to carry on the resistance work.

When, after the arrest and execution of Professor Kurt Huber, Jürgen Wittenstein helped to organize a collection for his widow and her children he came under suspicion, but managed to evade capture. He went back to the front where he was injured but he recovered and after the end of the Second World War he emigrated to America where he became a doctor in California.

Although the White Rose was a group of young students, it did have one older member, the Professor of Philosophy and psychology at the University of Munich, Kurt Huber. He was born in Chur in Switzerland on 24 October 1893, the son of German parents. His father was a teacher at the school in Chur. When Kurt was four years old the family came back to Germany and settled in Stuttgart where he was educated at the *Eberhard-Ludwig-Gymnasium* from the age of ten years. During his time at the grammar school his father died and his mother moved the family to Munich where Kurt studied musicology, philosophy and psychology at the university. He graduated in 1917 and three years later began teaching there. He became a full professor in 1926. In 1929 he married his fiancée, Clara Schlickenrieder. The couple had two children, a girl and a boy. By late 1942 Huber had joined his students in the White Rose. He listened to what they told him about their service in the army and the atrocities they had seen committed and he knew he could not keep silent any longer. Although an anti-Communist, he told them that it was much more important to bring about the downfall of the Nazi government than it was to oppose Communism. It was he who wrote the fifth and sixth of the White Rose leaflets, which were very different in tone from the previous four. Kurt Huber was a patriot and, although he believed that the downfall of the Nazis was a just aim, it bothered him to be seen to be challenging the government of his country. In his final leaflet he had included a line which said, 'Place yourselves tirelessly in the service of our glorious Wehrmacht.' The students, when they saw this line, immediately deleted it. They believed that the country, not just the regime, must be defeated for Germany to have a chance of survival after Hitler. That would seem to have been the only difference of opinion between the professor and his students.

Throughout the time that it was in existence the members of the White Rose worked unceasingly to write, produce and distribute their leaflets. They collected funds and checked telephone books for the names and addresses of those they thought would benefit from receiving a leaflet. They were always in danger as it was very difficult to carry large quantities of paper about unnoticed. They had to buy enormous amounts of stamps to post the leaflets and, although it only cost about eight pfennigs per letter, the amount that they sent out meant that they were spending a large sum of money. They also needed paper and duplicating facilities, and somewhere to store their material once it had been produced. They were able to use the studio of architect Manfred Eickemeyer for this purpose. They were pleased to find that a significant number of people were willing to help them.

The knowledge that there were large numbers of opponents to the government led them to believe that their aims of ridding the country of the Nazis would be better served if they were to unite with other resistance groups. In particular they were keen to establish contact with the *Rote Kapelle* (Red Orchestra) and with Pastor Dietrich Bonhoeffer and, in order to further their aims, they had met up with a thirty-year-old man, Falk Harnack, the brother of

Arvid, of the Red Orchestra, at his barracks in Chemnitz. The meeting had been arranged by a mutual friend, Lilo Ramdohr, and Hans Scholl and Alexander Schmorell met Harnack in November 1942.

Harnack had been a student at Munich University in the very early days of the Nazi regime. He and his friends had, like the White Rose, produced and distributed leaflets telling the population to oust Hitler and his bunch of thugs. At that time none of them believed that the Nazi regime could last for very long but by 1938 they were becoming worried and organized a student strike. It was a complete failure. People either did not care about the Nazis or they were too frightened to do anything about them. Harnack received his doctorate in theatre studies soon after the ill-fated strike attempt and left Munich to take up a position in Weimar.

Falk Harnack, Hans and Alexander met in the morning and talked all that November day and most of the night about how they could join forces with other resistance groups in their struggle for freedom. The two students had brought with them from Munich copies of the first four leaflets that they had produced and they gave them to Harnack to see what he thought. He told them that they were too academic to appeal to the masses and that it was obvious that intellectuals who didn't speak for the working man had written them. In spite of this criticism, Hans and Alexander were encouraged by what Harnack had to say about his vision for the uniting of different forces of resistance and they made an appointment for him to visit them in Munich the following February.

Harnack went to Munich at the beginning of February for a two-day visit and during that time met most of the members of the White Rose. While he was there he arranged with Hans Scholl to meet him three weeks later in Berlin so that he might introduce him to Pastor Bonhoeffer.

When the Scholls and Christoph Probst were arrested on 18 February 1943, after distributing their leaflets in the university buildings, the other members of the White Rose knew that they would be very lucky to avoid arrest themselves. They had planned that, should an arrest take place, whoever the unlucky person was would say that he or she had produced and distributed the leaflets alone and had had no help from anyone else. In this way they hoped to avoid mass arrests.

In spite of Hans, Sophie and Christoph sticking to their pledge to involve no one else, arrests were made, including that of Traute Lafrenz, Hans Scholl's girlfriend and the person who had taken the White Rose leaflets from Munich where she was studying, back to her home town of Hamburg, to continue the fight there. The students at the university were frightened and a few days after the three friends had had their heads cut off, a rally was organized to show solidarity with the Nazi government. Whether out of fear or genuine anger at the three White Rose martyrs, hundreds of students decried their sacrifice and loudly applauded the caretaker, Jakob Schmid, who had betrayed them to the Gestapo.

On the night of the execution, Willi Graf and his sister, Anneliese, were both arrested.

Alexander Schmorell had fled from Munich but was having no luck in escaping the country and so returned to the city to seek help from friends not involved in the White Rose movement. He sought out a former girlfriend on 24 February and found her in an air raid shelter at the height of a raid. Instead of helping him, she betrayed him. The Gestapo arrived and arrested him.

Professor Huber knew that he would be arrested and was pleased that his wife and young son were away in the country and so would not be involved. Unfortunately his twelve-year-old daughter, Birgit, was still in the city with him and in the early morning of 26 February it was she who opened the door to three men from the Gestapo.

After these arrests the families of the students and the wife of Professor Huber were all arrested in what was known as *Sippenhaft* (clan arrest). They remained in custody for varying amounts of time before being released. Only Robert Scholl, father of Hans and Sophie, was given a two-year sentence.

Falk Harnack had also been arrested in March 1943 when it was discovered that he had links with the White Rose. On 25 February he had waited for Hans Scholl at the Kaiser Wilhelm Memorial Church in Berlin but his young friend had not arrived. He did not know that he had been murdered three days before their appointment and did not find out until he returned to his barracks and found a letter from Lilo Ramdohr.

131

The trial of Willi Graf, Alexander Schmorell and Kurt Huber was set for 19 April 1943. In total there were fourteen defendants, including Hans Scholl's girlfriend, Traute Lafrenz, and Falk Harnack. The others, who were all accused of helping the group in their treasonous activities, were Eugen Grimminger, Heinz Bollinger, Helmut Bauer, brother and sister Hans and Susanne Hirzel, Franz Müller, Heinrich Guter, Gisela Schertling and Katharina Schüddekopf. Once again Roland Freisler presided over the trial. This time it lasted for fourteen hours, one hour for each defendant, proportionally slightly less time than the first trial (three and a half hours for three defendants).

Alexander Schmorell was dealt with first and suffered screaming abuse from Freisler. Willi Graf, who in comparison with Schmorell, came off lightly in terms of the ridicule he had to endure, followed him. Then came Professor Huber. He had engaged a defence lawyer who suddenly stood up in court and declared that he was unable to act for the defendant, as he could not bear to hear any insulting remarks about the Führer. He begged leave to be excused and Freisler was happy to comply. He immediately appointed another lawyer to represent Huber but declined to grant any time for him to familiarize himself with the case. Huber spoke in his own defence. In the final speech of his trial he said:

As a German citizen, as a German professor, and as a political person, I hold it to be not only my right but also my moral duty to take part in the shaping of our German destiny, to expose and oppose obvious wrongs.

What I intended to accomplish was to rouse the student body, not by means of an organization, but solely by my simple words; to urge them, not to violence, but to moral insight into the existing serious deficiencies of our political system. To urge the return to clear moral principles, to the constitutional state, to mutual trust between men. A state which suppresses free expression of opinion and which subjects to terrible punishment – yes, any and all – morally justified criticism and all proposals for improvement by characterizing them as 'Preparation for High Treason' breaks an unwritten law, a law which has always lived in the sound instincts of the people and which may always have to remain.

You have stripped from me the rank and privileges of the professorship and the doctoral degree, which I earned, and you have set me at the level of the lowest criminal. The inner dignity of the university teacher, of the frank, courageous protestor of his philosophical and political views – no trial for treason can rob me of that. My actions and my intentions will be justified in the inevitable course of history; such is my firm faith. I hope to God that the inner strength that will vindicate my deeds will in good time spring forth from my own people. I have done as I had to on the prompting of my inner voice.

While he spoke Freisler looked bored. Several times he interrupted to insult Huber. Finally Huber asked for some leniency for his family. Having been stripped of his professorship, he was no longer entitled to a pension and he was worried that his wife and children would be destitute. His request was met with a blank stare.

When each of the defendants had been tried Freisler and his stooges went off to decide their verdicts. When they returned they declared that Schmorell, Graf and Huber had been found guilty and were sentenced to death. The *Völkischer Beobachter* reported the outcome of the trial in an article on Wednesday, 21 April:

The People's Court of the German Reich, in session in Munich, dealt with a number of accused persons who were involved in the high treason of the brother and sister Scholl sentenced on February 22, 1943.

At the time of the arduous struggle of our people in the years 1942-43, Alexander Schmorell, Kurt Huber, and Wilhelm Graf of Munich collaborated with the Scholls in calling for sabotage of our war plants and spreading defeatist ideas. They aided the enemy of the Reich and attempted to weaken our armed security. These accused, having through their violent attacks against the community of the German people voluntarily excluded themselves from that community, were punished by death. They have forfeited their rights as citizens forever.

Eugen Grimminger of Stuttgart furnished funds in support of this action, though, to be sure, he was not fully aware of its details. The Court was unable to establish that he consciously gave aid to the enemy of the Reich. Furthermore, he gave considerable assistance to his employees who were serving in the armed forces, though on the other hand he was aware that the money might be used for purposes injurious to the state. He has been sentenced to ten years in prison.

Heinrich Bollinger and Helmut Bauer of Freiburg had knowledge of the treasonous acts of the above named accused but failed to report them, despite the fact that they are mature adults, and in contravention of the obligation of every German to report treasonous plans of this kind. In addition, they listened to enemy broadcasts. They have been sentenced to seven years in prison, and they have forfeited their honour as citizens for the same length of time.

Hans Hirzel and Franz Müller of Ulm, immature youths, aided in the distribution of the treasonous leaflets. In consideration of their youth they were sentenced to five years' imprisonment.

The accused Heinrich Guter of Ulm, likewise a young person who knew of the treasonous acts but failed to report them, was sentenced to eighteen months' imprisonment. Three girls [Traute Lafrenz, Gisela Schertling and Katharina Schüddekopf] who were guilty of the same act were sentenced to one year's imprisonment.

One other accused person [Susanne Hirzel], who assisted in the distribution of the leaflets but who did not know their content, was given a sentence of six months in prison because she failed to carry out her responsibility to apprise herself of the content of the leaflets.

There was no mention in the newspaper article of Falk Harnack, who was acquitted. This was not an act of clemency on the part of the Court, although it was stated that he was freed because so many members of his family had died. Rather it was so that the Gestapo could follow him and, hopefully, manage to catch other dissident groups that he might contact. Eventually, Harnack was sent to fight in Greece, where he disappeared following an order for his arrest signed by Heinrich Himmler. He surfaced again to fight for the Greek partisans against the German forces and managed to survive the war.

After the war he became a film director and between 1949 and

1951 he was the artistic director of the East German production company DEFA. He married the actress Käthe Braun and they moved to West Berlin where he worked on a number of television films. Falk Harnack died, following a long illness, in Berlin in 1991. He was seventy-eight years old.

After the trial the condemned men were taken to Stadelheim prison to await their execution. Although they had appealed against their sentences none of them had any hope that the appeals would be upheld. Two months after the trial they received word on their appeals. The document was personally signed by Adolf Hitler and stated, 'I reject all petitions for mercy.'

For Karl Huber the time between his trial and his execution was frantically busy. He had been writing a book about the German mathematician and philosopher Gottfried Leibniz and was anxious to finish it so that his family might benefit from the royalties. Even that was denied him and by the day of his death two chapters remained unfinished.

Clara Huber was allowed to visit her husband for a few short minutes on four occasions and, strangely enough, so was their daughter Birgit. The child was told that she could only see her father if she promised not to cry. She visited him for the last time and kept her promise.

The time for the execution was set for 5 pm on 13 July. Just before the appointed hour some SS men appeared at Stadelheim prison. They said that they had come to watch the hanging and were very annoyed when they discovered that the three men were going to be beheaded.

Later that evening first Alexander Schmorell and then Professor Kurt Huber went to the guillotine. Willi Graf was spared the knife that day because the authorities thought that they might be able to get more names of White Rose members from him. They never did manage to, in spite of daily interrogations from July until October. On 12 October 1943 he too lost his fight for life and was beheaded.

Following the execution of Kurt Huber, some members of the White Rose started a fund for his dependants. These included Jürgen Wittenstein in Munich and Hans Leipelt, who was originally from Hamburg.

Leipelt was the son of a Protestant father, Konrad, and a Jewish mother, Katharina, who had converted to Protestantism.

According to Nazi race laws that made Hans Leipelt half-Jewish and, as such, not eligible for any of the privileges reserved for Aryans. In 1941 he was thrown out of the University of Hamburg for being half-Jewish and the following year his sister, Maria, was made to leave school. His grandmother was arrested and sent to Theresienstadt concentration camp where she was murdered and not long afterwards his father died. For many people these tragedies would have meant the end of all hope but for Hans Leipelt they did not. He had enrolled at Munich University where Professor Heinrich Wieland at the Chemical Institute regularly ignored the Nazis' rules and allowed 'half-Jewish' students to study with him. While he was at Munich Leipelt met his fiancée Marie-Luise Jahn. Together they decided to take on some of the resistance work that had been started by the White Rose. They had one of the leaflets, the sixth, which they retyped on a portable typewriter many, many times so that it could be redistributed. At the top of the first page they typed a new heading, 'And their spirit lives on, despite all!'

The engaged couple wanted to do something to help Professor Huber's family and secretly began collecting money for them, both in Hamburg and in Munich. Although they didn't meet the family, they managed to get the money to them via a third party. Unfortunately the Gestapo found out about the collection and on 8 October 1943 Hans Leipelt and Marie-Luise Jahn were both arrested. Then Leipelt's mother and his sister were also arrested and taken into prison. On 9 December 1943 his mother died in Fuhlsbüttel prison in Hamburg.

Leipelt and Jahn were kept in custody for a year before coming to trial on 13 October 1944. The result of the trial was a foregone conclusion. Leipelt was sentenced to death and Jahn to twelve years in a maximum-security prison.

Hans Leipelt was executed like the other White Rose members, in Stadelheim prison in Munich on 29 January 1945, when the Nazis already knew that their days in office were numbered; another senseless waste of a young life.

Chapter Eleven

Conspiracy

The lukewarm attitude of most of the military, men such as General Franz Halder and his superior officer, Commander-in-Chief of the Army Field Marshal Walther von Brauchitsch, who purported to be anti-Nazi, must have been a great disappointment to those who genuinely felt the need to risk everything to rid the country of the Nazi scourge. It soon became clear to them that Hitler could only be deposed with the help of the army and that while the armed forces remained loyal to him there was no way for them to oust him.

One of the main problems with those who did try to work against Hitler and his government was that they all had their own agenda and never managed to form a cohesive resistance movement which would encompass the views of the many different groups. Instead of people with purely anti-Nazi beliefs forming resistance movements, the groups were made up of Communist resisters or Social Democratic resisters and so on, who each had their own idea of what life should be once the Nazis had been eliminated. Most were fighting a battle on two fronts – to depose the Nazis and, equally, to impose their own preferred government when the first task had been accomplished.

One group did manage to include members from different backgrounds and beliefs who genuinely sought to organize a proper resistance with stated objectives and workable plans for a new administration once the Nazis were gone. This group, which began its life in the early days of the Nazi government but became most active at the start of the Second World War, was known as the

Kreisau Circle. It took its name from the estate of the Moltke family in Kreisau in Silesia. The area in which it was situated is now called Krzyzowa and is part of Poland.

Count Helmuth James von Moltke and his friend Count Peter Yorck von Wartenburg were the leaders of the Kreisau Circle, which had about twenty permanent members. Others joined and left, or merely visited it as representatives of other resistance movements wishing to exchange ideas and information. They came from such varied backgrounds as education, philosophy, journalism, commerce and trade unionism.

Both von Moltke and von Wartenburg were from wealthy backgrounds and had travelled extensively, the former having spent time in South Africa, homeland of his mother Dorothy, who was the daughter of the South African Minister of Justice, and in the United States where, for a time, he was a journalist. When he returned to Germany he studied to become a lawyer and went to work in the legal department of the *Abwehr*. It was through his work that he met Peter von Wartenburg who was also a lawyer, and von Wartenburg's cousin, Colonel Klaus von Stauffenberg. All three detested Nazi ideals and looked forward to the day when Hitler would be ousted and Germany would return to a more sane form of government.

It became the aim of the Kreisau Circle to formulate a plan for a post-Hitler government. Although they wanted to get rid of Hitler as quickly as possible most of the members were against the idea of assassinating him, as assassination didn't fit well with their mainly Christian principles.

At first they were convinced that because Hitler was so obviously bad for Germany it would not take long for the people to realize this and vote him out of office. It soon became clear, however, that the people would not have the opportunity to rid themselves of Hitler by any conventional means if, indeed, they even wanted to. It was difficult for a group of intellectuals to understand exactly why the population seemed to be so impressed with the Nazi regime.

In spite of this they continued to meet and began to draw up their plans for a new government. It was to be loosely based on both Christian and socialist values. Primary schools were to be run mainly by the Church while higher education was to be independent. All adults over the age of twenty-one were to be given the vote and the head of each household would be given additional votes depending on how many children, under the age of twenty-one, he or she had. Local and provincial politicians were to be elected by the people but here the democratic process ended. All officials above local and provincial level were to be appointed rather than elected and administrative positions were to be taken only by university graduates.

Industry was to be nationalized and the group made provision for the involvement of both workers and management in the running of businesses. The collective wealth of the country was to be used for the benefit of all citizens and not just an elite few.

The Kreisau Circle's ultimate aim for Germany was that she should become a leading member of a community of European nations, which would also include the Soviet Union. These nations would have limited individual power but would, collectively, be a force for good and for peace. They proposed that the man who should become German Chancellor following the downfall of Hitler should be Karl Goerdeler.

Another group, which had formed links with various resistance movements including the Kreisau Circle and whose membership sometimes overlapped, was known as the Solf Circle. Strictly speaking the people who gathered at the home of Hanna Solf, widow of German Ambassador to Japan, Dr Wilhelm Solf, were not a resistance group. They were a group of intellectuals, diplomats, businessmen and former politicians who met to enjoy the company of likeminded people, safe in the knowledge that they were not in danger of being overheard and denounced by fanatical neighbours. They included Nikolaus von Halem, a lawyer and former civil servant, and Reichstag Legation Secretary Herbert Mumm von Schwartzenstein who both had links with Communist resistance leader Josef 'Beppo' Römer; diplomat Otto Kiep; Count Albrecht von Bernstorff, nephew of the German ambassador to the United States during the First World War; educationalist Elisabeth von Thadden who ran a school for girls near Heidelberg; Countess Hanna von Bredow, the granddaughter of Bismarck; Father Erxleben, a Jesuit priest, and Hanna Solf's daughter, Countess Ballestrem. Although their main purpose had not been to fight against Nazism they found that the mutual support they received did lead them to acts of resistance, mainly helping persecuted Jews.

Another member of the circle, Baron Karl-Ludwig von Guttenberg, had been publishing a Catholic magazine that he called *Weisse Blätter* (White Pages) since 1934. Although it was clearly an anti-Nazi magazine, it never actually mentioned the NSDAP by name and the writers were very careful to couch their opposition in diplomatic terms. Most of the Nazi censors were not well educated and did not pick up the subtle condemnations of the government in its pages and, since the magazine was directed at intellectuals it had no trouble in putting across its message.

Klaus Bonhoeffer, brother of Pastor Dietrich Bonhoeffer, often wrote articles for *Weisse Blätter,* as did former ambassador Ulrich von Hassell, who also worked with Karl Goerdeler and Ludwig Beck on the plans for the post-Hitler government. Goerdeler and Beck served as consultants for the magazine that was produced on a monthly basis until the start of the Second World War when paper shortages forced it to become a quarterly journal. In January 1943 these shortages put the magazine out of business altogether and it was greatly missed by its former subscribers who regarded it as the only sane voice in the insane times through which they were living.

On 10 September 1943 members of the Solf Circle were invited to tea at the home of Elisabeth von Thadden. There they were introduced to a Swiss doctor from the Charité Hospital in Berlin, Dr Paul Reckzeh. He was a personable young man and seemed to have the same opinions as those in the group about Hitler and the Nazis. Since a number of anti-Nazi Germans had managed to escape from Germany and were living in exile in Switzerland, Dr Reckzeh offered to take letters from the group members to them when he went back to Switzerland. Many in the group gladly accepted his offer, including Elisabeth von Thadden who sent a letter to Professor Friedrich Siegmund-Schultze who was connected to the World Council of Churches, which the Nazis believed had links to the resistance.

Soon after what became known as the Solf Tea Party Count Helmuth James von Moltke of the Kreisau Circle received word that the most prominent members of the Solf Circle had had their phones tapped. Since the two circles had close ties, von Moltke immediately got in touch with Otto Kiep, who was a personal friend, and with Hanna Solf to warn them that the group had been infiltrated. It transpired that the spy in their midst had been the young Swiss doctor, Paul Reckzeh. In fact he was a Gestapo informer who had delivered the letters given to him by the Solf Circle directly to the Gestapo and had suggested that the phones be tapped in order to trap as many members as possible. Through warning his friends, von Moltke himself was also brought to the attention of the Gestapo and, along with the members of the Solf Circle, he was arrested in January 1944.

With the exception of Hanna Solf and her daughter, all those who had been present at the tea party were executed. Frau Solf and Countess Ballestrem were sent to Ravensbrück concentration camp and then sent for trial, where they both received death sentences. However the Japanese ambassador to Germany intervened on behalf of the two women and the People's Court, under the direction of the notorious Roland Freisler, retried them in February 1945. While in the middle of this new trial on 3 February there was an air raid and an Allied bomb destroyed the courthouse. All the records relating to the women were destroyed. Hanna Solf and Countess Ballestrem remained in Moabit prison where they had been sent following their time in Ravensbrück, until they were released on 23 April 1945. Hanna Solf felt unable to stay in Germany and went to live in England while her daughter remained in Berlin until her untimely death at the age of forty-six.

Karl Goerdeler, the man the Kreisau Circle wanted as Chancellor of Germany, was born in Schneidemühl in Prussia on 31 July 1884. The town is now part of Poland and has been renamed Pila. He was the son of a district judge and he studied law before taking up a career in the civil service, becoming Mayor of Königsberg in 1922 and Lord Mayor of Leipzig in 1930. He accepted a position under the Nazi government of Reich Commissioner of Prices, a post he held for four years, but quickly discovered that Hitler, once he came to power, was not interested in improving local government and so resigned from this post.

Following the passing of the Nuremberg Laws depriving Jews of German citizenship, Goerdeler was instructed to remove the statue of German composer Felix Mendelssohn, who was Jewish, from opposite the *Gewandhaus* concert hall in Leipzig. He refused and declared that if the statue went then so would he. While he was abroad Nazi officials came and took down the statue. True to his word, on his return Goerdeler resigned as mayor and became a representative of the Bosch Company, on whose behalf he travelled all over Europe.

It was during his time with the Bosch Company that Goerdeler became involved in resistance to Hitler. As an overseas representative he was able to make contact with people in other countries and let them know what was happening in his homeland. He was tireless in his efforts to alert the world to the evils of Nazism and to enlist outside help in the overthrow of Hitler. He travelled all over Europe and went to the United States. He even had meetings with the man who, in 1940, would become British Prime Minister, Winston Churchill.

It was all to no avail. It seemed to Goerdeler that no one was interested in the plight of Germany, but he wouldn't give up trying to involve anyone he felt could be of assistance. Back in Germany Karl Goerdeler became, with General Beck, one of the leading figures in the resistance. He worked constantly on the plans for the new government and was confident that, once they had succeeded in deposing Hitler there was a bright new future for Germany.

In a letter he wrote to Field Marshal Günther von Kluge in July 1943 he tried, unsuccessfully, to recruit the Field Marshal into the resistance. His letter was somewhat incautious as he took pains to spell out exactly what he thought of the Nazi government when he said:

Do you know any means whereby, in the face of the frightful and ever increasing destruction of German cities, a victory can be won? Do you know any means whereby Russia can be repulsed from Europe and the United States and the British Empire can be forced to desist from these bombings and make peace? That is the political and military question with which we are faced. . . .

I have once again determined, and I will take the responsibility for this statement, that a possibility still exists for us to conclude peace on a favourable basis if we Germans make of ourselves a people with whom it is once again possible to deal. It is obvious that no statesman in the world can negotiate with criminals and fools, because none would recklessly entrust the fate of his nation to the hands of fools.

On 16 July 1944 Goerdeler received word from Colonel Klaus von Stauffenberg that a warrant had been issued for his arrest. He immediately went into hiding in Berlin. He stayed with various people until finally a forty-one-year-old Berlin housewife, Elisabeth Charlotte 'Lilo' Gloeden, sheltered him in the flat that she shared with her husband and her mother.

Goerdeler stayed with the Gloedens until 12 August when he was discovered and arrested. Lilo Gloeden and her family were also taken into custody. On 30 November Lilo, her mother and her husband were beheaded at two-minute intervals in Plötzensee prison in Berlin.

Ludwig Beck was born on 29 June 1880 in Biebrich in the Rhineland. A career army officer, he was very well thought of and in 1935 was appointed Chief of the Army General Staff. He held this position for three years and as such was entitled to make military decisions without reference to higher authority. He found it difficult to fulfil his proper role, however, as Hitler was always interfering with these military decisions.

When, on 30 May 1938, Hitler told him that he intended to invade Czechoslovakia, Beck protested strongly. Quite apart from any moral considerations, he felt that Germany was not in a position to go to war over Czechoslovakia, which was what he was sure would happen once Britain and France were made aware of what was happening. He tried in vain to rally the Chiefs of Staff and when, in August, he could see that he had failed to gain any significant support, he resigned.

Hitler was not sure that Beck was correct in his judgement of Britain and France. Nothing had happened a few months before when he had annexed Austria and he was convinced that he could hoodwink the naïve British and French leaders, Neville Chamberlain and Edouard Daladier, into believing that all he wanted was the return of the Sudetenland, the part of Czechoslovakia in which the population was mainly of German heritage.

Sadly for Beck, Hitler was right and the British and French leaders did not even bother to consult the Czech leadership; Czechoslovakia was virtually handed over to Hitler without a fight. It was not only a betrayal of Czechoslovakia and its government, and the people of Great Britain who would ultimately be drawn into a war they did not want, but also a betrayal of the members of the German resistance who had tried to pass on warnings about what was happening in their country and had been ignored.

From the moment of his resignation Ludwig Beck devoted himself entirely to the resistance movement and was generally regarded as being the most likely head of state in the post-Hitler government.

Hitler was again correct when he said of Beck, 'The only man in the world I fear is Beck. That man would be capable of acting against me.'

General Franz Halder replaced Beck as Chief of the Army General Staff on 27 August 1938. Although he and his superior officer, Commander-in-Chief Field Marshal Walther von Brauchitsch, at first opposed Hitler, mainly because of his interference in military matters, they eventually decided against an active resistance and went along with whatever Hitler wanted. Halder is said to have declared that 'A breach of my oath to the Führer is not justified.'

In spite of his loyalty to Hitler he was not spared arrest and spent the last part of the war in a concentration camp at Niederdorf, being released on 28 April 1945 by American troops.

In 1949 Franz Halder, speaking about the Nazi era, said that Hitler had hindered the Germany armed forces in all their efforts and that, although the country might not have won the war, at least it could have avoided the stigma of defeat. One would have thought that defeat was the least of his worries. Surely the knowledge that during the twelve years of Nazi rule millions of people had been senselessly slaughtered in the most horrific way by a psychopathic thug and his henchmen, and that he himself had done virtually nothing to stop it, would have been a far worse burden to carry than mere defeat.

Although military men such as Halder and von Brauchitsch were weak and ineffective when given the chance to put up a serious threat to Hitler, there were others who were not so cautious.

Small groups of resisters were now gathering, including men from the *Abwehr* and the armed forces, and various former politicians, diplomats, lawyers and theologians. They included

Admiral Wilhelm Canaris, Head of the *Abwehr*; his deputy, Colonel Hans Oster; Oster's deputy, lawyer Hans von Dohnanyi; Field Marshal Erwin von Witzleben, the second highest military figure in the resistance after Beck and earmarked as Commander-in-Chief elect, in a post-Hitler government; General Friedrich Olbricht, Head of the Army Central Administration Office; General Erich Hoepner, a former tank commander on the Russian front and commander of the Wuppertal Panzer Division which was based near Munich; Colonel Klaus von Stauffenberg, who, along with the previous two officers, would be in charge of the Ministry of Defence in the new government; Lieutenant Colonel Henning von Tresckow, Reich Police Minister elect; Lieutenant Werner von Haeften, von Stauffenberg's ADC; Lieutenant Ludwig Freiherr von Hammerstein, Beck's ADC elect in a post-Hitler government; Colonel Rudolf-Christoph von Gersdorff; Lieutenant Fabian von Schlabrendorff, a lawyer and close associate of von Tresckow; Lieutenant Colonel Friedrich Heinz of the Military Division of the OKW *(Oberkommando der Wehrmacht)*; Lieutenant Ewald von Kleist-Schmenzin; Hans Bernd Gisevius, a lawyer and Chief of Special Projects for the OKW; Fritz-Dietlof von Schulenburg, a member of the Kreisau Circle and former Deputy President of the Berlin Police; Dr Julius Leber, Social Democrat politician, von Stauffenberg's choice for Chancellor but actually designated Vice Chancellor elect; Professor Dr Adolf Reichwein, Social Democrat politician and associate of Leber; Wilhelm Leuschner, trade union leader, friend of Leber and the conspirators' choice as Reich President; Adam von Trott zu Solz, lawyer and diplomat; Ulrich von Hassell, diplomat, former German Ambassador to Rome and Foreign Minister elect; Lieutenant of the Naval Reserve Hans-Bernd von Haeften, lawyer, Foreign Office official and brother of Werner; Eugen Gerstenmaier, Protestant theologian and member of the Kreisau Circle, and Professor Dr Johannes Popitz, who was the Prussian Finance Minister between 1933-1944 and would become Reich Finance Minister in the new government.

Although there were other groups still trying to oust Hitler, it was these men that now conspired to assassinate the Führer.

At first there had been some argument as to whether or not Hitler should be killed. There were those who thought this would just make him a martyr and would only serve to solidify support for the

Nazis. Others objected to assassination on religious grounds. General Beck, Field Marshal von Witzleben and Admiral Canaris wanted Hitler to be arrested and tried for his crimes against the German people. Hans von Dohnanyi wanted Hitler to be declared insane and sent to an institution for an indefinite period. Eventually, however, it was decided that the only way to rid themselves of the Nazis would be to remove Hitler permanently since no one in the rest of Europe seemed to be interested in helping them overthrow their government.

The first attempt at a coup was during the Czechoslovakian crisis in 1938 and, although the conspirators made very careful and detailed plans, they depended largely on the reactions of the British and the French to the German plan to annexe the Sudetenland. When British Prime Minister Neville Chamberlain did nothing to stop Hitler's expansionist policy, the attempted coup collapsed.

In July 1940 Fritz-Dietlof von der Schulenburg and fellow Kreisau Circle member, Eugen Gerstenmaier, decided to shoot Hitler while he was in Paris attending a parade. The parade was due to take place on 20 July and the two made their plans for the assassination. On the appointed day Hitler failed to attend. Perhaps because he realized that he had many enemies, he often changed his plans at the last moment and on this occasion he did just that. Instead of going to the parade, he arrived in the city just after dawn, visited some of the tourist attractions, had a few photos taken and then left again as quietly as he had arrived. It may have been that he thought there would be more chance of something happening to him in an occupied country than in Germany. Whatever his reason he did not seem to suspect either von der Schulenburg or Gerstenmaier.

Then next attempt on Hitler's life was organized by Erwin von Witzleben nearly a year after the first. He had put together a team of four snipers to shoot the Führer during yet another military parade. Again the attempt failed because Hitler failed to attend.

Chief of Staff at the Army Group Centre on the Eastern front, Lieutenant Colonel Henning von Tresckow, decided in March 1943 that the time had come for him to make an attempt on the life of the Führer. He made elaborate arrangements including two fallback plans should the first not succeed. His preferred method of execution was with a gun as he thought other methods ungentlemanly, but the final alternative plan did involve the use of a bomb. The first plan was to have Hitler's escorts shoot him during a motorcade. If this did not work then von Tresckow and some colleagues would shoot Hitler once he arrived at the officers' mess at Army Group Centre headquarters. If this also failed then he planned to put a bomb on to Hitler's personal aeroplane, a Focke-Wulf FW200 Kondor.

On 13 March Hitler arrived in Smolensk for his visit to the Army Group Centre. The cavalry group chosen to escort Hitler to the headquarters building was under the command of Captain Georg von Boeselager, who was aware of the assassination plan and was willing to give the order to shoot. He never had a chance to act. As soon as Hitler settled into his car it took off at great speed, escorted not only by von Boeselager's cavalry but also by SS troops on motorcycles. The conspirators decided to revert to their second plan and shoot Hitler while he was in the mess. This attempt also failed, as he was never far enough away from anyone else to allow a clear shot to be taken. Reluctantly they decided to put the bomb on to Hitler's aircraft.

When von Tresckow and his associates had been deciding how to assemble the bomb they had been concerned about using a German explosive device. Although they obviously worked, they made a loud hissing noise once they had been armed and the conspirators felt that the bomb would be discovered and dismantled long before it detonated. Luckily for them Colonel Rudolf-Christoph von Gersdorff had managed to procure a British bomb which they could use. It had been taken from supplies dropped by the British to the resistance in France and was particularly useful to the conspirators as, once set, it made no noise at all. It was set by pressing a small button, which broke a bottle containing a corrosive substance. This ate through a wire that held a spring and once the spring had been released it pressed a striker that hit the bomb's detonator and set off the explosion.

Von Tresckow's colleague, Fabian von Schlabrendorff, disguised the bomb as two bottles of brandy and during the meal that was served at the headquarters building, von Tresckow struck up a conversation with Colonel Heinz Brandt who was in Hitler's party and would be accompanying him on the next part of his trip to his own headquarters, the so called 'Wolf's Lair' near

147

Rastenburg in East Prussia. He asked Brandt if he would mind taking two bottles of brandy as a present for his friend General Helmuth Stieff. Brandt agreed to carry the bottles for him and so von Schlabrendorff set the bomb and von Tresckow passed it over to Colonel Brandt.

The timer had been set to work about thirty minutes after the plane took off, when it should have been over Minsk. The conspirators were confident that a mid-air explosion would remove all traces of the bomb and that the crash would just be regarded as an unfortunate accident.

They went back to their headquarters to await the news of the explosion. Thirty minutes passed, then an hour. After ninety minutes they were beginning to get very worried and then, two hours after Hitler's aircraft had taken off from Smolensk, they received word that it had landed safely at Rastenburg. They were filled with horror. Not only had they failed to kill the Führer, but very soon their plot would be discovered and with it would come their arrests and those of many of their colleagues.

Von Schlabrendorff and von Tresckow began frantically to think how they could recover the situation. Eventually, a few hours later, von Tresckow telephoned Colonel Brandt in Rastenburg. He asked if he had managed to deliver the brandy to General Stieff. Brandt apologized, saying that he had not yet had the time. Von Tresckow told him that he was very relieved, as he had given him the wrong parcel. He told Brandt that von Schlabrendorff would be coming to Rastenburg the following day for a short visit and that he would ask him to bring the correct parcel so that it could be swapped with the one that Brandt was holding. Luckily it didn't occur to Brandt to ask why von Schlabrendorff hadn't been given the task of delivering the brandy to General Stieff in the first place. He cheerfully agreed to meet von Schlabrendorff the next day and swap over the parcels.

Von Schlabrendorff flew to Rastenburg the next morning and handed over two bottles of brandy to the unsuspecting Brandt. He later spoke of his ordeal:

> I can still recall my horror when Brandt handed me the bomb and gave it a jerk that made me fear a belated explosion. Feigning a composure I did not feel, I took the bomb, immedi-

148

ately got into a car and drove to the neighbouring railway junction of Korschen.

Once on the train to Berlin he dismantled the bomb and discovered that everything had worked except the detonator. It was believed that the explosive had failed to blow up because the bomb had been stored in the hold of the aircraft and had become too cold.

By now the conspirators were becoming increasingly desperate, as nothing that they planned seemed to work. Von Gersdorff decided that he would make an attempt to kill Hitler and that it would be a suicide attack. This he thought would ensure that there would be no mistakes. He planned to put two small bombs in the pockets of his greatcoat. He would arm them and, at the last moment, grab Hitler and hold on to him until the bombs killed them both. The occasion he chose for his suicide mission was the visit that Hitler planned to make to the Berlin Armoury, where he was due to be shown captured Soviet weapons. The visit was meant to last about fifteen minutes, which von Gersdorff believed would give him plenty of time to carry out his mission. Hitler arrived at the Armoury, but before von Gersdorff had the chance to do anything, he abruptly turned round and hurried out again. No explanation was given for his departure, but it almost seemed as if he could sense danger in the air.

The next attempt, which was masterminded by von Tresckow, involved putting a bomb into the water tower at the Wolf's Lair. This attempt also failed when the bomb failed to explode. It did, however, explode some weeks later when all it served to do was alert Hitler to the vulnerability of his headquarters and ensure that future security measures were increased.

Baron Axel von dem Bussche-Streihorst, an army major, was the next person to contemplate a suicide bombing. Hitler was due to inspect a new winter army uniform and the Major had been chosen to model it for the Führer. He decided that he would also hide a bomb within the new uniform and kill himself and Hitler when the latter came to inspect the uniform. Incredibly, this attempt also failed because the train in which the new uniforms were being transported was hit and destroyed by an Allied bomb the night before the proposed fashion show. With nothing to see, Hitler did not bother to turn up.

One year after von Tresckow's first attempt to kill Hitler he was becoming too busy with his army duties to contribute much to the resistance. The situation on the Eastern front had deteriorated rapidly and it took all his attention to try to hold things together. He had, however, managed to recruit some more conspirators one of whom, Captain Eberhard von Breitenbuch, volunteered to shoot Hitler during one of his briefings. He knew that he would be gunned down himself but was willing to sacrifice his life for the cause in which he believed so strongly. Like the others who tried to get rid of Hitler, von Breitenbuch also failed because it was suddenly decreed that officers of his rank were no longer entitled to attend briefings.

The time had come for someone different to try to accomplish what the other conspirators had failed to do. That person was Klaus von Stauffenberg.

Chapter Twelve

Operation Valkyrie

Klaus Philip Schenk von Stauffenberg was born on 15 November 1907 at Greifenstein Castle in the region of Oberfranken (Upper Franconia) to the north of Munich. His father, Count Alfred Schenk von Stauffenberg, was Marshal of the Court to the last King of Württemberg, Wilhelm II, who abdicated on 29 November 1918, the last of the German kings to do so. His mother, Countess von Uxkull-Gyllenbrand, was a granddaughter of Field Marshal Count August-Wilhelm Neidhardt von Gneisenau, who fought at the Battle of Waterloo. The family were strict Roman Catholics whose interests included art, literature and horses. Klaus shared these interests and was also keen on sport.

In 1926 he joined the army and became an officer cadet in the 17th Bamberg Cavalry Regiment. By 1936 he had been transferred to the War Academy in Berlin. At the start of the Second World War he was a staff officer in the 6th Panzer Division commanded by General Erich Hoepner and when Operation Barbarossa began was sent to Russia where he spent the next eighteen months. During this time his distaste for the Nazis was intensified when he witnessed the atrocities committed by the SS. He met Henning von Tresckow and Fabian von Schlabrendorff while in Russia and his links with the resistance began.

At the beginning of 1943 he went to Tunisia as Operations Officer of the 10th Panzer Division in the dying days of the Battle of Kasserine. In April his car drove into a minefield while it was being attacked by Allied aircraft. Von Stauffenberg was badly hurt, losing his right hand and two fingers on his left hand. He was also blinded in his left eye and had wounds to his ears and knees. He was evacuated from Tunisia and sent back to Germany where he spent the next few months in a Munich hospital.

While in hospital he told his wife, Nina, that the time had come for him to save Germany. She, seeing his severe injuries, thought he was joking, as at that point he was not in a fit state to do anything at all.

By September Lieutenant Colonel von Stauffenberg had become Chief of Staff to General Olbricht in Berlin and his involvement with the resistance movement began in earnest.

In 1942 General Olbricht had managed to convince Hitler that a plan should be put in place in case of attempts against the Nazi government. Hitler agreed that this would be an excellent idea and gave instructions for such a plan to be formulated. It was given the code name Operation Valkyrie.

The plan made provision for martial law to be declared in the event of a coup and the securing of government and civil service buildings. Olbricht's purpose in setting up Operation Valkyrie was for the exact reason that he had told Hitler. The only thing that he had not made clear was that it *was* actually the plan for the take-over of the government and was to be put into action by the conspirators when Hitler had been assassinated.

Once Hitler was dead they would issue a statement saying that members of the Nazi party had killed the Führer and that the army had therefore taken control of the country to avoid any further action by the rebels. In that way they hoped to stop any interference in their plans from people who still supported the Nazis. They would arrest all the key members of the government, secure government buildings and break all communication links with the Wolf's Lair in Rastenburg so that those who were with Hitler could not contact the outside world. With this in mind they also planned to take over radio stations and telephone exchanges. Part of their plan relied on Himmler being killed at the same time as Hitler so that he could not assume control.

However, in February 1944 the resistance movement received a severe blow when *Abwehr* chief Wilhelm Canaris was dismissed from his post and imprisoned in Lauenstein fortress.

Following the Solf Tea Party in January 1944 Count von Moltke had been arrested after his attempt to warn his friend Otto Kiep that the Solf Circle had been infiltrated. Kiep had another friend, Erich Vermehren, who was an *Abwehr* agent and an anti-Nazi. Both he and his wife, Countess Elisabeth von Plettenberg, had been sent to Turkey as agents, but when Kiep was arrested they, as his associates and close friends, were called back to Berlin to be interrogated. Fearing for their safety they instead decided to defect to Great Britain and so contacted the British Secret Service and were flown from Turkey to Egypt and then on to England.

When he heard about the defection Hitler flew into one of his famous rages and ordered that Admiral Canaris be dismissed and that the functions of the *Abwehr* be taken over by the *Reichssicherheitshauptamt* (Reich Central Security Office) under the control of Heinrich Himmler. It was a blow to the conspirators for many reasons, not least of which was the fact that Canaris was a meticulous keeper of records and also kept his own personal diary, which the others feared would give details of everything they had been planning.

Hans von Dohnanyi, who had worked with Canaris and had himself been arrested in April 1943, had kept a huge dossier on Nazi atrocities which he hoped would be able to be used in court cases against the Nazis once Hitler had been deposed. This dossier had been placed in a safe in an office at army headquarters in Zossen, a town twenty miles to the south-east of Berlin. It was a damning document for all those in the resistance group, but while Canaris was still in charge at the *Abwehr* it posed no problems. With the functions of the *Abwehr* having been passed to Himmler on Canaris's dismissal, however, they all knew that it was just a matter of time before they were discovered. This meant that they had very little time left to assassinate the Führer.

Stauffenberg was worried that if he used a bomb to kill Hitler and Himmler, other people would also be killed. As a Christian, it troubled his conscience very much, but he reluctantly decided that there was no other way to be sure of a successful outcome. Consequently he began to carry a bomb in his briefcase so that, should the opportunity arise, he would be ready.

On 1 July 1944 Stauffenberg was promoted to Colonel and became Chief of Staff to the Commander of the Reserve Army, General Friedrich Fromm. This new role gave him access to Hitler at numerous conferences, which he attended either with Fromm or as his stand-in. He was quite open with Fromm about his feelings towards Hitler and his plans for the future, but was unable to interest his new boss in joining the conspirators. Fromm, however, did nothing to betray von Stauffenberg's intentions.

Ten days after his promotion von Stauffenberg was called to Hitler's home and headquarters in Bavaria, the Berghof at Berchtesgaden. He took with him his briefcase containing the bomb, but on his arrival discovered that Himmler was not present. Making an excuse, he left the conference room and telephoned to General Beck and Field Marshal von Witzleben in Berlin. In a coded message he told them that Himmler was not present and asked if they thought that the assassination attempt should go ahead regardless. They told him under no circumstances to do anything that would leave Himmler available to take over from Hitler.

On 15 July von Stauffenberg was once again called to a conference with Hitler, this time at the Wolf's Lair in Rastenburg, East Prussia. He again took the bomb and again was disappointed to learn that Himmler was missing. He made another telephone call to General Beck and received the same advice – to do nothing with Himmler not present. This time, however, he decided to telephone General Olbricht in Berlin and, after a brief discussion, they decided to go ahead with the assassination in spite of Himmler's absence.

Von Stauffenberg went back to the conference room and was horrified to find that the conference was over and that he would be unable to do anything that day. He rushed back to the telephone and called Olbricht, telling him to abandon the attempt. However, Olbricht had already issued the order to begin Operation Valkyrie and the army units in Berlin were on standby. Realizing that if he did not act immediately everything would be lost, Olbricht jumped into his car and drove to all the garrisons in turn telling them to stand down. When Fromm heard what had happened he was furious and reported the matter to Field Marshal Wilhelm Keitel, Chief of the OKW (Oberkommando der Wehrmacht). Keitel demanded to know why Olbricht had issued the order at all and why he had not sought the permission of his superior officer, Fromm, if he believed that the order was necessary. Olbricht thought fast and told Keitel that he had made the order to instigate a full 'rehearsal' to ensure that, should the real thing ever be necessary, everyone would be ready for action. His quick thinking paid off and his superior officers, although annoyed that they had not been consulted, believed his story.

By now the conspirators were becoming very nervous about the entire situation. They had wanted to complete their task while Germany was still an independent nation so that, if they succeeded, they would be in a position to negotiate an end to the war with the Allies, but time was rapidly running out. It was already over a month since the Allied landings in Normandy and, in spite of the best German efforts, the Allies were gaining ground. The conspirators knew that they must act at the next opportunity. Now that they had nearly spoilt their chances by calling for Operation Valkyrie to begin before they were sure that the coup was underway there was no more time left to ensure that they assassinated Himmler as well. As Henning von Tresckow wrote in a message to von Stauffenberg:

> The assassination must be attempted, at any cost. Even should that fail, the attempt to seize power in the capital must be undertaken. We must prove to the world and to future generations that the men of the German Resistance movement dared to take the decisive step and to hazard their lives upon it. Compared with this, nothing else matters.

Ever since Canaris had been dismissed and the functions of the *Abwehr* had been transferred to the *Reichssicherheitshauptamt* the noose had been tightening around the conspirators. On 5 July the Social Democrat politician, and von Stauffenberg's choice as chancellor following Hitler's demise, Dr Julius Leber, was arrested. Then, on 16 July, General Alexander von Falkenhausen, the military governor for Belgium, who had promised his support to the conspiracy, was dismissed from his post.

Von Falkenhausen's friend, Field Marshal Erwin Rommel, leader of the legendary Afrika Korps, had also decided to join the conspirators. In February 1944 he said of Hitler:

> I know that man. He will neither resign nor kill himself. He will fight, without the least regard for the German people, until there isn't a house left standing in Germany. . . . I believe it is my duty to come to the rescue of Germany.

Although there were those who believed that Rommel was changing sides to ensure that he was among the victors, he didn't get the chance to make a difference to the resistance. The day after his friend von Falkenhausen was dismissed Rommel was badly injured in an attack on his car by Allied fighter aircraft.

When, on 16 July, von Stauffenberg heard of the arrest warrant for Karl Goerdeler he knew that they could wait no longer. Whether or not Himmler was present, the very next time that he was with the Führer he would set his bomb and Operation Valkyrie would begin. His chance came when he was called to attend a conference at the Wolf's Lair on 20 July.

In the meantime the other conspirators were getting ready to act once the confirmation had been received that Hitler was dead. Eleven orders had been prepared and were to be telexed to various military units detailing such things as the imposition of martial law, the identities of the people who should be arrested, including the commandants and guards of all the concentration camps and the buildings to be secured (see appendix 4). In addition, three speeches had been written to be delivered over the radio. Two of the speeches were to be directed to the armed forces and were to be delivered by General Beck and Field Marshal von Witzleben. The other was addressed to the German people and would be given by Karl Goerdeler, who would come out of hiding once the coup had been confirmed. In Rastenburg General Fritz Fellgiebel, Chief of Signals of the OKW and himself a conspirator, prepared to shut down all communications from the Wolf's Lair for a few hours following the assassination attempt and in Paris General Karl-Heinrich von Stülpnagel, the military governor of France, arranged for the troops under his command to arrest all Gestapo and SS officers. It was now up to von Stauffenberg to play his part.

Early on the morning of 20 July 1944 Klaus von Stauffenberg, with Lieutenant Werner von Haeften acting as his ADC, left Rangsdorf airport in Berlin bound for Rastenburg. He was due to brief Hitler on the *Volksgrenadier* divisions on the Eastern Front at approximately 1.00 pm. In his briefcase he carried a captured British bomb similar to the one that had been placed on Hitler's aeroplane in 1943. The flight took three hours to reach Rastenburg and the aeroplane was to wait for the return of von Stauffenberg and von Haeften.

Upon arriving at the Wolf's Lair von Stauffenberg went to find General Fellgiebel. He emphasized the need for Fellgiebel to send a message to Berlin the moment they knew that Hitler was dead and to then shut down all communications for as long as was possible to allow him to get back to Berlin and assume control of the coup. Fellgiebel confirmed that he was ready to act.

Von Stauffenberg then found Field Marshal Wilhelm Keitel, Chief of the OKW, who would be accompanying him into the conference room. Keitel gave him the unwelcome news that his briefing time had been brought forward by half an hour to 12.30 pm as Hitler was expecting a visit from the Italian leader, Benito Mussolini, that afternoon.

Just before 12.30 pm as Keitel and von Stauffenberg prepared to enter the conference room, the latter made an excuse to leave Keitel for a moment so that he could set the bomb. The wire that would be corroded by the chemical was extremely thin, giving only ten minutes from setting to detonation. It was, therefore, crucial that von Stauffenberg set the bomb just as he was about to go into the conference room. When he returned Keitel was annoyed and said that they were now late for the briefing but von Stauffenberg managed to keep calm and chatted happily to the Chief of the OKW without rousing the suspicions of the latter. As they went into the conference room the young Colonel told a guard at the door that he was expecting an urgent phone call from Berlin concerning one aspect of his report for the Führer and asked that he be alerted as soon as the call came through.

Inside the conference room von Stauffenberg was briefly introduced and told to wait while another officer completed his report. He put his briefcase on the floor under the table at which Hitler was sitting, no more than a few feet from Hitler's legs. There were now just minutes before the bomb was due to explode and so von Stauffenberg slipped, unnoticed, out of the room and hastily found his ADC, Werner von Haeften. The pair hurriedly went across to the office of Fellgiebel from where a few moments later they witnessed a huge explosion. Von Stauffenberg was elated. Smoke and flames were pouring through the remains of the building and bodies had been blasted out of the windows. He was sure that no one could survive the explosion, least of all someone who was as close to the bomb as Hitler had been. What he did not know was that Colonel Heinz Brandt who, the previous year, had taken the brandy bottle bomb on board Hitler's aircraft, had pushed von Stauffenberg's briefcase out of the way to enable him to get closer to the Führer. Brandt paid for this action with his life but, in doing so, he saved Adolf Hitler.

Von Stauffenberg and von Haeften bade a hasty farewell to Fellgiebel, who promised to contact Berlin immediately to inform them that the assassination attempt had worked, and then they made their way out of the Wolf's Lair to retrace their steps to Rastenburg airport. They had some problems leaving the compound because the security guards had also heard the explosion, but eventually managed to bluff their way through the checks and drove at top speed to the airport where they boarded their aircraft and took off at once for Rangsdorf airport in Berlin.

Fellgiebel contacted Berlin and told the conspirators that the bomb had exploded. The telephone line, however, was bad and they had trouble hearing him and so were not sure whether or not Hitler was alive. Fearing a repeat of the situation when Olbricht had set Operation Valkyrie in motion prematurely, they decided to wait until von Stauffenberg arrived back in Berlin to take control of the coup before doing anything. Thus the coup was delayed by three vital hours.

On landing at Rangsdorf, von Stauffenberg was distraught to learn that nothing at all had been done and, in a telephone call to General Olbricht, he urged him to begin Operation Valkyrie with immediate effect.

The Chief of Signals, General Fritz Fellgiebel, had been true to his word and had managed to cut communications from Rastenburg for the time that it took von Stauffenberg to return to Berlin. However, he could not block them indefinitely and, after three hours, confident that von Stauffenberg was once more in Berlin and in control, the lines of communication were restored. It was, therefore, an easy matter for General Fromm to contact Keitel in Rastenburg and discover that, although there had been an explosion, Hitler was only slightly injured. Fromm then knew that he would not join the conspirators but would act against them in an effort to absolve himself of any blame.

When von Stauffenberg arrived back in his office in Bendlerstrasse his first action was to contact Paris and inform von

158

Stülpnagel what had happened so that he could carry out his part of the plan. Ultimately this was to be the only part of the conspiracy plan that worked as meant. Von Stülpnagel had made his arrangements very carefully and within a short time the troops under his command had rounded up and arrested the 1,200 Gestapo and SS officers in Paris. Later, when it was obvious that the coup attempt had failed, von Stülpnagel was forced to release all his prisoners.

Von Stauffenberg then went to the office of General Fromm and tried to persuade him to join them. Fromm was furious that, once again, the order to begin Operation Valkyrie had been given without reference to him and, although von Stauffenberg insisted that Hitler had not survived the bomb blast, Fromm could not be persuaded to join the conspirators and instead declared them to be under arrest. A fight began at the end of which it was Fromm who was placed under arrest. Von Stauffenberg then realized that they had forgotten to secure government buildings and so word was sent immediately to a detachment of the Guard Battalion *Grossdeutschland* under the command of Major Otto Remer. Remer began to alert his battalion at once and before long the Reich ministry offices in Wilhelmstrasse were secured, along with the SS Security Main Office. He was then given the task of arresting Josef Goebbels.

At this point, with the communications between Rastenburg and Berlin restored, Hitler made a call to his propaganda minister, told him what had happened and instructed him to make a radio broadcast to announce to the country that he was safe. When Remer arrived at Goebbels' office to arrest him the propaganda minister reminded him of the oath he had made to the Führer and told him that Hitler was, in fact, alive and still in control. He then telephoned to Rastenburg and let Remer speak to Hitler. Remer immediately knew that he would not be able to arrest Goebbels and promptly changed sides.

At 6.30 pm a broadcast on the German radio station, *Deutschlandsender*, was made which told the whole of Europe that there had been an attempt on the life of Adolf Hitler but that it had failed and he was alive. Von Stauffenberg tried to convince everyone that the broadcast was a lie, but it had had its effect and some of the conspirators began to falter. Von Witzleben, in spite of having been named Commander-in-Chief of the Wehrmacht, had still not arrived in Berlin to take up his duties and when he did arrive at around 8.00 pm and saw that the coup was failing he turned tail and returned to his office in Zossen, where he had wasted precious time that afternoon. From there he went home. He was arrested at his estate the following day.

At 9.00 pm an announcement was made on *Deutschlandsender* which stated that Hitler would make a broadcast to the people of Germany later that evening and the conspirators realized that it would take nothing short of a miracle to enable them to retrieve the situation. It was at this point that General Hoepner made the fatal mistake. When General Fromm asked to be allowed to go to his own office rather than remain in the office of his adjutant where he had been arrested and gave his word that he would not make contact with anyone or try to escape, Hoepner agreed. He even sent him some food and a bottle of wine to make his detention a little more pleasant.

Shortly afterwards a group of Olbricht's officers decided that the coup had failed and that they did not want to be associated with it any longer. They obtained some guns and went to Olbricht's office where they arrested him. Von Stauffenberg tried to escape, but was shot in the arm and the others – General Ludwig Beck, Lieutenant Werner von Haeften, Colonel Albrecht Ritter Mertz von Quirnheim, who had succeeded von Stauffenberg as Chief of Staff to Olbricht, and General Erich Hoepner – were all arrested and put into Fromm's office.

They then freed Fromm who decided that, to save himself from being implicated in the coup, he would have the main conspirators shot. He allowed General Beck to draw his gun and told him to make sure that he only aimed it at himself. The General pulled the trigger but only succeeded in giving himself a flesh wound in the head. Covered with his own blood, the General asked for another gun and then shot himself once more. He still didn't manage to kill himself and was eventually dispatched by one of the soldiers in the room with a single shot. Fromm left the room and returned to say that there had been a court martial and that von Quirnheim, Olbricht, von Haeften and von Stauffenberg had all been sentenced to death for treason. The four were immediately taken down into the courtyard and executed by firing squad. General Hoepner was taken to Moabit prison.

Just after midnight the promised broadcast by Adolf Hitler began. In it he said:

My German Comrades,
If I speak to you today it is first in order that you should hear my voice and should know that I am unhurt and well, and secondly, that you should know of a crime unparalleled in German history.

A very small clique of ambitious, irresponsible and, at the same time, senseless and stupid officers had concocted a plot to eliminate me and, with me, the staff of the High Command of the Wehrmacht.

The bomb, which was planted by Colonel von Stauffenberg, exploded two metres to the right of me. It seriously injured a number of my true and loyal collaborators, one of whom has died. I, myself, am completely unhurt apart from a few minor scratches, bruises and burns. I interpret this as confirmation that Providence wishes me to continue my life's mission as I have in the past. For I can solemnly state in the presence of the entire nation that since the day I moved into the Wilhelmstrasse my sole thought has been to carry out my duty to the best of my ability. And from the time when I realized that the war was unavoidable and could no longer be delayed, I have known nothing but worry and hard work; and for countless days and sleepless nights have lived only for my People!

At the very moment when the German armies are engaged in a most difficult struggle, a small group formed in Germany, as happened in Italy, which thought that as in 1918 it could now deliver the stab in the back. However, this time they totally miscalculated. The claim by these usurpers that I am no longer alive is at this very moment proven false, for here I am talking to you, my dear fellow countrymen. The circle of these usurpers is very small and has nothing in common with the spirit of the German Wehrmacht and, above all nothing to do with the German people. It is a very small gang composed of criminal elements, which will now be destroyed without mercy. I therefore give the following orders with immediate effect:

161

1. That no civilian agency is to obey an order from a government agency, which these usurpers claim that they command.
2. That no military installation, no commander of a unit, no soldier is to obey any order by these usurpers.

I also order that it is everyone's duty to arrest, or, if they resist, to shoot at sight, anyone issuing or handling such orders.

In order to restore complete order, I have appointed Minister of the Reich Himmler to be Commander of the Home Forces. I have drafted into the General Staff General Guderian to replace the Chief of the General Staff who is at the moment absent due to illness, and have appointed a second proven leader from the Eastern Front to be his aide.

In all the other agencies of government within the Reich everything remains unchanged. I am convinced that with the departure of this small gang of traitors and conspirators, we will finally create the atmosphere here at home, too, which the soldiers at the Front need. For it is intolerable that at the Front hundreds of thousands and millions of brave men are willing to make the ultimate sacrifice, while here at home a small gang of ambitious, despicable creatures constantly tries to undermine this attitude.

Once again I take this opportunity, my old comrades in arms, to greet you, joyful that I have once again been spared a fate which, while it held no terror for me personally, would have had terrible consequences for the German People. I interpret this as a sign from Providence that I must continue my work, and therefore I shall continue it.

This time we will settle accounts with them in the manner to which we National Socialists are accustomed. I am convinced that at this time every decent officer, every honest soldier will understand that.

In spite of Hitler's claims not to have been hurt he did receive some injuries in the bomb blast. His personal doctor, Theodor Morrel, made the following report:

Right forearm badly swollen, prescribed acid aluminium acetate compress. Effusion of blood on right shinbone has

162

subsided. On back of third and fourth finger of left hand there is a large blister. Bandage. Occiput *(back of the head)* partly and hair completely singed, a palm-sized second-degree burn on the middle of the calf and a number of contusions and open flesh wounds. Left forearm has effusion of blood on interior aspects and is badly swollen; he can move it only with difficulty. He is to take Optalidons at once, and two tablespoons of Brom-Nervacit before going to sleep.

Hitler's retribution began immediately. On 21 July, in spite of his treachery to the conspirators, General Fromm was arrested. He was imprisoned at the Gestapo prison on Prinz Albrecht Strasse and sent for trial in February 1945 where he was sentenced to death for cowardice. He was executed by firing squad on 19 March 1945.

The first of the many trials of the conspirators began on 7 August 1944 when Judge Roland Freisler of the People's Court sentenced Hoepner, von Witzleben and von Wartenburg, among others, to death. The trial ended the following day and the sentence was carried out immediately. The condemned men were all taken to Plötzensee prison where, following Hitler's orders that they be strung up like animals, they were hanged with piano wire attached to meat hooks. The entire gruesome scene was filmed. An eye-witness described the execution:

Imagine a room with a low ceiling and whitewashed walls. Below the ceiling a rail was fixed. From it hung six big hooks, like those butchers use to hang their meat. In one corner stood a movie camera. Reflectors cast a dazzling, blinding light. At the wall there was a small table with a bottle of cognac and glasses for the witnesses of the execution. The hangman wore a permanent leer, and made jokes unceasingly. The camera worked uninterruptedly, for Hitler wanted to see and hear how his enemies died. He had the executioner come to him, and had personally arranged the details of the procedure. 'I want them to be hanged, hung up like carcasses of meat.' Those were his words.

Julius Leber, who had been arrested before the assassination attempt, was sentenced to death at the People's Court on 20 October, as was his friend Adolf Reichwein, who was executed the same day. Leber had to wait until 5 January 1945 to be hanged at Plötzensee. Ulrich von Hassell, who had also been arrested prior to the attempted coup was tried on 8 September and executed at Plötzensee. Hans Oster was arrested on 21 July and sent to Flossenbürg concentration camp. Wilhelm Leuschner escaped arrest, but when his wife was caught in August 1944 he gave himself up and was executed at Plötzensee on 29 September.

In September, following a tip-off, a police inspector discovered the secret dossier held in the safe at Zossen. The safe also contained some pages of Admiral Wilhelm Canaris's diary. From that moment his fate was also sealed. In February 1945 Canaris was transferred to Flossenbürg concentration camp. At the beginning of April the rest of his diaries were found in Zossen and were taken to Berlin to be shown to Hitler. The following day Hitler, in a towering rage after reading the diaries, ordered that the remaining conspirators be 'destroyed'. On 8 April a trial was held at Flossenbürg and Canaris was sentenced to death. That evening he tapped out a message to a Danish officer, Colonel Hans Lunding, held in an adjoining cell, which said that he would die with a clear conscience, as he was not a traitor. The next day Canaris was hanged along with Hans Oster, Dietrich Bonhoeffer, Captain Ludwig Gehre of the Abwehr and military judge, Karl Sack.

Henning von Tresckow was at the Eastern Front at the time of the attempted coup. He knew that he would be implicated and so committed suicide by blowing his head off with a grenade.

General von Stülpnagel, whose prompt actions in Paris had resulted in the arrest and imprisonment of all the Gestapo and SS officers there, was recalled to Berlin by Hitler. On the way through France by car, he stopped where, during the First World War, he had fought in the Battle of Verdun and told his guard and driver that he wanted to look at the battlefield. Soon after he left the car they heard a gunshot and found von Stülpnagel in a nearby canal. In attempting suicide he had blinded himself in one eye and so badly damaged the other that it had to be removed in the military hospital in Verdun. While he was semi-conscious following his operation, von Stülpnagel was rambling and one of the names he mentioned was that of Erwin Rommel. It alerted the Nazis to the possibility that Germany's most popular general might have been involved in the attempt on Hitler's life.

Back in Berlin Lieutenant Colonel Caesar von Hofacker, who had liaised between the conspirators in Berlin and von Stülpnagel in Paris, was arrested. He was taken to the Gestapo cells in Prinz Albrecht Strasse where he was tortured until he confessed that Rommel had told him, 'Tell the people in Berlin they can count on me'.

Rommel was, at this time, still recovering from the attack by Allied aircraft on his car when he had suffered a fractured skull and other head injuries. Following his discharge from hospital he returned to his home near Ulm. On 14 October 1944 he received a visit from two men, Wilhelm Burgdorf and Ernst Maisel, who had been sent by Hitler with an ultimatum. They told him that they had sufficient evidence to implicate him in the 20 July plot and that the Führer had given him the choice of being charged with treason and tried by the People's Court or of committing suicide. Burgdorf had brought along some poison should Rommel choose the latter option. He was informed that if he did take the poison he would be given a state funeral and his family would not be harmed. Rommel felt that he had no choice and told his wife and his son, Manfred, that he was going to commit suicide. He told them to expect a phone call from the hospital in Ulm to say that he had had a brain embolism as a result of the injuries he had received in July and that he had died. He then said goodbye to his family and went off with the two men. Burgdorf gave him the poison, which he took, and a few seconds later he was dead.

Adolf Hitler, the instigator of this terrible deed, had the gall to send a telegram to Frau Rommel in which he said:

Accept my sincere sympathy for the heavy loss you have suffered with the death of your husband. The name of Field Marshal Rommel will be forever linked with the heroic battles in North Africa.

Von Stülpnagel, meanwhile, had not escaped Hitler's wrath. In spite of his terrible injuries he was taken to the People's Court on a stretcher where he was tried by Freisler, who treated him to his usual ignorant abuse before condemning him to death. Like the other main conspirators von Stülpnagel was hanged in Plötzensee prison on 30 August.

Karl Goerdeler was sent to trial at the People's Court where, on

8 September 1944, he was sentenced to death. He was held in the Plötzensee prison for the next five months and was constantly tortured and interrogated about the attempts on Hitler's life. He eventually disclosed details of the conspirators and, being of no further use to the Nazis, was hanged in Plötzensee on 2 February 1945.

Adam Trott zu Solz and Count Helmuth James von Moltke, both leading members of the Kreisau Circle, were executed. The former was hanged in Plötzensee prison on 25 August 1944, the latter on 23 January 1945, in spite of not having been at all involved in Operation Valkyrie.

Of all the main conspirators the only one who survived the hangman's noose was Fabian von Schlabrendorff. He was arrested the day after Operation Valkyrie and was sent to both Flossenbürg and Dachau concentration camps. He came up for trial in front of People's Court judge Roland Freisler on the same day as Hanna Solf and her daughter, Countess Ballestrem. In the bombing raid that destroyed the records of the women from the Solf Circle, Freisler was himself killed. His death meant that von Schlabrendorff's trial was postponed until the following month when, under a new judge, he was acquitted. After the war he went on to become a judge himself in the Federal Republic of Germany.

In total nearly 5,000 people were executed as a direct result of the assassination attempt and the implementation of Operation Valkyrie. It was a tragedy from which the remaining members of the resistance movement never recovered.

Hitler and his government continued to rule Germany for another nine months until, with the Russian troops advancing on Berlin, Hitler showed himself for the true coward he had always been and committed suicide.

Chapter Thirteen

The Forgotten Few

In the years following the demise of the Nazi regime and the end of the Second World War the men and women of the various German resistance movements were almost forgotten. The German people had more pressing problems to occupy their minds than remembering the relatively few people who had fought against Nazism or tried to overthrow their government.

They were faced with hunger, poverty and an infrastructure that lay in ruins. They were forced to acknowledge that the regime and the leader they had so enthusiastically supported for twelve years had committed horrendous atrocities in their name and that the rest of the world would find it hard ever to forgive them. They had to suffer both the occupation of their country and its division into two separate states. They also had to face the shame of the International War Crimes Tribunal and the knowledge that, had they acted sooner they may have been able to prosecute the criminals themselves rather than have foreign lawyers and judges do it for them.

Although the Allies had been aware for some years that the concentration camps existed, they were totally unprepared for what they found when they liberated them at the end of the war. Towards the end of April 1945 CBS reporter Ed Murrow made a report on the liberation of Buchenwald by American troops. In part he said:

> There surged around me an evil-smelling stink, men and boys reached out to touch me. They were in rags and the remnants of uniforms. Death already had marked many of them, but

they were smiling with their eyes. I looked out over the mass of men to the green fields beyond, where well-fed Germans were ploughing . . . .

As we walked out into the courtyard, a man fell dead. Two others, they must have been over 60, were crawling toward the latrine. I saw it, but will not describe it. . . .

Murder had been done at Buchenwald. God alone knows how many men and boys have died there during the last 12 years. Thursday, I was told that there were more than 20,000 in the camp. There had been as many as 60,000. Where are they now?

I pray you to believe what I have said about Buchenwald. I reported what I saw and heard, but only part of it. For most of it, I have no words.

If I have offended you by this rather mild account of Buchenwald, I'm not in the least sorry.

The Allies who saw sights like this could not understand how a government could sanction such behaviour or how the people could allow it. Some of the liberating troops made the Germans who lived near to the camps visit them and see for themselves what Hitler and his bunch of thugs had done. Most of them were visibly shocked; many collapsed in tears at what they were made to see. And the question was asked, time and time again: why did you not do anything to stop this? More often than not the answer they gave was that they did not know it was happening. That is rather hard to understand.

Just after the end of the First World War the fledgling Nazi party had bought its own newspaper, the anti-Semitic *Münchener Beobachter*, whose name they changed to the *Völkischer Beobachter*. Although the name was changed the tone of its editorials was not and, as an NSDAP mouthpiece, it was even more anti-Semitic than before. Did the general public not notice this?

After the failed 1923 *putsch*, Hitler spent time in Landsberg prison where he dictated his book *Mein Kampf* to Rudolf Hess. Not only did this chronicle his own anti-Semitism, it also put forward his plans for Germany and his own 'ideals'. It was a clear indication to everyone of what Germany would become under Nazi rule. It would be easy to suppose that no one had bothered to read the book – it is a rather tedious, self-satisfied work – but for the fact that its sales made Hitler a lot of money. Surely the large numbers of copies that were sold were not left unread on their owners' bookshelves?

The fact that during the 1920s the NSDAP continued to gain public support would seem to indicate that a proportion of the population at least was in favour of Nazi policies. Nor did they object when Dachau, the first of the German concentration camps, was built in 1933 soon after the Nazis came to power, or when subsequent camps were set up. In Germany alone there were thirteen camps with 565 sub-camps. It would be difficult to hide such a huge number of evil places, and yet still people denied knowledge of their existence. Thousands of people were incarcerated in these hellholes. Surely at least some of them must have had neighbours or work colleagues who noticed that they had suddenly gone missing. Did no one wonder what had happened to them all?

There were at least thirty-three companies conducting their business in Germany who used slave labour from the concentration camps to supplement their own work forces. Were their employees really unaware of what was going on or did they simply not care?

Perhaps the real question should be, not whether or not the population knew about what was happening in their own country but rather, why a resistance movement was necessary and why it even existed if in fact no one knew of any problems?

It was, perhaps, easy for those of us from the Allied nations to criticize the Germans for not doing anything to stop one of the most evil regimes of all time. We, however, did not have to live under the conditions that they did and so were not really in a position to judge.

Worse, we did nothing to help them in their fight for freedom, in spite of many pleas for Allied assistance. The German resistance movement was the only one not to receive any help from the Allies and yet the enemy they were fighting was the same one as all the others, who were given money, personnel, training and weapons.

And there were those among our own people who held Hitler in high regard, including our own king, Edward VIII, by then Duke of Windsor, and his American wife, Wallis Simpson. Who knows what would have happened to Great Britain had Edward VIII not abdicated in order to be able to marry Mrs Simpson?

Unity Valkyrie Mitford, socialite daughter of the second Baron Redesdale, was a devoted supporter of Hitler and spent much time in his company. When Britain declared war on Germany in 1939 she was distraught and tried to commit suicide by shooting herself. Hitler visited her in hospital before she was sent back to England. She never really recovered and died in 1948.

American Ambassador to Great Britain, Joseph P. Kennedy, the father of President John F. Kennedy, could not see what problems the Nazis were causing and regularly sent misleading reports back to Franklin D. Roosevelt in the White House. His information became so unreliable that the President was forced to circumvent him in an effort to obtain real information. John H. Davis, in his book *The Kennedy Clan*, said of the ambassador:

> Joe Kennedy never fully realized the extent of the Nazi menace especially in regard to the Jews. He admired the Germans' capacity for hard work and their efficiency and thought they were the logical leaders of Europe.

He went on to detail the criticisms made of Joe Kennedy and reported that:

> Meanwhile telegrams and letters from all over the United States poured into the White House complaining of Joseph P. Kennedy. Among the many (which are now on file in the FDR Library in Hyde Park) was one from John Boettiger, the President's son-in-law, about a film Kennedy had advised the Hollywood producers not [to] make because it might offend Hitler and Mussolini.

Roosevelt is said to have called Kennedy to his estate at Hyde Park and after a ten minute meeting told the First Lady, 'I never want to see that son of a bitch as long as I live. Take his resignation and get him out of here.'

Even aviation pioneer Charles Lindbergh did not seem to realize the full extent of the danger posed by Nazi Germany. At one point he and his wife were planning to live in Berlin. He seemed to feel that the Allied view of Hitler was exaggerated when he said:

> the potentially gigantic power of America, guided by un-informed and impractical idealism, might crusade into Europe

to destroy Hitler without realizing that Hitler's destruction would lay Europe open to the rape, loot, and barbarism of Soviet Russia's forces, causing possibly the fatal wounding of Western civilization. . . . I was far from being in accord with the philosophy, policy, and actions of the Nazi government, but it seemed to me essential to France and England, and even to America, that Germany be maintained as a bulwark against the Soviet Union.

Perhaps his views were coloured by the almost paranoid fear and mistrust with which most Americans regarded Communism at that time. It is difficult to see how the 'rape, loot, and barbarism' of the Nazis would be any better than that of the Soviets. Atrocities are still atrocities whoever commits them.

Resistance in Germany manifested itself in a number of forms. Many people fought against the regime's insane directives regarding Jews by helping to protect Jewish friends and neighbours. Others sheltered the resisters themselves. Still others produced leaflets and information about what the Nazis were doing. Most of the resistance was in this vein and there were only a few who tried physically to bring down the government and assassinate Hitler. Whatever they did, the result was usually the same if they were caught; arrest, a show trial and a death sentence.

This begs the question, 'Why bother with leaflets when physically removing Hitler was no more risky?' Perhaps the answer relates directly to how Hitler came to be in such a strong position in the first place and brings me back to the point that the German people, as a whole, are law-abiding and disciplined. Whatever they thought of Hitler and the Nazis, he had been elected to office and to remove him, or even attempt to remove him, would be unlawful.

In some respects the military men were in a worse position. They had all been forced to swear an oath of allegiance to the person of Hitler rather than to his position and to attempt to remove him would be in breach of that oath. I find it hard to think of any other people who, when faced with the tyranny and horror of the twelve years of Nazi rule, would find it more honourable to uphold an oath rather than remove the perpetrator of these crimes against humanity.

The coup attempt on 20 July 1944 could have worked. Although von Stauffenberg's bomb did not kill Hitler, he was severely shaken and in the few minutes following the blast the conspirators were able to inform Berlin, shut down the communications from the Wolf's Lair and make their escape back to Berlin. When von Stülpnagel was given the information in Paris, he acted immediately and was able to arrest all the Gestapo and SS officers in the French capital. Had those officers overseeing the operation in Berlin acted with equal haste, they would surely have been able to make their arrests and secure buildings as von Stülpnagel had done. It would seem, however, that, although they were anxious to rid themselves of Hitler, many of them were still unwilling to break their oaths of allegiance. Waiting for von Stauffenberg to arrive back in Berlin, not issuing any orders and, in some cases, not even coming in to the city until many hours later, cost them their coup and, ultimately, their lives. Had von Stauffenberg been in a position to lead the coup in Berlin rather than plant the bomb, the officers who wavered could quite legitimately have been able to say that they were obeying his orders. Without a leader of his calibre not one of them managed to put aside his inbuilt sense of honour.

Unless the lessons that history teaches us are learnt, that history will almost certainly be repeated. Following the defeat in the First World War, the victorious nations were so vindictive in their quest for retribution that they left the way open for a man such as Hitler to step in. In the eyes of the vanquished nation things could not be worse and the rise of Nazism gave them hope that things could indeed be a lot better.

When Edouard Daladier and Neville Chamberlain did nothing to stop Hitler annexing Austria or marching in to Czechoslovakia and seizing the Sudetenland the message they sent was that, in spite of the terms of the peace treaty having been broken, they were unwilling to do anything about it and that Hitler had, in fact, *carte blanche* to do as he wished. He soon put the theory to the test when he invaded the rest of Czechoslovakia and then Poland. Had the French and British leaders been more forceful, perhaps Hitler might have thought twice about taking matters into his own hands in the way he did.

Just as the First World War – the War to end all Wars – resulted in only twenty years of peace, so the Second World War did nothing to stop other tyrants from oppressing their own people. One only has to think of the genocide in Rwanda, the ethnic cleansing in Kosovo and the mass murders of the Iraqi Kurds and other Iraqi nationals to know that this is true. At the end of the Second World War the people of the Allied nations were scathing in their criticism of the Germans for failing to remove a tyrant. Nearly sixty years later the same nations were critical of their own governments' attempts to get rid of another evil dictator. It makes one wonder if the human race has ever learnt anything at all.

Epilogue

Hitler's pilot

Hitler was one of the first European heads of state to travel regularly by air. He had his own air transport squadron and a number of pilots, the chief of whom was Hans Baur.

Baur had been a pilot during the First World War and had been decorated as a war hero. After the war he made flying his career and was a commercial pilot in the early days of civil aviation. He joined the Nazi party in the 1920s, long before membership was the only way to secure a good job, and became Hitler's personal pilot in 1932. During the Second World War Hitler usually flew over foreign territory at least twice a month and was always piloted by Baur, a number of other pilots travelling in reserve. It is believed that the other pilots were employed by Baur and answered to him. The aeroplane in which Hitler often flew was a Focke-Wulf FW200 Kondor. In the summer of 1940 it was believed to have been observed flying over the United Kingdom at a high altitude and with a large fighter escort.

In early December 1940 a Bulgarian named Kiroff went to the British Embassy in Sofia and asked to speak to someone in the strictest confidence about a very delicate matter. The attaché to whom he spoke could hardly believe his ears as the story that Kiroff had come to tell unfolded.

Kiroff claimed he was Hans Baur's father-in-law. He said that Baur, who had lost two brothers during the war, was tired and 'fed up'. He had been working extremely long hours with hardly a break and had decided that he could no longer continue. He was

175

disillusioned with the Nazi regime and was prepared to defect to England, bringing with him the Führer and other top-ranking party members.

The account that Kiroff gave was passed on to the Royal Air Force since they would be coordinating the operation should the defection actually take place. The then Deputy Chief of the Air Staff, Air Vice Marshal Arthur Harris, who would later become Commander-in-Chief, Bomber Command, wrote in late February 1941 to Air Marshal W. Sholto Douglas, Commander-in-Chief, Fighter Command, at his headquarters in Stanmore, Middlesex, giving him details of what was proposed. He himself found the story very hard to believe but assured Douglas that:

> I will not go into the various measures we took to test this apparently fantastic story, but, with one or two exceptions, the story has run true to form and the present position is that Kiroff, who all along has not asked for money, has left Bulgaria and was, on the 18th, in Belgrade, with the object of getting a German visa on his Yugoslav passport, since he had found it impossible, in the present troubled state of Bulgaria, to get an entry permit to Germany from Bulgaria. The Attaché, therefore, has handed written instructions, bearing no trace of origin, to Kiroff, who has said that he will convey them to his son-in-law Bauer [sic] and hopes to bring his daughter [Bauer's wife] and her family, out of Germany to Belgrade, before Bauer makes the flight which might have so much importance for all of us.

Harris then went on to discuss with Douglas what arrangements were being made to ensure Hitler's safe arrival in England. The aerodrome that had been chosen was Lympne, seven miles west of Folkestone in Kent. Baur had been instructed that he was to make a very steep approach into the airfield with his undercarriage down. He had been told that he must fire at least four red flares at thirty-second intervals when approached by British fighter aircraft and that as soon as he had landed he was to stop the engines and put them out of action. It was thought unlikely that the flight would be made at night, so Douglas was asked to provide fighter cover during daylight hours in the immediate area around Lympne. He was also told to make sure that no fighter aircraft attack the German intruder, in spite of the worry that the defection story might be a trick. Harris suggested that, for reasons of secrecy, it might be prudent to say that 'a German deserter' was expected, but finished his instructions to Douglas by saying:

> The vital necessity to confine this story to the smallest circle will be apparent to you and in any case I think there should be no mention to *anybody* of the possible occupants of the aircraft, whose arrival we hope for but do not expect.

On 7 March 1941 Harris again wrote to Douglas, giving him an update on the progress of the operation. Kiroff had been to Belgrade for his visa and had returned to Sofia, having first made a brief visit to see his son-in-law who was, at that time, in Vienna. The message he brought back from Vienna gave more information about the proposed defection but also raised some problems over the way the Royal Air Force had intended to handle the flight. Baur told Kiroff that, because he was always accompanied by at least three other aircraft, he did not want to fire the red flares and alert the other pilots as to what was happening. He suggested instead that, once over the airfield at Lympne, he would drop a number of small yellow metal plaques bearing the letters 'AB'. He told his father-in-law that he had already had a number of the plaques made specifically for this purpose. He gave no explanation as to why he picked the letters 'AB'. As regards when the defection might occur, he said that it was likely to be on or after 25 March and would be within a narrow time frame of 5 to 6 am or 6 to 8 pm.

Harris was still doubtful about the whole thing and ended his letter to Douglas by saying:

> The story seems so fantastic that one is tempted to look for snags, but I can find none, with the possible exception of the time factor, since blackout on the 25th March is at 6.23 in the morning and 7.21 in the evening. Bauer [*sic*] may be speaking of Central European time which would of course make his suggested times less unlikely.

The week before the date proposed for Baur's arrival in England Douglas received another letter from Harris in reply to his request for some definite instructions should the event happen. Harris told him:

> I feel that it will be essential to get the prize, (or prizes if there are more than one 'of great price'), away from the scene of 'the accident' at the earliest possible moment in case of any immediate attempt at interference by an escort or by hastily summoned air support. I consider, therefore, that the booty should be brought straight up to the Air Ministry by car under armed escort, and would be glad if you will give orders to that effect. Sanders has arranged for a Ford V.8 box-body touring car with driver, and two motor cycles and D.Rs., to be sent down to the Station for this particular purpose, all of which will arrive there today.
>
> If there is a large bag, only the biggest birds need be sent in the Ford, the number being limited to a maximum of two so as to allow for an adequate close escort. Any others could be dealt with later.
>
> As it would be most undesirable to extend the circle of those already in the know, I do not propose to lay on any special arrangements this end unless and until we hear that something is in the net. It will be essential therefore that a telephone message should be got through at highest priority either to me, to Sanders, or to Boyle, if anything occurs at the coast.
>
> Will you arrange this too?

The appointed day, 25 March, came and went. Nothing happened. No German aircraft were spotted in the vicinity of Lympne and eventually the authorities accepted that they would not be receiving a visit from 'a German deserter'. Nor does there appear to have been any further correspondence between Air Vice Marshal Harris and Air Marshal Douglas on the subject.

Hitler remained in Germany and Hans Baur continued to fly the Führer on his constant trips through Europe. Hitler trusted Baur implicitly, valuing his opinions on aerial warfare and sometimes seeking his advice on subjects he felt would not be properly considered by Reichsmarschall Herman Goering. Whether his trust had been misplaced remains a subject for conjecture. Baur stayed with the Führer until the end, going with him eventually to the bunker in Berlin where, in April 1945, Hitler took his own life. Baur left the bunker but was shot and captured by Russian troops while escaping. His injuries were so severe that he eventually had to have one of his legs amputated and he remained a prisoner for ten years, being held in a number of Soviet prisons.

After his release from captivity, Baur returned to Germany where he wrote a book about his life and the time spent in the service of the Third Reich. He called it *Hitler at my Side*. There was, of course, no mention of a planned defection in the early part of 1941. Hans Baur died in 1993 at the age of ninety-six. He is buried in Westfriedhof in Munich.

Was Hans Baur really ready to betray Hitler in 1941? It is difficult to imagine what Kiroff could have gained by inventing such a story. As Harris said in his letter to Douglas in February 1941, Kiroff had not asked for any money and, as far as I have been able to ascertain, was not offered any inducement to encourage Baur to defect with Hitler in tow. Nor have I been able to discover anything else about this curious tale. But it does make one wonder what would have happened had the story been true. Perhaps the war might have ended four years earlier than it did, and thousands, maybe millions, of lives might have been saved if Baur really had been a traitor to Adolf Hitler.

Appendix 1

The Twenty-Five Points of the *Deutsche Arbeiterpartei,* which, in 1920, became the *Nationalsozialistische Deutsche Arbeiterpartei* (NSDAP).

The programme of the German Workers' Party is limited as to period. The leaders have no intention, once the aims announced in it have been achieved, of setting up fresh ones, merely in order to increase the discontent of the masses artificially, and so ensure the continued existence of the party.

1. We demand the union of all Germans to form a Great Germany on the basis of the right of self-determination enjoyed by nations.
2. We demand equality of rights for the German people in its dealings with other nations, and abolition of the peace treaties of Versailles and Saint-Germain.
3. We demand land and territory (colonies) for the nourishment of our people and for settling our excess population.
4. None but members of the nation may be citizens of the state. None but those of German blood, whatever their creed, may be members of the nation. No Jew, therefore, may be a member of the nation.
5. Anyone who is not a citizen of the state may live in Germany only as a guest and must be regarded as being subject to foreign laws.

6. The right of voting on the leadership and legislation is to be enjoyed by the state alone. We demand therefore that all official appointments, of whatever kind, whether in the Reich, in the country, or in the smaller localities, shall be granted to citizens of the state alone. We oppose the corrupting custom of Parliament of filling posts merely with a view to party considerations, and without reference to character or capacity.

7. We demand that the state shall make its first duty to promote the industry and livelihood of citizens of the state. If it is not possible to nourish the entire population of a state, foreign nationals (non-citizens of the state) must be excluded from the Reich.

8. All non-German immigration must be prevented.

9. All citizens of the state shall be equal as regards rights and duties.

10. It must be the first duty of each citizen of the state to work with his mind or with his body. The activities of the individual may not clash with the interests of the whole, but must proceed within the frame of the community and be for the general good. We demand therefore:

11. Abolition of incomes unearned by work.

12. In view of the enormous sacrifice of life and property demanded of a nation by every war, personal enrichment due to a war must be regarded as a crime against the nation. We demand therefore ruthless confiscation of all war gains.

13. We demand nationalization of all businesses.

14. We demand that the profits from wholesale trade shall be shared.

15. We demand extensive development of provision for old age.

16. We demand creation and maintenance of a healthy middle class, immediate communalization of wholesale business premises, and their lease at a cheap rate to small traders, and that extreme consideration shall be shown to all small purveyors to the state, district authorities, and smaller localities.

17. We demand land reform suitable to our national requirements.

18. We demand ruthless prosecution of those whose activities are injurious to the common interest. Sordid criminals against the nation, usurers, profiteers, etc., must be punished with death, whatever their creed or race.

19. We demand that the Roman Law, which serves the materialistic world order, shall be replaced by a legal system for all Germany.

20. With the aim of opening to every capable and industrious German the possibility of higher education and of thus obtaining advancement, the state must consider a thorough reconstruction of our national system of education.

21. The state must see to raising the standard of health in the nation by protecting mothers and infants, prohibiting child labour, increasing bodily efficiency by obligatory gymnastics and sports laid down by law, and by extensive support of clubs engaged in the bodily development of the young.

22. We demand abolition of a paid army and formation of a national army.

23. We demand legal warfare against conscious political lying and its dissemination in the press. In order to facilitate creation of a German national press we demand – (a) that all editors of newspapers and their assistants, employing the German language, must be members of the nation; (b) that special permission from the state shall be necessary before non-German newspapers may appear. These are not necessarily printed in the German language; (c) that non-Germans shall be prohibited by law from participation financially in or influencing German newspapers. It must be forbidden to publish papers which do not conduce to the national welfare. We demand legal prosecution of all tendencies in art and literature of a kind likely to disintegrate our life as a nation, and the suppression of institutions which militate against the requirements above mentioned.

24. We demand liberty for all religious denominations in the state, so far as they are not a danger to it and do not militate against the moral feelings of the German race. The party, as such, stands for positive Christianity, but does not bind itself in the matter of creed to any particular confession. It combats the Jewish-materialist spirit within us and without us.

25. That all the foregoing may be realized we demand the creation of a strong central power of the state; unquestioned authority of the politically centralized Parliament over the entire Reich and its organizations; and the formation of chambers for classes and occupations for the purpose of carrying out the general laws promulgated by the Reich in the various states of the confederation.

The leaders of the party swear to go straight forward – if necessary to sacrifice their lives – in securing fulfilment of the foregoing points.

Evidence from a report made by Kurt Gerstein on 26 May 1945

In Lublin, SS *Gruppenfuehrer* Globocnik was waiting for us. He said: 'This is one of the most highly secret matters there are, perhaps the most secret. Anybody who speaks about it is shot dead immediately. Two talkative people died yesterday.' Then he explained to us that, at the present moment – August 17, 1942 – there were the following installations:

1. Belzec, on the Lublin-Lvov road, in the sector of the Soviet Demarcation Line. Maximum per day: 15,000 persons. (I saw it!)
2. Sobibor, I am not familiar with the exact situation, I did not visit it. 20,000 persons per day.
3. Treblinka, 120 km. NNE of Warsaw, 25,000 per day, saw it!
4. Majdanek, near Lublin, which I saw when it was being built.

Globocnik said: 'You will have very large quantities of clothes to disinfect, 10 or 20 times as much as the "Textiles Collection", which is only being carried out in order to camouflage the origin of the Jewish, Polish, Czech and other items of clothing. Your second job is to convert the gas chambers, which have up to now been operated with exhaust gases from an old Diesel engine, to a more poisonous and quicker means, cyanide. But the Führer and Himmler, who were here on August 15, the day before yesterday that is, gave orders that I am myself to accompany all persons who visit the installations.' Professor Pfannenstiel replied, 'But what does the Führer say?' Then Globocnik, who is now Higher SS and Police Leader in Trieste on the Adriatic Coast, said: 'The whole *Aktion* must be carried out much faster.' Ministerial Director Dr Herbert Lindner [Linden] of the Ministry of the Interior suggested, 'Would it not be better to incinerate the bodies instead of burying them? Another generation might perhaps think differently about this?' Then Globocnik, 'But, Gentlemen, if we should ever be succeeded by so cowardly and weak a generation that it does not understand our work, which is so good and so necessary, then, Gentlemen, the whole of National Socialism will have been in vain. On the contrary, one should bury bronze plaques [with the bodies], on which is inscribed that it was we, we who had the courage to complete this gigantic task.' Hitler said to this, 'Well, my good Globocnik, you have said it, and that is my opinion, too.'

The next day we moved on to Belzec. There is a separate little station with two platforms, at the foot of the hill of yellow sandstone, due north of the Lublin-Lvov road and rail line. To the south of the station, near the main road, there are several office buildings with the inscription 'Belzec Office of the *Waffen*-SS' [Military Unit of the SS]. Globocnik introduced me to SS *Hauptsturmführer* Obermeyer from Pirmasens, who showed me the installations very much against his will. There were no dead to be seen that day, but the stench in the whole area, even on the main road, was pestilent. Next to the small station there was a large barrack labelled 'Dressing Room,' with a window that said 'Valuables,' and also a hall with 100 'Barber's Chairs.' Then there was a passage 150 m. long, in the open, enclosed with barbed wire on either side, and signs inscribed 'To the Baths and Inhalation Installations.' In front of us there was a house, the bathhouse, and to the right and left large concrete flowerpots with geraniums or other flowers. After climbing a few steps there were three rooms each, on the right and on the left. They looked like garages, 4 by 5 m. and 1.90 m. high. At the back, out of sight, there were doors of wood. On the roof there was a Star of David made of copper. The front of the building bore a notice 'Heckenholt Institution.' That is all I saw that afternoon.

Next morning, a few minutes before 7 o'clock, I was told that the first train would arrive in 10 minutes. And in fact the first train from Lvov arrived a few minutes later. There were 45 carriages with 6,700 persons, of whom 1,450 were already dead on arrival. Through small openings closed with barbed wire one could see yellow, frightened children, men, and women. The train stopped, and 200 Ukrainians, who were forced to perform this service, tore open the doors and chased the people from the carriages with whips. Then instructions were given through a large loudspeaker: The people are to take off all their clothes out of doors and a few of them in the barracks, including artificial limbs and glasses. Shoes must be tied in pairs with a little piece of string handed out by a small four-year-old Jewish boy. All valuables and money are to be handed in at the window marked 'Valuables,' without any document or receipt being given. The women and girls must then go to the barber, who cuts off their hair with one or two snips. The hair disappears into large potato sacks, 'to make something special for the submarines, to seal them and so on,' the duty SS *Unterscharführer* explained to me.

Then the march starts: barbed wire to the right and left and two dozen Ukrainians with rifles at the rear. They came on, led by an exceptionally pretty girl. I myself was standing with Police Captain Wirth in front of the death chambers. Men, women, children, infants, people with amputated legs, all naked, completely naked, moved past us. In one corner there is a whimsical SS man who tells these poor people in an unctuous voice, 'Nothing at all will happen to you. You must just breathe deeply, that strengthens the lungs; this inhalation is necessary because of the infectious diseases, it is good disinfection!' When somebody asks what their fate will be, he explains that the men will of course have to work, building streets and houses. But the women will not have to work. If they want to, they can help in the house or the kitchen. A little glimmer of hope flickers once more in some of these poor people, enough to make them march unresisting into the death chambers. But most of them understand what is happening; the smell reveals their fate! Then they climb up a little staircase and see the truth. Nursing mothers with an infant at the breast, naked; many children of all ages, naked. They hesitate, but they enter the death chambers, most of them silent, forced on by those behind them, who are driven by the whip lashes of the SS men. A Jewish woman of about 40, with flaming eyes, calls down [revenge] for the blood of her children on the head of the murderers. Police Captain Wirth in person strikes her in the face five times with his whip, and she disappears into the gas chamber.

Appendix 3

The White Rose Leaflets

First Leaflet

Nothing is so unworthy of a civilized nation as allowing itself to be *governed* without opposition by an irresponsible clique that has yielded to base instinct. It is certain that today every honest German is ashamed of his government. Who among us has any conception of the dimensions of shame that will befall us and our children when one day the veil has fallen from our eyes and the most horrible of crimes – crimes that infinitely outdistance every human measure – reach the light of day? If the German people are already so corrupted and spiritually crushed that they do not raise a hand, frivolously trusting in a questionable faith in lawful order of history; if they surrender man's highest principle, that which raises him above all other God's creatures, his free will; if they abandon the will to take decisive action and turn the wheel of history and thus subject it to their own rational decision; if they are so devoid of all individuality, have already gone so far along the road toward turning into a spiritless and cowardly mass – then, yes, they deserve their downfall. Goethe speaks of the Germans as a tragic people, like the Jews and the Greeks, but today it would appear rather that they are a spineless, will-less herd of hangers-on, who now – the marrow sucked out of their bones, robbed of their centre of stability – are waiting to be hounded to their destruction. So it seems – but it is not so. Rather, by means of gradual, treacherous, systematic abuse, the system has put every man into a spiritual prison. Only now, finding himself lying in fetters, has he become aware of his fate. Only a few recognized the threat of ruin, and the reward for their heroic warning was death. We will have more to say about the fate of these persons. If everyone waits until the other man makes a start, the messengers of avenging Nemesis will come steadily closer; then even the last victim will have been cast senselessly into the maw of the insatiable demon. Therefore every individual, conscious of his responsibility as a member of Christian and Western civilization, must defend himself as best he can at this late hour, he must work against the scourges of mankind, against fascism and any similar system of totalitarianism. Offer passive resistance – resistance – wherever you may be, forestall the spread of this atheistic war machine before it is too late, before the last cities, like Cologne, have been reduced to rubble, and before the nation's last young man has given his blood on some battlefield for the hubris of a sub-human. Do not forget that every people deserves the regime it is willing to endure!

From Friedrich Schiller's *The Lawgiving of Lycurgus and Solon*:

Viewed in relation to its purposes, the law code of Lycurgus is a masterpiece of political science and knowledge of human nature. He desired a powerful, unassailable start, firmly established on its own principles. Political effectiveness and permanence were the goal toward which he strove, and he attained this goal to the full extent possible under the circumstances. But if one compares the purpose Lycurgus had in view with the purposes of mankind, then a deep abhorrence takes the place of the approbation which we felt at first glance. Anything may be sacrificed to the good of the State except that end for which the State serves as a means. The State is never an end in itself; it is important only as a condition under which the purpose of mankind can be attained, and this purpose is none other than the development of all man's power, his progress and improvement. If a state prevents the development of the capacities which reside in man, if it interferes with the progress of the human spirit, then it is reprehensible and injurious, no matter how excellently devised, how perfect in its own way. Its very permanence in that case amounts more to a reproach than to a basis for fame; it be comes a prolonged evil, and the longer it endures, the more harmful it is. . . .

At the price of all moral feeling a political system was set up, and the resources of the State were mobilized to that end. In Sparta there was no conjugal love, no mother love, no filial devotion, no friendship; all men were citizens only, and all virtue was civic virtue.

A law of the State made it the duty of Spartans to be in-humane to their slaves; in these unhappy victims of war humanity itself was insulted and mistreated. In the Spartan code of law the dangerous principle was promulgated that men are to be looked upon as means and not as ends – and the foundation of natural law and of morality were destroyed by that law . . . .

What an admirable sight is afforded, by contrast, by the rough soldier Gaius Marcius in his camp before Rome, when he renounced vengeance and victory because he could not endure to see a mother's tears! . . .

The state [of Lycurgus] could endure only under the one condition: that the spirit of the people remained quiescent. Hence it could be maintained only if it failed to achieve the highest, the sole purpose of a state.

From Goethe's *The Awakening of Epimenides*, Act II, Scene 4.

SPIRITS:
Though he who has boldly risen from the abyss
Through an iron will and cunning
May conquer half the world,
Yet to the abyss he must return.
Already a terrible fear has seized him;
In vain he will resist!
And all who still stand with him
Must perish in his fall.

HOPE
Now I find my good men
Are gathered in the night,
To wait in silence, not to sleep.
And the glorious word of liberty
They whisper and murmur,
Till in unaccustomed strangeness,

191

On the steps of our temple
Once again in delight they cry:
Freedom! Freedom!

Please make as many copies of this leaflet as you can and distribute them.

Second Leaflet

It is impossible to engage in intellectual discourse with National Socialist Philosophy, for if there were such an entity, one would have to try by means of analysis and discussion either to prove its validity or to combat it. In actuality, however, we face a totally different situation. At its very inception this movement depended on the deception and betrayal of one's fellow man; even at that time it was inwardly corrupt and could support itself only by constant lies. After all, Hitler states in an early edition of 'his' book (a book written in the worst German I have ever read, in spite of the fact that it has been elevated to the position of the Bible in this nation of poets and thinkers): 'It is unbelievable, to what extent one must betray a people in order to rule it.' If at the start this cancerous growth in the nation was not particularly noticeable, it was only because there were still enough forces at work that operated for the good, so that it was kept under control. As it grew larger, however, and finally in an ultimate spurt of growth attained ruling power, the tumour broke open, as it were, and infected the whole body. The greater part of its former opponents went into hiding. The German intellectuals fled to their cellars, there, like plants struggling in the dark, away from light and sun, gradually to choke to death. Now the end is at hand. Now it is our task to find one another again, to spread information from person to person, to keep a steady purpose, and to allow ourselves no rest until the last man is persuaded of the urgent need of his struggle against this system. When thus a wave of unrest goes through the land, when 'it is in the air,' when many join the cause, then in a great final effort this system can be shaken off. After all, an end in terror is preferable to terror without end.

We are not in a position to draw up a final judgment about the meaning of our history. But if this catastrophe can be used to further the public welfare, it will be only by virtue of the fact that we are cleansed by suffering; that we yearn for the light in the midst of deepest night, summon our strength, and finally help in shaking off the yoke which weighs on our world.

We do not want to discuss here the question of the Jews, nor do we want in this leaflet to compose a defence or apology. No, only by way of example do we want to site the fact that since the conquest of Poland *three hundred thousand* Jews have been murdered in this country in the most bestial way. Here we see the most frightful crime against human dignity, a crime that is unparalleled in the whole of history. For Jews, too, are human beings – no matter what position we take with respect to the Jewish question – and a crime of this dimension has been perpetrated against human beings. Someone may say that the Jews deserve their fate. This assertion would be a monstrous impertinence; but let us assume that someone said this – what position has he then taken toward the fact that the entire Polish aristocratic youth is being annihilated? (May God grant that this program has not yet fully achieved its aim as yet!) All male offspring of the houses of the nobility between the ages of fifteen and twenty were transported to concentration camps in Germany and sentenced to forced labour, and all the girls of this age group were sent to Norway, into the bordellos of the SS! Why tell you these things, since you are fully aware of them – or if not of these, then of other equally grave crimes committed by this frightful sub-humanity? Because here we touch on a problem which involves us deeply and forces us all to take thought. Why do German people behave so apathetically in the face of all these abominable crimes, crimes so unworthy of the human race? Hardly anyone thinks about that. It is accepted as fact and put out of mind. The German people slumber on in their dull, stupid sleep and encourage these fascist criminals; they give them the opportunity to carry on their dep-redations; and of course they do so. Is this a sign that the Germans are brutalized in their simplest human feelings, that no chord within them cries out at the sight of such deeds, that they have sunk into a fatal consciencelessness from which they will never, never awake? It seems to be so, and will certainly be so, if the German does not at last start up out of his stupor, if he does not protest wherever and whenever he can against this clique of criminals, if he shows no sympathy for these hundreds of thousands of victims. He must evidence not only sympathy; no, much more: a sense of *complicity* in guilt. For through his apathetic behaviour he gives these evil men the opportunity to act as they do; he tolerates this 'government' which has taken upon itself such an infinitely great burden of guilt; indeed, he himself is to blame for the fact that it came about at all! Each man wants to be exonerated of a guilt of this kind, each one continues on his way with the most placid, the calmest conscience.

But he cannot be exonerated; he is *guilty, guilty, guilty*! It is not too late, however, to do away with this most reprehensible of all miscarriages of government, so as to avoid being burdened with even greater guilt. Now, when in recent years our eyes have been opened, when we know exactly who our adversary is, it is high time to root out this brown horde. Up until the outbreak of the war the larger part of the German people was blinded; the Nazis did not show themselves in their true aspect. But now, now that we have recognized them for what they are, it must be the sole and first duty, the holiest duty of every German to destroy these beasts.

> *If the people are barely aware that the government exists, they are happy. When the government is felt to be oppressive they are broken.*
>
> *Good fortune, alas! builds itself upon misery. Good fortune, alas! is the mask of misery. What will come of this? We cannot foresee the end. Order is upset and turns to disorder; good becomes evil. The people are confused. Is it not so, day in, day out, from the beginning?*
>
> *The wise man is therefore angular, though he does not injure others; he has sharp corners, though he does not harm; he is upright but not gruff. He is clear minded, but he does not try to be brilliant.*
>
> *Lao-Tzu*

> *Whoever undertakes to rule the kingdom and to shape it according to his whim – I foresee that he will fail to reach his goal. That is all.*
>
> *The kingdom is a living being. It cannot be constructed, in truth! He who tries to manipulate it will spoil it, he who tries to put it under his power will lose it.*
>
> *Therefore: some creatures go out in front, others follow, some have warm breath, others cold, some are strong, some weak, some attain abundance, others succumb.*
>
> *The wise man will accordingly forswear excess, he will avoid arrogance and not overreach.*
>
> *Lao-Tzu*

Please make as many copies as possible of this leaflet and distribute them.

Third Leaflet

Salus publica suprema lex

All ideal forms of government are utopias. A state cannot be constructed on a purely theoretical basis; rather, it must grow and ripen in the way an individual human being matures. But we must not forget that at the starting point of every civilization the state was already there in rudimentary form. The family is as old as man himself, and out of this initial bond man, endowed with reason, created for himself a state founded on justice, whose highest law was the common good. The state should exist as a parallel to the divine order, and the highest of all utopias, the *civitas dei*, is the model which in the end it should approximate. Here we will not pass judgment on the many possible forms of the state – democracy, constitutional monarchy, and so on. But one matter needs to be brought out clearly and unambiguously. Every individual human being has a claim to a useful and just state, a state which secures freedom of the individual as well as the good of the whole. For, according to God's will, man is intended to pursue his natural goal, his earthly happiness, in self-reliance and self-chosen activity, freely and independently within the community of life and work of the nation.

But our present 'state' is the dictatorship of evil. 'Oh, we've known that for a long time,' I hear you object, 'and it isn't necessary to bring that to our attention again.' But, I ask you, if you know that, why do you not bestir yourselves, why do you allow these men who are in power to rob you step by step, openly and in secret, of one domain of your rights after another, until one day nothing, nothing at all, will be left but a mechanized state system presided over by criminals and drunks? Is your spirit already so crushed by abuse that you forget it is your right – or rather, your *moral duty* – to eliminate this system? But if a man no longer can summon the strength to demand his right, then it is absolutely certain that he will perish. We would deserve to be dispersed through the earth like dust before the wind if we do not muster our powers at this late hour and finally find the courage which up to now we have lacked. Do not hide your cowardice behind a cloak of expediency, for with every new day that you hesitate, failing to oppose this offspring of Hell, your guilt, as in a parabolic curve, grows higher and higher.

Many, perhaps most, of the readers of these leaflets do not see clearly how they can practise an effective opposition. They do not see any avenues open to them. We want to try to show them that everyone is in a position to contribute to the overthrow of this system. It is not possible through solitary withdrawal, in the manner of embittered hermits, to prepare the ground for the overturn of this 'government' or bring about the revolution at the earliest possible moment. No, it can be done only by the cooperation of many convinced, energetic people – people who are agreed as to the means they must use to attain their goal. We have no great number of choices as to these means. The only one available is *passive resistance*. The meaning and the goal of passive resistance is to topple National Socialism, and in this struggle we must not recoil from any course, any action, whatever its nature. At *all* points we must oppose National Socialism, wherever it is open to attack. We must soon bring this monster of a state to an end. A victory of fascist Germany in this war would have immeasurable, frightful consequences. The military victory over Bolshevism dare not become the primary concern of the Germans. The defeat of the Nazis must *unconditionally* be the first order of business, the greater necessity of this latter requirement will be discussed in one of our forthcoming leaflets.

And now every convinced opponent of National Socialism must ask himself how he can fight against the present 'state' in the most effective way, how he can strike it the most telling blows. Through passive resistance, without a doubt. We cannot provide each man with the blueprint for his acts, we can only suggest them in general terms, and he alone will find the way of achieving this end:

Sabotage in armament plants and war industries, sabotage at all gatherings, rallies, public ceremonies, and organizations of the National Socialist Party. Obstruction of the smooth functioning of the war machine (a machine for war that goes on solely to shore up and perpetuate the National Socialist Party and its dictatorship). *Sabotage* in all the areas of science and scholarship which further the continuation of the war – whether in universities, technical schools, laboratories, research institutes, or technical bureaus. *Sabotage* in all cultural institutions which could potentially enhance the

197

'prestige' of the fascists among the people. *Sabotage* in all branches of the arts which have even the slightest dependence on National Socialism or render it service. *Sabotage* in all publications, all newspapers, that are in the pay of the 'government' and that defend its ideology and aid in disseminating the brown lie. Do not give a penny to public drives (even when they are conducted under the pretence of charity). For this is only a disguise. In reality the proceeds aid neither the Red Cross nor the needy. The government does not need this money; it is not financially interested in these money drives. After all, the presses run continuously to manufacture any desired amount of paper currency. But the populace must be kept constantly under tension, the pressure of the bit must not be allowed to slacken! Do not contribute to the collections of metal, textiles, and the like. Try to convince all your acquaintances, including those in the lower social classes, of the senselessness of continuing, of the hopelessness of this war; of our spiritual and economic enslavement at the hands of the National Socialists; of the destruction of all moral and religious values; and urge them to passive resistance!

Aristotle, *Politics*: ' . . . and further, it is part [of the nature of tyranny] to strive to see to it that nothing is kept hidden of that which any subject says or does, but that everywhere he will be spied upon, . . . and further, to set man against the privileged and the wealthy. Also it is part of these tyrannical measures, to keep the subjects poor, in order to pay the guards and soldiers, and so that they will be occupied with earning their livelihood and will have neither leisure nor opportunity to engage in conspiratorial acts . . . . Further, [to levy] such taxes on income as were imposed in Syracuse, for under Dionysius the citizens gladly paid out their whole fortunes in taxes within five years. Also, the tyrant is inclined constantly to foment wars.'

Please duplicate and distribute!

Fourth Leaflet

There is an ancient maxim that we repeat to our children: 'He who won't listen will have to feel.' But a wise child will not burn his fingers the second time on a hot stove. In the past weeks Hitler has chalked up successes in Africa and in Russia. In consequence, optimism on the one hand and distress and pessimism on the other have grown within the German people with a rapidity quite inconsistent with traditional German apathy. On all sides one hears among Hitler's opponents – the better segments of the population – exclamations of despair, words of disappointment and discouragement, often ending with the question: 'Will Hitler now, after all . . . ?'

Meanwhile, the German offensive against Egypt has ground to a halt. Rommel has to bide his time in a dangerously exposed position. But the push into the East proceeds. This apparent success has been purchased at the most horrible expense of human life, and so it can no longer be counted an advantage. Therefore we must warn against *all* optimism.

Neither Hitler nor Goebbels can have counted the dead. In Russia thousands are lost daily. It is the time of the harvest, and the reaper cuts into the ripe grain with wide strokes. Mourning takes up her abode in the country cottages, and there is no one to dry the tears of the mothers. Yet Hitler feeds with lies those people whose most precious belongings he has stolen and whom he has driven to a meaningless death.

Every word that comes from Hitler's mouth is a lie. When he says peace, he means war, and when he blasphemously uses the name of the Almighty, he means the power of evil, the fallen angel, Satan. His mouth is the foul-smelling maw of Hell, and his might is at bottom accursed. True, we must conduct a struggle against the National Socialist terrorist state with rational means; but whoever today still doubts the reality, the existence of demonic powers, has failed by a wide margin to understand the metaphysical background of this war. Behind the concrete, the visible events, behind all objective, logical considerations, we find the irrational element: the struggle against the demon, against the servants of the Antichrist. Everywhere and at all times demons have been lurking in the dark, waiting for the moment when man is weak; when of his own volition he leaves his place in the order of Creation as founded for him by God in freedom; when he yields to the force of evil, separates himself from the powers of a higher order; and after voluntarily taking the first step, he is driven on to the next and the next at a furiously accelerating rate. Everywhere and at all times of greatest trial men have appeared, prophets and saints who cherished their freedom, who preached the One God and who by His help brought the people to a reversal of their downward course. Man is free, to be sure, but without the true God he is defenceless against the principle of evil. He is a like rudderless ship, at the mercy of the storm, an infant without his mother, a cloud dissolving into thin air.

I ask you, you as a Christian wrestling for the preservation of your greatest treasure, whether you hesitate, whether you incline toward intrigue, calculation, or procrastination in the hope that someone else will raise his arm in your defence? Has God not given you the strength, the will to fight?   We *must* attack evil where it is strongest, and it is strongest in the power of Hitler.

So I returned, and considered all the oppressions that are done under the sun: and behold the tears of such as were oppressed, and they had no comforter; and on the side of their oppressors there was power; but they had no comforter. Wherefore I praised the dead which are already dead more than the living which are yet alive. Ecclesiastes 4

True anarchy is the generative element of religion. Out of the annihilation of every positive element she lifts her gloriously radiant countenance as the founder of a new world. . . .   If Europe were about to awaken again, if a state of states, a teaching of political science were at hand! Should hierarchy then . . .   be the principle of the union of states? Blood will stream over Europe until the nations become aware of the frightful madness which drives them in circles. And then, struck by celestial music and made gentle, the approach their former altars all together, hear about the works of peace, and hold a great celebration of peace with fervent tears before the smoking altars. Only religion can reawaken Europe, establish the rights of the peoples, and instal Christianity in new splendour visibly on earth in its office as guarantor of peace. Novalis

We wish expressly to point out that the White Rose is not in the pay of any foreign power. Though we know that National Socialist power must be broken by military means, we are trying to achieve a renewal from within of the severely wounded German spirit. This rebirth must be preceded, however, by the clear recognition of all the guilt with which the German people have burdened themselves, and by an uncompromising battle against Hitler and his all too many minions, party members, Quislings, and the like. With total brutality the chasm that separates the better portion of the nation from everything that is opened wide. For Hitler and his followers there is no punishment on this Earth commensurate with their crimes. But out of love for coming generations we must make an example after the conclusion of the war, so that no one will ever again have the slightest urge to try a similar action. And do not forget the petty scoundrels in this regime; note their names, so that none will go free! They should not find it possible, having had their part in these abominable crimes, at the last minute to rally to another flag and then act as if nothing had happened! To set you at rest, we add that the addresses of the readers of the White Rose are not recorded in writing. They were picked at random from directories.

We will not be silent. We are your bad conscience. The White Rose will not leave you in peace!

Fifth Leaflet

A Call to All Germans!

The war is approaching its destined end. As in the year 1918, the German government is trying to focus attention exclusively on the growing threat of submarine warfare, while in the East the armies are constantly in retreat and invasion is imminent in the West. Mobilization in the United States has not yet reached its climax, but already it exceeds anything that the world has ever seen. It has become a mathematical certainty that Hitler is leading the German people into the abyss. *Hitler cannot win the war; he can only prolong it.* The guilt of Hitler and his minions goes beyond all measure. Retribution comes closer and closer.

But what are the German people doing? They will not see and will not listen. Blindly they follow their seducers into ruin. *Victory at any price!* is inscribed on their banner. 'I will fight to the last man,' says Hitler, but in the meantime the war has already been lost.

Germans! Do you and your children want to suffer the same fate that befell the Jews? Do you want to be judged by the same standards as your traducers? Are we to be forever a nation which is hated and rejected by all mankind? No.

Dissociate yourselves from National Socialist gangsterism. Prove by your deeds that you think otherwise. A new war of liberation is about to begin. The better part of the nation will fight on our side. Cast off the cloak of indifference you have wrapped around you. Make the decision *before it is too late.* Do not believe the National Socialist propaganda which has driven the fear of Bolshevism into your bones. Do not believe that Germany's welfare is linked to the victory of national Socialism for good or ill. A criminal regime cannot achieve a German victory. Separate yourselves *in time* from everything connected with National Socialism. In the aftermath a terrible but just judgment will be meted out to those who stayed in hiding, who were cowardly and hesitant.

What can we learn from the outcome of this war – this war that never was a national war?

The imperialist ideology of force, from whatever side it comes, must be shattered for all time. A one-sided Prussian militarism must never again be allowed to assume power. Only in large-scale cooperation among the nations of Europe can the ground be prepared for reconstruction. Centralized hegemony, such as the Prussian state has tried to exercise in Germany and in Europe, must be cut down at its inception. The Germany of the future must be a federal state. At this juncture only a sound federal system can imbue a weakened Europe with a new life. The workers must be liberated from their condition of downtrodden slavery under National Socialism. The illusory structure of autonomous national industry must disappear. Every nation and each man have a right to the goods of the whole world!

Freedom of speech, freedom of religion, the protection of individual citizens from the arbitrary will of criminal regimes of violence – these will be the bases of the New Europe.

Support the resistance. Distribute the leaflets!

Sixth Leaflet

Fellow Fighters in the Resistance!

Shaken and broken, our people behold the loss of the men of Stalingrad. Three hundred and thirty thousand German men have been senselessly and irresponsibly driven to death and destruction by the inspired strategy of our World War I Private First Class. Führer, we thank you!

The German people are in ferment. Will we continue to entrust the fate of our armies to a dilettante? Do we want to sacrifice the rest of German youth to the base ambitions of a Party clique? No, never! The day of reckoning has come – the reckoning of German youth with the most abominable tyrant our people have ever been forced to endure. In the name of German youth we demand restitution by Adolf Hitler's state of our personal freedom, the most precious treasure we have, out of which he has swindled us in the most miserable way.

We grew up in a state in which all free expression of opinion is unscrupulously suppressed. The Hitler Youth, the SA, the SS have tried to drug us, to revolutionize us, to regiment us in the most promising young years of our lives. 'Philosophical training' is the name given to the despicable method by which our budding intellectual development is muffled in a fog of empty phrases. A system of selection of leaders at once unimaginably devilish and narrow-minded trains up its future party bigwigs in the 'Castles of the Knightly Order' to become Godless, impudent, and conscienceless exploiters and executioners – blind, stupid hangers-on of the Führer. We 'Intellectual Workers' are the ones who should put obstacles in the path of this caste of overlords. Soldiers at the front are regimented like schoolboys by student leaders and trainees for the post of Gauleiter, and the lewd jokes of the Gauleiters insult the honour of the women students. German women students at the university in Munich have given a dignified reply to the besmirching of their honour, and German students have defended the women in the universities and have stood firm .... That is a beginning of the struggle for our free self-determination – without which intellectual and spiritual values cannot be created. We thank the brave comrades, both men and women, who have set us brilliant examples.

For us there is but one slogan: fight against the party! Get out of the party organization, which is used to keep our mouths sealed and hold us in political bondage! Get out of the lecture rooms of the SS corporals and sergeants and the party bootlickers! We want genuine learning and real freedom of opinion. No threat can terrorize us, not even the shutting down of the institutions of higher learning. This is the struggle of each and every one of us for our future, our freedom, and our honour under a regime conscious of its moral responsibility.

Freedom and honour! For ten long years Hitler and his coadjutor have manhandled, squeezed, twisted, and debased these two splendid German words to the point of nausea, as only dilettantes can, casting the highest values of a nation before swine. They have sufficiently demonstrated in the ten years of destruction of all material and intellectual freedom, of all moral substance among the German people, what they understand by freedom and honour. The frightful bloodbath has opened the eyes of even the stupidest German – it is a slaughter which they arranged in the name of 'freedom and honour of the German nation' throughout Europe, and which they daily start anew. The name of Germany is dishonoured for all time if German youth does not finally rise, take revenge, and atone, smash its tormentors, and set up a new Europe of the spirit. Students! The German people look to us. As in 1813 the people expected us to shake off the Napoleonic yoke, so in 1943 they look to us to break the National Socialist terror through the power of the spirit. Beresina and Stalingrad are burning in the East. The dead of Stalingrad implore us to take action. 'Up, up, my people, let smoke and flame be our sign!'

Our people stand ready to rebel against the National Socialist enslavement of Europe in a fervent new breakthrough of freedom and honour.

Appendix 4

The telexes which formed the orders to implement Operation Valkyrie.

1.
FRR-HOKW 02150 20.7.44, 16.45 FRR to corps area HQ XII –
secret – Domestic unrest.

I. An unscrupulous clique of non-combat party leaders has tried to
exploit the situation to stab the deeply committed front in the back,
and to seize power for selfish purposes.

II. In this hour of highest danger, the Reich government has
proclaimed a state of martial law, and has at the same time dele-
gated supreme executive power of the armed forces to me.

III. Accordingly I order the following.
1. I delegate the executive power – with the right of further dele-
gation by those named to the territorial commanders – in the Zone
of the Interior to the commander of the replacement army,
appointing him at the same time Commander-in-Chief in the Zone
of the Interior.
In the occupied west areas, to the Commander-in-Chief West
(Commander-in-Chief of army group D), in Italy to the
Commander-in-Chief South-West (Commander-in-Chief of army
group C), in the south-east area to the Commander-in-Chief South-
East (Commander-in-Chief of army group F), in the occupied east
areas to the Commanders-in-Chief of army groups south Ukraine,
north Ukraine; to the Middle, north and the armed forces east

commanders for their respective command areas; in Denmark and in Norway, to the commanders of the armed forces.

2. To the holders of executive power are subordinated:

(a) All offices and units of the armed forces, including the armoured SS, the Reich Labour Service and the Organization Todt, that are within their command area.

(b) All public authorities (of the Reich, the states and the communities), in particular the entire police forces, including forces for keeping order, for security, for administration.

(c) All office holders and formations of the National Socialist party and its affiliated units.

(d) Traffic and supply organizations.

3. The entire armoured SS is incorporated into the army, with this order to take effect immediately.

4. The holders of executive power are responsible for maintenance of order and public safety. In particular they are charged with:

(a) The security of the signal installations.

(b) The elimination of the SD. Any resistance to the military executive supremacy must be broken regardless of consequences.

5. In this hour of highest danger for the Fatherland, solidarity of the armed forces and maintenance of full discipline is the highest order.

Therefore I charge all commanders in the army, the navy and the air force with supporting the bearers of executive power in carrying out their difficult task with all means at their disposal, and with ensuring obedience of their orders by subordinate offices. The German soldier is facing an historic task. On his determination and bearing will depend whether Germany is to be saved.

The same responsibilities apply to all territorial commanders, the Commanders-in-Chief of the segments of the armed forces and the command authorities of the army, navy and air force that are directly subordinate to the Commanders-in-Chief.

Signed: Field Marshal Erwin von Witzleben

Commander-in-Chief of the Armed Forces

2.

I. Under the authority given to me by the Commander-in-Chief of the armed forces, I transfer the executive power in the corps areas to the deputy commanding generals and corps area commanders. Together with the executive power, the authority of the Reich defence commissioners passes over to the corps area commanders.

II. The following direct measures are to be taken:
(a) Signal installations: The principal buildings and installations of the post and armed forces signal net (including radio installations) are to be made militarily secure. The forces assigned to this task must be strong enough to prevent interference and sabotage. Principal signal installations are to be occupied by officers. These in particular are to be made secure: amplifying stations, communications exchanges of the army operations network, high-power transmitters (broadcasting stations), telephone and telegraph officers insofar as major telephone lines run through them, amplifier and battery rooms, antennas, emergency power supplies, and operating rooms. The communication net of the railways is to be protected in agreement with the transport offices. Radio network is to be kept operative from own resources.
(b) Arrests: The following are to be removed from their posts without delay and are to be held in individual arrest: all district leaders, Reich governors, ministers, chief presidents, police presidents, senior SS and police leaders, Gestapo leaders and chief of SS officers, chief of propaganda offices and area leaders. Exceptions are to be ordered by me.
(c) Concentration camps: The concentration camps are to be occupied speedily, the camp commanders arrested, the guards disarmed and confined to barracks. The political prisoners are to be informed that they must abstain from all rallies and individual measures until their discharge.
(d) Armed SS: If doubts exist as to the obedience of leaders of armed SS units or of senior armed SS officers, or if they seem unsuitable for further command, they are to be taken into protective custody and replaced by officers of the army. Units of the armed SS whose unlimited obedience is in doubt are to be disarmed ruthlessly. This is to be accomplished energetically with superior forces, to avoid bloodshed as far as possible.
(e) Police: The offices of the Gestapo and of the SD are to be occupied. Regular police are to be utilized for relief of the armed forces.

Police orders are to be issued through the chief of German police via police command.

(f) Navy and Air Force: Connection is to be established with commanders of navy and air force. Common action is to be achieved.

III. For the administration of all political matters that arise under the state of martial law, I appoint a political commissioner for each corps area. Until further notice he is to discharge the tasks of the chief of administration. He is to advise the commander of the corps area in all political matters.

IV. The staff for domestic operations is the executive authority of the Commander-in-Chief in the Zone of the Interior in all executive matters. He appoints a liaison officer to the corps commanders for the purpose of mutual information about the situation and intentions. (VO OKH).

V. No arbitrary actions or actions based on vengeance are to be tolerated in the exercise of the executive power. The population must be made aware that the executive power distances itself from the arbitrary methods of the previous rulers.

The Commander-in-Chief in the Zone of the Interior
No.31 160/44, SECRET.
Signed: General Erich Hoepner, Colonel Count Klaus von Stauffenberg

3.

I. Valkyrie, 2nd stage, for corps area HQ XIII, XVII, XVIII, XX, XXI. With application to all reserves of field and replacement army. If necessarily, with application also to reserves of ordnance and motor maintenance departments.
X-hour, 20 July 1944, 18:00
II. Weapons, heavy equipment and vehicles of the army high command reserves that are taken from ordnance and motor maintenance departments must be reported immediately to the general army office, Staff I-B, by teletype.
III. Formations, strengths and places of origin of mobilized units are to

be reported to the general army office, Staff I by 21 July, 12:00 hours. IV. Measures taken in corps area HQ Bohemia-Moravia and in corps area HQ of Governor-General are to be reported correspondingly. Units that are mobilized are to be reported according to (3) above.

4.

Martial Law Regulation No. 1
I decree for the entire area of the Reich:

I. Parades, rallies and the assembling of groups in streets and squares, as well as assemblies indoors, are prohibited.

II. Only the armed forces and the police acting under their orders, along with the units that have been entrusted with military or pretective tasks, are entitled to bear arms. All persons not entitled to bear arms under this provision are required to report the possession of arms of any kind, within 24 hours of publication of this order, at the appropriate police stations; or, insofar as these do not exist, at the office of the local police authority.

III. Production and distribution of leaflets is prohibited.

IV. Anyone who violates the above orders is subject to proceedings of martial law.
The Commander-in-Chief of the Zone of the Interior.
Signed: General Erich Hoepner

5.

Martial Law Regulation No. 2
I. All economic activities and transportation services are to be continued.
II. The offices of the Reich Agricultural Board and the organizations of commercial life are to continue functioning, under my supervision and that of the corps area commanders.
III. The offices of the National Socialist People's Welfare organization are to continue functioning. Their leadership is taken over by the community, district, province and state. At the same time,

the duties of the National Socialist People's Welfare organization are returned to these local entities.

IV. The Todt Organization, the Labour Service and the National Socialist Motorized Corps will continue to function, subordinated to me and to the corps area commanders.

V. The German Labour Front is to continue to function. I shall appoint a new provisional leadership.

VI. Officials, employees and workmen are to continue their functions, insofar as they receive no other instructions from me.

VII. All vacations for officials and employees of the Reich, of the states and the communities are cancelled, with the exception of sick leaves. Officials are to be on call by their superiors, within and outside of office hours.

VIII. Anyone who ceases his work contrary to the preceding orders, or who fails to carry out instructions based on the state of martial law will be subject to proceedings under martial law.

The Commander-in-Chief of the Zone of the Interior.

Signed: General Erich Hoepner

6.

Martial Law Regulation No. 3

I

For office-holders in the party (NSDAP), its formations and its affiliated units: any and all activities assigned to them by the party are forbidden. Insofar as they continue active, within the framework of the instructions provided by me, they are to obey the orders given under the state of martial law.

II

In order to make them secure, the entire movable and immovable assets of the NSDAP and of its formations and affiliated units (Labour Service and Todt Organization are excepted under this provision) are confiscated temporarily. All party accessories and assets are similarly confiscated, including all demand notes, shares, ownership rights and assignments of interest of any kind, and in particular all files.

2.Under this confiscation, the individuals who hitherto held the right of disposition of these assets lose any power of disposition over the confiscated items.

3.The regulations of the 7th code of civil law regarding attachment are applied where appropriate to the confiscations.

III

The following will be subject to proceedings under martial law:

(a) Anyone who acts contrary to the above regulations.

(b) Anyone who wilfully destroys, conceals, intercepts, damages or falsifies a document, a record, files, or any other item that belongs to the assets of the NSDAP and its formations and affiliated units; or any item that is located within the jurisdiction of these entities.

The Commander-in-Chief of the Zone of the Interior

Signed: General Erich Hoepner

7.

I

1.Sentences of up to 15 years in the penitentiary, or, in particularly grave cases, of life terms in the penitentiary or death, apply to:

(a) Anyone who acts contrary to the order of the Commander-in-Chief of the Armed Forces, the Commander-in-Chief of the Zone of the Interior, or the armed forces commanders, or who endangers the effectiveness of prescribed measures, or who incites to disobedience of or interference with orders.

(b) Anyone who publicly incites another person or persons to commit an act of violence against an individual or to acts of violence in general against persons or property.

(c) Anyone who loots.

2. In less severe cases, prison terms of a minimum of three years may be decreed.

3. Besides penitentiary sentences or death sentences, confiscation of property is permissible.

II

Courts-martial are formed to adjudicate the offences under (I) above.

III

1.The courts-martial are also competent to try members of the armed forces.

2.The courts-martial are also competent in cases of crimes or offences that, while under their jurisdiction, at the same time involve other crimes or misdemeanours. Similarly, the courts-martial are competent to proceed if a crime or offence under another jurisdiction also falls within the jurisdiction of the courts-martial.

IV

1. Seats and areas of jurisdiction of the courts-martial are determined by the Commander-in-Chief of the Zone of the Interior. Until this determination has been made, the courts-martial are appointed by the armed forces commanders.

2. Commanders of mobile units of the armed forces, down to and including the battalion level, are authorized to establish courts-martial with jurisdiction within their areas.

V

1.The courts-martial are to pass judgment as three-member bodies. One of these shall possess, insofar as practicable, the qualifications of judgeship.

2.The charge is to be presented and prosecuted by an officer appointed for this purpose, or who has qualifications for judgeship. The Commander-in-Chief of the Zone of the Interior and, within their respective areas, the armed forces commanders, may appoint a chief prosecutor. The prosecutors must follow the official instructions of the chief.

VI

1.The courts-martial will decide the form of proceedings, under their discretion, using as a model the principles of the Reich code of criminal procedure. They will summon the defendant, afford him legal hearing, interrogate witnesses if appropriate, and pass sentence immediately.

2.The armed forces commanders are authorized to initiate proceedings before the courts-martial established at the corps area HQ.

VII

The sentences of the court-martial are final and are to be carried out without delay.

The Commander-in-Chief of the Zone of the Interior.

Signed: General Erich Hoepner

8.

I

Martial Law Regulation No. 5

1.For the purpose of safeguarding them, certain assets will be temporarily confiscated. These include the total movable and immovable assets, with all physical equipment, all demand notes, shares, rights and assignments of any kind, and in particular all files:

(a) Of the Reich leader, Gauleiter, and all other persons who are holding or have held an official position down to and including district leader in the NSDAP, its formations and affiliated units (excepting the Labour Service and Todt Organization).

(b) Of persons and corporate persons authorized to hold or created to hold property of persons detailed under (a), or in whose governing bodies half or more of the voting representatives consisted of persons detailed under (a).

2. Under this confiscation, persons who hitherto were entitled to dispose of such items lose any power of disposition over the confiscated goods and properties.

3. The regulations of the civil code in regard to attachment are applicable as appropriate to the acts of confiscation.

II

Certain crimes call for a quick atonement, as they have aroused the special indignation of the people. The jurisdiction of the courts-martial is extended to offences involving murder, extortion, bribery in connection with public office, and misuse of authority against defenceless people or for personal enrichment.

III

1. The courts-martial also have jurisdiction over the following offences if they are committed deliberately and during the state of martial law:

(a) Sedition (Nos.80-85 Reich criminal code)

(b) High treason (Nos.89-93 Reich criminal code)

(c) Resistance to state authority (Nos.10-122-B Reich criminal code)

(d) Crimes and offences against public order (Nos.123-143, with the exception of Nos.134-8 Reich criminal codes)

(e) Offences against religions (Nos.166-68 Reich criminal code)

(f) Crimes and offences against life (Nos.211-5 Reich criminal code)

(g) Crimes und offences against??? (No.239 Reich criminal code)

(h) Robbery and extortion (Nos.249-256 Reich criminal code)

(i) Damage to property (Nos.303-305 Reich criminal code)

(k) Crimes dangerous to the public (Nos.306-320-C Reich criminal code)

(l) Crimes and offences against the law on use of explosives in a criminal manner or in a way endangering public safety, of 9 June 1884.

(m) Crimes under Nos.1 and 2 of the regulation of 5 December 1939, on crimes of violence.

2.The preceding offences, insofar as their gravity exceeds the previously provided penalties, can be punished with penitentiary sentences up to 15 years, with life imprisonment, or with death.

3.Besides penitentiary sentences and death sentences, confiscation of property is permissible.

The Commander-in-Chief of the Zone of the Interior.

Signed: General Erich Hoepner

9.

I. The offices and quarters of the party, of its formations and of its affiliated units are to be closed immediately, and to be made secure so that files cannot disappear.

II. The continuation of the functions of those organizations and formations designated in Martial Law Regulation No.2 is to be safeguarded.

III. Regarding the continuation of function of organizations and party formations under Martial Law Regulation No.2, in the event that present leaders are not able to assure that continuation, especially commissioned leaders are to be appointed in their place. The state labour offices and local labour offices are available to the German Labour Front to help in this process.

IV. Those persons active in the party, its formations and affiliated units who are not absolutely required for the continuation of functions under Martial Law Regulation No.2 are to be drafted as soon as possible, by lifting all statutes of indispensability, so that they can be conscripted for work-service.

The Commander-in-Chief of the Zone of the Interior

Signed: General Erich Hoepner

10.

Regulation on private travel, telephone and telegraphic communications, and closing times.

I. Private long-distance travel is forbidden immediately, for a period of three days. The authorized authorities may give written permission for urgent official trips.

Journeys that have been started at the time this regulation is issued may continue to the destination stated on the ticket or travel paper.

II. All telephone communication is to be blocked for the time being, except for local telephone calls and for calls to and from government and armed forces offices, which are to be made by giving the names of the person who is calling and the person being called. Telegraphic communication is subject to stoppage, except for official use, until this order is recalled.

III. Closing hours are uniformly fixed at 9 p.m.

The Commander-in-Chief of the Zone of the Interior
Signed: General Erich Hoepner

11.

Order concerning arrests

I. The regulation proclaiming a state of martial law in the Zone of the Interior enables corps area commanders and the subordinate police units to make all arrests that seem necessary to them. Rather too much than too little use is to be made of this authorization.

II. The following persons are to be removed from their offices without delay, and brought into secure solitary confinement-possibly individually confined in a barracks:

(a) As a matter of basic principle:

All Gauleiter, Reichsstatthalter, chief presidents, police presidents, higher SS and police leaders, Gestapo leaders, leaders of the SD offices and of the propaganda offices and district leaders.

(b) According to the decision of the individual corps area commanders:

Other hitherto political leaders (for example, SS leaders, Gauleiter and district leaders and local group leaders presidents of the administrative districts, district presidents, mayors) who have shown themselves to be miscarriers of justice or scoundrels.

(c) I reserve to myself personally the issuing of exemptions from arrest under (II-a) above, by special order. Corps area commanders can grant exemption from arrest only to persons of a rank no higher than that of district leaders, and then only after making reports of the individual instances to me.

III. Whoever has offended against law and decency must face the consequences. I expect these persons to be ascertained, so that justice may be satisfied, with the accused to be judged in orderly proceedings. To accomplish this, politically clear, experienced and uncompromisingly efficient officers are to be carefully selected and entrusted with preparing for this action, gathering all necessary forces to accomplish it, and carrying out the process with speed and determination.

IV. First priority is to be given to those arrests that serve the restoration of justice and the sense of decency.

Bibliography

Benz, Wolfgang and Peble, Walter H., eds., *Encyclopedia of German Resistance to the Nazi Movement*, Continuum, New York, 1997

Berg, A. Scott, *Lindbergh*, G.P. Putnam's Sons, 1998

Craig, Gordon A., *Germany 1866-1945*, Oxford University Press, 1978

Davis, John H., *The Kennedy Clan*, Sidgwick & Jackson, 1985

Dulles, Allen W., *Germany's Underground*, The Macmillan Company, New York, 1947

Dumbach, Annette E. and Newborn, Jud, *Shattering the German Night, The Story of the White Rose*, Little, Brown and Company, 1986

Ferrell, Robert H., ed., *The Twentieth Century: an Almanac*, Harrap, 1986

Fest, Joachim, *Plotting Hitler's Death: The German Resistance to Hitler 1933-1945*, Weidenfeld & Nicolson, 1996

Friedländer, Saul, *Counterfeit Nazi*, Weidenfeld & Nicolson, 1969

Gill, Anton, *An Honourable Defeat*, Heinemann, 1994

Gilfond, Henry, *The Reichstag Fire*, Franklin Watts, Inc., 1973

Gisevius, Hans Bernd, *To the Bitter End*, Jonathan Cape, 1948

Hamerow, Theodore S., *On the Road to the Wolf's Lair*, The Belknap Press of Harvard University Press, 1999

Hitler, Adolf, *Mein Kampf*, Hutchinson, 1974

Hoffmann, Peter, *German Resistance to Hitler*, Harvard University Press, 1988

Kershaw, Ian, *Hitler*, Longman, 1991

Koch, H.W., *In the Name of the Volk, Political Justice in Hitler's Germany*, I.B. Tauris Publishers, 1997

Mann, Erika, *School for Barbarians*, Modern Age Books, 1938

Matanle, Ivor, *The Hitler Years: A photographic documentary*, Colour Library Books Ltd., 1983

McConkie, Bruce R., *Mormon Doctrine*, Bookcraft, Salt Lake City, Utah, 1979

Meding, Dorothee von, *Courageous Hearts: Women and the Anti-Hitler Plot of 1944*, Berghahn Books, 1997

Rogasky, Barbara, *Smoke and Ashes, The story of the Holocaust*, Oxford University Press, 1988

Schoenberner, Gerhard, *The Yellow Star*, Corgi Books, 1969

Scholl, Inge, *The White Rose, Munich 1942-1943*, Wesleyan University Press, 1988

Shirer, William L., *The Rise and Fall of the Third Reich*, Pan Books, 1964

Snyder, Louis L., *Encyclopedia of the Third Reich*, Wordsworth Editions, 1998

Tillion, Germaine, *Ravensbrück, an Eyewitness account of a Women's Concentration Camp*, Anchor Books, 1975

Townsend, Colin and Eileen, *War Wives*, Grafton Books, 1990

Traverso, Enzo, *Understanding the Nazi Genocide*, Pluto Press, 1999

Vat, Dan van der, *The Good Nazi: The life and lies of Albert Speer*, Houghton Mifflin Company, 1997

Wheal, Elizabeth-Anne and Pope, Stephen, *The Macmillan Dictionary of the Second World War*, Macmillan, 1997

Other sources

There are numerous Internet sites which are both interesting and informative including –
www.nizkor.org
www.joric.com
www.us-israel.org
ww2.klup.info

Index

222